TRADING SECRETS

TRADING SECRETS

R. Foster Winans

St. Martin's Press

NEW YORK

Design by M. Paul

Library of Congress Cataloging in Publication Data

Winans, R. Foster.
    Trading secrets.

    1. Wall Street. 2. Wall Street journal. 3. Dow
Jones & Co. I. Title.
HG4572.W547 1986   364.1'68   86-12700
ISBN 0-312-81227-2

First Edition

10 9 8 7 6 5 4 3 2 1

For David

Apart from the substantial eyewitness recollections of David Carpenter, Ken Felis and me, the facts in this book were largely drawn from documents, depositions, and other materials filed with the courts in both the civil and criminal proceedings against us. In most cases, dialogue was reconstructed and double-checked against the recollections of the parties so that it would accurately reflect both the sense and spirit of the speaker and the circumstance. Peter Brant declined, through his attorney, to speak with me prior to publication. I relied for his point of view on his testimony at our trial and the recollection of those with whom he associated, including his secretaries, who also testified at our trial, and the testimony of David Clark, before the Securities and Exchange Commission.

Contents

Acknowledgments

This book was a labor of love, pain, and introspection: a punctuation mark at the end of an unhappy chapter in my life. I would have written it without a publisher but I'm glad I didn't have to. For this I owe my deepest gratitude to the group of editors and executives at St. Martin's Press who believed in this book when it seemed no one else would.

I am also grateful to those who read the manuscript during its metamorphosis and helped keep my eye on the goal—to tell a simple, compelling story well. These include (alphabetically): Ken Felis; Darrell Gossett; Mickey Harris; Ed Leefeldt; Toni Lopopolo, my editor at St. Martin's; Al Lowman, my agent; Doug Meurs; Kevin Ottem; Christopher Winans, my brother; Ellen Harris Winans, my mother; and Robert F. Winans, my father.

Many people, especially on Wall Street and at *The Wall Street Journal*, who offered encouragement and research assistance would be uncomfortable or embarrassed being identified here. They know who they are: thanks.

One who I can and frequently do name: Don D. Buchwald, my lawyer and good friend.

For a variety of reasons, I am grateful to the following people (in no particular order) for the spiritual and/or practical help they provided: Paul Franklin, Gigi Franklin, Howard Avery, Kenneth H., Dan Dorfman, Jane B., E. Michael Bradley, Kenny and Rhea Gross, Hank Bryant, "Tilt" Stryker-Meyer, Gerry Hughes, Pat Read, Rob Fisher, Kathy Winans, Mitzi Evans, Bill Evans, Howard W. Goldstein, Jed S. Rakoff, Steve Grover, Rena Caref, Scott J. Bieler, Caroline A. Riggio, Catherine Curran, Thomas Souther, Marc M. Harris, Bob Wilson, Bob Cecchi, S. Miller and Mary Louise Harris, Len Kessler, Fred Holub, Jim Fixter, Jon and Ari Holub, Alan Kaufman, Frank Davis, Jr., Margarete Hardy, Jack Caravela, Francie Schwartz, Tom Stieghorst, Jim Keller, Howard

Zucker, Sam Earle, Bill Mahoney, Nancy Rosin, Jose Binet, Henry and Virginia Martin, Martha Winans, Jeffrey W. Mays, Martha Nagy, Don Nute, Ruben Macaya, Vince Schiraldi, David Rothenberg, Denise Turner, Alden Thayer, Eddie Sanchez, Audrey Miller, Tony Proscio, Morgan Pinney, Joe DiSabato, Michael Gravois, Gerry Robinson, Stu Rose, Jodine Mayberry, Morton and Roz Rosen, Lucia Valeska, Kevin and Nancy Hauser, Claire Muhlbauer, Jim Hughes, and anyone else whose name I have overlooked.

Cast of Characters

The Main Characters

Peter N. Brant . . . . Kidder, Peabody stockbroker

David W. C. Clark . . . . . Peter Brant's social squire and investment partner, and a lawyer with the New York firm of Appleton, Rice & Perrin

Kenneth P. Felis . . . . Peter Brant's business partner and best friend

R. Foster Winans . . . . *Wall Street Journal* "Heard on the Street" columnist

At The Wall Street Journal

George Anders . . . . "Heard on the Street" columnist who preceded Foster Winans

Barnie Calame . . . . Chief of the Los Angeles bureau

Charles Elia . . . . "Heard" columnist who preceded George Anders

Everett Groseclose . . . . . . Managing editor of the Dow Jones News Service (the ticker) who hired Foster Winans

Harry . . . . A senior editor at the ticker

Vic Hillery . . . . Reporter who wrote the "Abreast of the Market" column

Georgette Jasen . . . . An editor on the spot news desk in the New York bureau

Monica Langley . . . . A reporter in the New York bureau

Larry O'Donnell . . . . Managing editor of the *Journal* when Foster Winans was hired

Norman Pearlstine . . . . .O'Donnell's successor as managing editor
Stew Pinkerton . . . . .Chief of the New York bureau
Gary Putka. . . . . .Coauthor with Foster Winans of the "Heard"
Dean Rotbart . . . . .Gary Putka's successor as "Heard" columnist
Dick Rustin . . . . .Editor in charge of the markets columns when Foster Winans was hired to cowrite the "Heard"
Bob Sack. . . . . .Chief outside attorney to Dow Jones & Co., publisher of *The Wall Street Journal*
Paul Steiger . . . . .Successor to Richard Rustin as editor in charge of the "Heard" and other market columns
Chris Winans . . . . .Foster Winans's brother and a copy editor at *The Wall Street Journal*
Bernie Wysocki . . . . . . .Former chief of the Philadelphia bureau and an executive editor in the *Journal*'s New York office

In the Life of Peter N. Brant

Paul Barber . . . . .His personal banker at Morgan Guaranty Trust
Morton Bornstein . . . . . .His father, an insurance salesman and, later, a lawyer
Chuckie Bornstein. . . . . .His brother, an orchestra conductor
Peter Noel Bornstein. . . .The name he was born with
Lynn Brant. . . . . .His wife
Van Cliburn . . . . .The concert pianist who hired Peter one summer during college to work as his valet
Ken Felis . . . . .His best friend from September 1972 through March 1984
John Gerweck . . . . .A member of the dormitory clique he belonged to at Babson College
Garrison du Pont Lickle His friend and attorney—of Palm Beach

Jesse L. Livermore . . . . .Notorious stock-market operator of the
late 19th and early 20th centuries
whose exploits influenced Peter
Ricardo . . . . .His chauffeur

In the Life of R. Foster Winans

David J. Carpenter . . . . .His lover, with whom he lived for more
than a decade. Also a news clerk at
The Wall Street Journal

At Kidder, Peabody

Casey . . . . .One of Peter Brant's two secretaries
David W. C. Clark . . . . .A wealthy globetrotting lawyer who
became Peter's biggest client and his
trading and investment partner
Evan Collins. . . . . .Manager of the branch office at 101 Park
Avenue in which Peter worked
Diane . . . . .The other of Peter's two secretaries
Robert Goldhammer. . . .A high-ranking sales executive and an
important sponsor of Peter's career at
the firm
Nancy Huang . . . . .A customer of Peter's
William Kennedy. . . . . .New York regional sales executive
Robert Krantz . . . . .Chief inside counsel to the firm
Robert J. Turner . . . . . .A garment-industry executive in whose
rented cottage Peter lived for a time.
Also a customer
Western Hemisphere
Trading Corporation #2 A dummy company, registered in Costa
Rica and domiciled in Switzerland,
set up to further the trading scheme
with Foster Winans
Roger W. Wilson . . . . . .Son of an oil-industry executive and a
trust-account client of David Clark's.
Also one of Peter Brant's customers

For the Government

Joseph Cella . . . . Lead investigator for the Securities and
Exchange Commission in the matter
of trading by David W. C. Clark

Vincent DiCarlo . . . . An investigator with the SEC

John Fedders . . . . Chief of the Enforcement Division of
the SEC

Peter J. Romatowski . . . . An assistant United States attorney
assigned to prosecute in the case of
United States versus Foster Winans, et al.

The Judge

Hon. Charles E. Stewart The district court judge who heard
and decided *U.S. v. Winans, et al.*

For the Defense

E. Michael Bradley . . . . . Ken Felis's attorney, of Brown, Wood,
Ivey, Mitchell & Petty in New York

Don D. Buchwald . . . . . . Foster Winans's attorney, of Buchwald
& Kaufman in New York

Howard W. Goldstein. . . David Carpenter's attorney, of Mudge,
Rose, Guthrie, Alexander & Ferdon
in New York

Alan R. Kaufman . . . . . . Foster Winans's attorney, of Buchwald
& Kaufman in New York

Jed S. Rakoff . . . . David Carpenter's attorney, of Mudge,
Rose, Guthrie, Alexander & Ferdon
in New York

The Chorus

Dan Dorfman. . . . . Syndicated stock market columnist,
television commentator, and a former
"Heard" writer

Alex Jones . . . . *New York Times* reporter

Robert Metz. . . . . *New York Times* stock market columnist

Vartanig G. Vartan . . . . . *New York Times* stock market columnist

TRADING
SECRETS

1
Let's Make
a Deal

I would have accepted without question the information that Gatsby sprang from the swamps of
Louisiana or from the lower East Side of New
York. That was comprehensible. But young men
didn't—at least in my provincial inexperience I
believed they didn't—drift coolly out of nowhere
and buy a palace on Long Island Sound.
                    —Nick Carraway, in *The Great Gatsby*

It was a day to hate New York. Wind-driven rain splattered in
sheets on the buckled asphalt of the financial district and the gutters
ran full all afternoon. It was impossible to stay dry. As night came,
the wet streets reflected headlights, store neons, and fluorescent-lit
windows. In high-rise towers eager young executives, clerks rack-
ing up overtime, night-shift workers, and cleaning crews kept the
oil burning.

I had just gotten off work at *The Wall Street Journal*, where I co-
authored a daily gossip column covering the stock market. I was
late for an appointment. It had been my turn that day to write the
column, "Heard on the Street," for the next day's edition. Deadline
was about 5:30 or so. As usual, I left the office trembling slightly
from the adrenaline rush and my customary overdose of coffee and

cigarettes. The column that was being set in type that night at a printing plant 300 miles away had been a joint effort with a young reporter in the *Journal*'s London office, George Anders, a friend and my predecessor on the "Heard" column. Between us we'd learned that investors in the States were snapping up shares of Imperial Chemical Industries PLC, a London-based chemicals conglomerate, about as fast as the Brits could dump them. The cross fire between British stock analysts telling us what a lousy company Imperial was and their Yank counterparts putting the bull on the stock made for interesting reporting. But the transatlantic detective work and the five-hour time lag from London made for a tight deadline. By lunch in New York, most London businessmen were already home with their families or in a pub draining a glass of ale.

The homebound street crowds had thinned by the time I left my office at 6:30. I half-ran the block between the back door of the building in which I worked to the nearest entrance to the World Trade Center. I was supposed to meet Peter that night at his club in midtown and the time had gotten away from me. I looked forward to trading market gossip and a couple of tasteless jokes with him. I might even get the germ of an idea for a column. I'd be home by 9 o'clock.

Peter was among the richest and most successful retail stock-brokers on the Street. He entered my life during a boom cycle in the stock market. I had wanted to profile him in a front-page feature for the *Journal* or for the "Heard" column—an insider's view of how a broker hits the jackpot. The idea had been rolling around in my head for almost five months now, although everything I knew about Peter had come from him. He was handsome, poised, and natty. At the age of thirty he had accumulated the traditional icons of success: a yacht, a large home on Long Island's gilded North Shore, and a corner office at Kidder, Peabody & Co.'s branch on Park Avenue. From his mahogany desk Peter could prop his Guccis on the credenza and contemplate an unobstructed, 42nd-story view of the East River and the hazy suburbs of Queens. His clients ranked among the rich and super-rich. Their names appeared in social registers and volumes of *Who's Who*. That summer he had flown in the Concorde to London to attend a dinner party at an old English manor house owned by a member of the Astor family. Peter owned horses and played polo. He commuted thirty miles or so to and from work, weather permitting, in a helicopter. He'd reaped a fortune in the stock market for himself and his clients. He had a high opinion of his investment abilities, which struck me as perfectly reasonable.

He and I had spoken on the phone earlier that afternoon to confirm our meeting.

"You see what the weather's like outside," he said.

"I haven't been outside and I don't have a window," I said. "Is it still raining?"

"Oh, yeah! It's pouring cats and dogs. You want me to send Ricardo down to pick you up?" Ricardo drove Peter's black Cadillac.

My other line began to ring. It would always start to ring right in the middle of another call. I was expecting callbacks from sources I needed to interview if I hoped to finish the column on time. I used to dream about telephones.

"Hold on, Peter. Let me put this other line on hold." I stabbed the hold button, picked up the other call, put it on hold, and punched Peter back on the line.

"Um, I don't think so. I'll just jump on the subway. It's no problem."

I had been in a limousine only once before—Peter's—and found it to be an illicit pleasure compared to the dank and gritty subway tunnels where I usually did my commuting. But today it seemed a waste of time and energy to send a car all the way downtown to pick me up. In thirty minutes I could get from my office to Peter's club by subway. It would take Ricardo that long and maybe longer, because of the rain, just to get down to Wall Street.

"Are you sure?" he pressed. "The weather's awful and there's no sense your getting wet if you don't have to."

I hemmed and hawed for a few seconds while I debated. The limo won out. But no way was I going to climb into a black limousine, with Ricardo in his chauffeur's suit holding an umbrella in one hand and the door in the other, in front of the *Journal*'s offices. Someone from the paper might spot me, a *Journal* reporter, earning $575 a week and wearing scuffed-up loafers and a $28 navy-blue blazer from a seconds store, stepping into a limo at the *Journal*'s front door. The only person I knew at the paper entitled to commute in a limo was Warren Phillips, and he was the chairman of Dow Jones & Co., which owned the *Journal*. I was supposed to be writing about the silk-stocking crowd, not emulating it. Besides,

I was embarrassed by ostentatiousness. "I'll accept the invitation, Peter, but I don't want to meet Ricardo out front here. Can he meet me at the Vista Hotel? It's just across the street at the Trade Center."

"Sure, no problem." he said. "I understand. Where should he look for you?"

"Um, tell him I'll wait at the West Street entrance. There's a pull-in there for cabs and I can wait out of the rain. I'll be there about 6:30. Are you sure this isn't a hassle? The subway's a lot faster."

"No, no, no! Six-thirty at the Vista on West Street. I'll see you at the club when you get uptown."

There really weren't any anonymous spots for me in the financial district. Even the marble steps of the hotel, where I waited for Ricardo, held the potential of yielding a familiar face or two. The Vista boasted one of the few first-class restaurants in the area that suited the expense-account crowd. It was where Dow Jones executives frequently fed *Journal* editors, where *Journal* editors fed their reporters and where reporters fed their news sources, especially businessmen and Wall Street hotshots who long ago graduated from noisy coffee shops. I ate there maybe fifty times while I wrote for the *Journal*, mostly breakfasts with money managers, analysts, and businessmen hoping to get their names, or their favorite stocks, mentioned in the paper. I ran into so many of my coworkers at the Vista that we dubbed it the Dow Jones executive dining room.

Only strangers entered and left the hotel entrance that night as I waited. Peter's Cadillac, Ricardo at the wheel, finally emerged from the darkness and swung its nose into the loading area like a docking cruise ship. I let myself in the back door before Ricardo could dash around the hood and open it for me. I have always felt squeamish about being served. I had an aunt and uncle who employed a stout black woman who for thirty years or more brought them dinner on silver platters, the food served from the left and the empty plates removed from the right. It always felt like this demeaned the server and falsely exalted me. I gave Ricardo directions for the best route to Park Avenue and 51st Street, where I was to meet Peter at the Racquet and Tennis Club. I used to drive a cab in New York and always tried to help other drivers beat the traffic.

That night, October 12, 1983, was the second time I'd been in the Racquet Club, both times as Peter's guest. The first was in June, four months earlier. The three-story building resembled a bank, with its marble facade, high arched windows, and second-story columns defending a small patio overlooking Park Avenue. It was an elegant relic of old New York imbedded in a neighborhood of glass and steel high-rises. The gray stone was streaked with decades of urban soot. On my previous visit I had scanned a list of past and present members on a large plaque that hung in the lobby. I thought I might recognize a few captains of industry or maybe some Wall Street characters I knew from my work on the column. None rang a bell, but I noted there were one or two names I would identify as Jewish-sounding; I assumed they were descendants of German Protestants. It's the kind of thing a Jewish reporter would notice about an old exclusive men's club.

The Racquet Club was a prosperous village of ruddy-faced gentlemen, tucked away in a corner of the city. Members could purchase their meals and drinks, socialize with other successful or highborn white men, receive and post mail, send out laundry, store and retrieve personal stocks of cigars and pipe tobacco from a walk-in humidor, sleep, or play a number of indoor sports like squash or tennis without once touching shoe leather to concrete. All in fairy-tale elegance. The rooms and ceilings, including a library full of overstuffed chairs, were of concert-hall proportions. Walls were paneled in dark wood and bathed in a soft yellow light from brass sconces and crystal chandeliers. Broad staircases shouldered by polished wood banisters connected the three floors. A nearly palpable hush that spoke to me of discreet old money and privilege permeated the place. The atmosphere fit Peter like his tailored Brooks Brothers suits and monogrammed shirts.

He sprang from an old green-leather club chair in the lobby when he saw me.

"How you doin', buddy," he said, flashing a half-smile and extending a hand. Peter seasoned his vocabulary with words like "buddy" and "pal," producing a language pattern I found both eccentric and endearing. In another era he would have addressed me as "old sport." Peter was tall, and in close conversation with others he tilted his head forward to speak and to the side to listen. This habit tended to exaggerate the impression of his height and had another distinct advantage as well. He seemed to be intent on what you were saying, to have something to say that he wanted only you to hear. It was an element of my overall fascination with Peter, the kind of fascination adults have with precocious teenagers. Through them we vicariously relive our own youthful fantasies of success, fame, and fortune.

Peter was precocious and more. He was Gatsby: mysterious, charming, with a powerful charisma he could turn upon you like a brilliant spotlight. The beam emanated from that crooked half-smile, lips slightly parted to reveal a row of perfect teeth. That smile projected qualities of reassurance, confidence, and good-humored mischief. When he concentrated all his attention on you, he reflected only the best impression you had of yourself. He was unlike any other Wall Street types I'd met in my work. Most of them either were selling something—their ideas or themselves—or looking to acquire information. I couldn't pigeonhole Peter. Not until that night.

I checked my soft-leather shoulder bag with the cloakroom clerk (I didn't own a raincoat or an overcoat). Peter chattered aimlessly as we climbed to the club's large dining room and bar on the second floor. We settled into a semi-circular banquette on the wall opposite the bar. Each table had a small service bell in the center. Peter rang, and a white-jacketed waiter appeared to take our order.

"So, did you make any money today?" I asked, fishing in my pocket for a cigarette.

"Oh, boy," he said, shaking his head, flashing a half-smile and rubbing his hand across his mouth in contemplation. "It's tough. It's tough. The liquidity in the market is drying up. We're in a plateau in here until the market starts to take off again."

Wall Street buzz words. Liquidity. Plateau. I knew what Peter meant. The stock market, ground down inch by inch in the early 1980s by a devastating recession, awoke from its slumber with a bang in August 1982, just as I was starting my job as a "Heard" columnist. For the next eight or nine months, the law of gravity was repealed. Stock prices rose on a flood of trading volume as investors, big and small, lined up to get a piece of the free money. This record-breaking share volume provided liquidity. In other words, there was a good balance of buyers and sellers so that nobody had to wait very long to get his price on even the largest quantities of stock. Investors who a year earlier were worried about a devastating worldwide depression had turned greedy. Fearful they might miss out on a sure thing, they hungrily snapped up shares of big respectable companies and tiny one-man operations with equal gusto, paying ever higher prices.

By June 1983, just as Peter and I were getting acquainted, the bull was beginning to show early signs of fatigue. Too many people had made too much money in too little time. The smart money, the big boys who play the game all the time, stopped buying and either sat back or started selling and taking profits. The little guys, the individual investors who got to the party late, loaded up on all that expensive stock. When they ran out of money the Dow Jones Average of thirty industrial stocks stopped climbing and began to describe a narrow sawtooth path on a high plateau. The Dow rose or fell in a tight band, nudging and occasionally just poking through its previous highs.

The shares of some *five thousand* companies are traded on U.S. exchanges. Underneath the serene surface of the thirty Dow Industrials in the summer and early fall of 1983 an undertow developed that swept away a big chunk of the profits of many who had invested in smaller high-growth companies. Volume—the liquidity Peter talked about—tapered off. A stock trader who could have sold a barge load of stock in the rising tide of eager buyers a few months earlier now found barely enough water to get his knees wet. If he was in a hurry, the price of his stock had to be discounted, substantially in some cases, to attract buyers.

Peter was convinced that the market would soon reach the other side of this plateau where a fresh tide would again carry prices higher. The Dow had inched ahead to a new high just two days earlier. But he fancied the technology and small-company stocks that had been getting hammered for more than three months. I had interviewed him in August when his favorite stock, Digital Switch, abruptly plunged on a ruling by the Federal Communications Commission about the breakup of AT&T. I had quoted him, anonymously, saying, "If this keeps up, I'll be wiped out." This, I was sure, was just bravado. But it was a great quote befitting a stock that had fallen 42 percent in less than four months. A man about to be wiped out, I thought, has dark circles under his eyes, his hands shake, and he drinks a lot. Peter barely drank, his hands were steady, and he was the picture of health and self-confidence. After all, a man who is literally about to be wiped out doesn't brag about it. It was the kind of inspired superlative I expected from a rich young stockbroker who'd had a couple of bad days in the market and saw his net worth drop a few hundred thousand.

Peter and I chatted in the Racquet Club lounge about the market until our drinks arrived, mine Campari and soda, his a domestic low-calorie beer. Then, almost imperceptibly, like a sailboat coming about in a mild breeze on a calm ocean, the direction of the conversation shifted.

"So, how is it writing the 'Heard' column?" Peter asked. "Do you like what you're doing?"

"In some ways it's as though I died and went to heaven." Just two and a half years earlier I had been working in the "slave pit" at the *Trentonian*, a small daily tabloid newspaper in Trenton, New Jersey, writing up obituaries and rewriting press releases. I had burned out on small-town newspapers and especially at this one where I had long ago exhausted the challenge. I hadn't known nor cared to know the difference between a stock and a bond in those days. But I took a job at Dow Jones (which owns the *Journal*) on a whim and, overnight, found myself intimate with the gospel of capital formation. I had been forced to learn such unfamiliar terms as dividends, price-earnings ratios, and net income. Now I was a fly on the wall of possibly the biggest crap game in the world and I loved it.

"The column is the most exciting job I've ever had," I said. It was something different every day, I explained. Instead of covering the same personalities at the same government agency or corporation every day like I had in previous jobs, I now bumped into a completely fresh set of facts and characters with each column. "There's something exciting and intriguing about the markets that I find hard to explain. Maybe it's real people playing hardball with real money. The pressure is intense."

"And you're terrific at it," he offered. "Like the column on Apple Computer. You were right on top of the action in the stock while it was happening."

I had spoken to Peter a month or so earlier when I was tracking the spoor of the Apple story. The stock had been hit by panic selling that trimmed the price by as much as 12 percent in a few hours. The sell-off followed a gloomy profit forecast issued that morning by an analyst at Hambrecht & Quist, the San Francisco-based securities firm thought to have the inside story on Apple. Peter and I had talked on the phone that day about Apple, noting the violent swing in the price. The next day he called to tell me that, by coincidence, he had been short the stock.* As we sipped our drinks in the Racquet Club, he reminded me of this happy conjunction of interests.

"That was incredible. We talked on the phone that day about Apple and a bunch of things. I was short the stock. And the next day there it is in the column. I laughed when I saw the paper."

Apple's price sank again the day my column appeared and Peter was able to buy back, or "cover," his short sale at a profit. He linked the column to the price action.

"That's a tremendous amount of responsibility you have writing that column," Peter said. "You have a lot of power. Look what happened to Apple. A lot of people read that column and follow it."

The *Journal*'s readership surveys found that about half of the six million or so daily readers start with the stock market columns on the next-to-last page of the paper. These include the "Heard on the Street," which was must reading each morning among Wall Street professionals because of its perceived clout in the market.

The Racquet Club lounge was nearly empty. Pairs of older men in dark suits sipping highballs occupied just two other tables. Peter's booming, enthusiastic voice seemed to ricochet around the cavernous room.

"Yeah, it's mainly a lot of hard work," I said. My radar was picking up an unusual vector to the conversation and I grew wary. Many sources asked me the standard questions about myself— professional background, wife, kids, and stuff like that. Sometimes

---

*To short stock means to sell shares you don't own—to be "out of" or short the stock (as opposed to buying or being "long" the stock). It is a common and accepted way of betting that a stock price will fall. The short-seller's account is credited with the sale of shares he borrows, usually from his brokerage firm. If he is right and the stock price declines he can buy the stock in the open market at a lower price, return the borrowed shares, and pocket the difference. It is probably the riskiest of all investments. In theory, at least, a stock price can rise to infinity instead of falling. If an investor is short the stock and it rises instead, he may ultimately have to buy the stock and take a loss. An investor who buys a stock risks losing his entire investment—100%—but no more. An investor who shorts a stock that triples, for example, shows a loss equal to twice his original investment with unlimited potential for added losses.

I lied and said that I was a single. It was easier than explaining the relationship I had been in for ten years. Sometimes I told the truth. None of the many people I spoke to as sources for the "Heard" column had ever quizzed me like this about its power. It was kind of unseemly. The subject made me a little uneasy. I never imagined myself a genius, either as a reporter or a stock-picker. The column tried to follow the action in the market as closely and as quickly as possible. If Apple started sinking fast, we tried to ferret out why people were trashing the stock and say so in the column. Sometimes we were right and sometimes we shot ourselves in the foot. Mainly I suffered a raging case of self-doubt about my abilities. After all, I had no training in finance and less than three years' experience covering the markets.

The "power" I enjoyed was the same gratification that marries most reporters to their work: I got a real bang out of seeing my name in bold print at the top of my stories. It was nice to know, since I wasn't getting rich and didn't expect to in the newspaper business, that maybe a couple million people around the world at least glanced at what I wrote.

Like Peter, many of the sources with whom I spoke when I was reporting on a stock for the column imagined they had made money on the impact they believed the "Heard" had on stock prices. Often enough stock prices fell the morning a negative column appeared and vice versa. I didn't begrudge these people their profits. After all, they took the risk and there were no guarantees that the investing public would see wisdom in the points of view expressed in our columns.

"What are they paying you to write the column?"

Another question I had never been asked by a source. As a reporter it often was my job to ask people personal questions about their finances. This was the first time the tables had been turned. I had nothing to hide.

"I think it works out to about $28,000 a year or something like that," I said. "This isn't a get-rich business."

"That's all?" he asked. His eyes widened and he shook his head. "Oh boy, that's terrible! How can they do that?"

"Well, I'm not thrilled about it but that's the way the paper works. The *Journal* hires a lot of youngsters out of college for cheap and molds them in its image. They can do it because a lot of them would happily work at the *Journal* for free. It's the top of the newspaper heap. The other guy who I write the column with makes a lot more but I'm the new boy on the block. Besides," I said, "it's great training for something else. Lots of *Journal* reporters leave after a couple of years to make real money in other lines of work."

I told Peter I had been in San Francisco the month before at an investment conference. A senior partner at one of the firms out there told me to come and see him in a year about a job. He said I could write and edit research reports. I assumed the pay would be spectacular.

In fact, I had begun to think seriously about a career move. I hadn't done anything about it, but the invitation to San Francisco had intrigued me and ideas were beginning to roll around in my head. I didn't admit it to Peter, but I was pretty miserable about my salary, which, by New York City standards, made me feel like a college student. I knew plenty of people in New York paying $1,000 to $1,500 a month—50 percent and more of their income— to live in a tiny, bug-infested studio with a view through a grimy window of a brick wall streaked with pigeon droppings. New York is a great place to be a millionaire stockbroker or a schizophrenic homeless person. It offers those in between a smorgasbord of unaffordable delights, from Broadway shows that cost fifty dollars a seat to nightclubs where a beer could set you back five bucks.

Earlier that year an executive recruiter had tried to talk me into writing about tax shelters for E. F. Hutton for $60,000 a year. The work sounded deadly boring and I never seriously considered it.

The pace of cowriting the column was punishing. Other reporters wrote stories when news broke on their beats. On off days, they did their laundry or worked on feature stories. But the "Heard" was a hungry beast that had to be fed every day, whether or not I had clean underwear or the face of history had changed. I started most days at breakfast with a source in some overpriced hotel restaurant, and most days ended late. My constant companion was fear—that one day at deadline I'd have nothing to write about.

Peter's next words are burned into my memory like a cattle brand. "You know, we could make a lot of money," he boomed, "if I

knew the day before what was going to be in the column." The
half-smile dissolved into a mischievous, crooked grin that was
conspiratorial and seductive.

Whenever I am embarrassed or caught off guard like that I
react by laughing—like the time I was driving a taxi in New York in
the mid-1970s and a well-dressed man got in the cab and asked me
if he could pull down his pants and ride around until the meter
reached ten dollars. I laughed at him and said, "Hop in!"

This occasion hit me as no less outrageous. I laughed and
reached for another cigarette. I had been cowriting the "Heard"
column for more than a year. I knew that sources sometimes
speculated on what we were going to write about the next day. I
also knew that some of them would have done backflips to know in
advance. It was the stuff of fantasy, like having your own time
machine, roughly the equivalent in their minds of knowing the
winning horse in the fifth race at Belmont before post time. Peter
was the first person I'd met with the nerve to talk about it out loud.

What he was suggesting, however, was even more outrageous
than a man in a suit riding around in the back seat of a cab with his
pants around his ankles. For one thing, my editor had verbally
cuffed me early on for innocently telling sources the nature of the
columns I planned to write. He had overheard me on the phone
doing what I used to do before I covered the stock market—telling
the person I was interviewing the nature and content of my story. I
thought I'd get a better interview and more specific commentary.
But the *Journal* wanted to avoid anyone knowing in advance what
would be in the paper. At times this was impossible. There
frequently were rumors in the market about stories in the hopper at
Forbes or some other publication and the rumors usually proved to
be accurate. Secrets have a short life expectancy on Wall Street.
News or gossip that might affect a stock price is worth too much
money fresh, and too little stale, to hold on to it. I was sure of a
couple of instances where sources ran out and bought or sold stock
because my half-hour interview of them convinced them a story
was coming.

Peter's thinly-veiled invitation should have offended me. Reporters aren't supposed to accept even a bottle of booze at Christmas let alone cloak an undisclosed interest in the things they write
about, although it happens often enough. George Will, the conservative columnist, wrote a piece praising Ronald Reagan for his

performance in an election debate with Jimmy Carter. He didn't tell his readers that he had helped Reagan prepare for the debate. He might have written the column the same way had he not been Reagan's adviser. But since he was, he had an obligation to his readers to disclose his interest so they could evaluate his argument while in possession of all the facts.

I sat on the banquette stunned and spellbound, nervously picking at a seam in the upholstery. But I wasn't offended, and my embarrassed laughter only emboldened Peter.

"Look," he said, leaning closer to me, "if I knew the day before which stock you're writing up, I buy or sell and the next day we close the transaction and clip a quarter or a half point."

His husky voice grew evangelical. He had been giving my ego the stroking of its life and it felt great. Peter was never a more romantic figure in my professional life than he was that night: younger, more handsome, and richer than most of my Wall Street contacts. He was one of the few with whom I imagined I could identify. He was a person I could have become. We were contemporaries, although I was four years older and certainly not in his financial league. I got a kind of perverse pleasure out of the irony of this: being courted by someone who clearly needed nothing. It was part of the overall perversity that would come to dominate and consume our friendship. I envied Peter, mature beyond his years, driven by unblinking self-confidence and singularity of purpose. I wanted to be close to his light, to let its glow fall on me.

"Wouldn't you like to be a millionaire?"

"Sure," I said. Stupid question.

"It's simple, no problem. We'll both become millionaires." A sheepish look flitted across his face. "Well," he said, half apologetically, "I'm already a millionaire. But you'll become one too. Then you won't have to ride around in subways or buses with other people."

It had occurred to me that a whole lot of people were making a whole lot of money on Wall Street and that I wasn't one of them. I'd heard a few months earlier that a *Journal* editor had purchased a $400,000 co-op apartment for cash with profits from stock trading. I was mesmerized by the possibilities and curious to learn more of the mystery of Peter and the stock market. His proposal triggered no ethical skirmish in my mind. I knew it was wrong. I wanted to hear more but Peter's loud voice was making me jumpy. He might as well have been screaming at the top of his lungs in the *Journal* newsroom.

"Peter," I hissed, lowering my head and shielding my eyes with my hand. "Keep your voice down for Christ's sake!"

He looked around the room as though realizing for the first time where he was.

"Okay, okay. But what do you think?" The half-smile again. I laughed. "Uh, look," I said, "this isn't the place for this kind of conversation. And I don't know what I think. Let me give it some private time and, uh, we can talk again."

"I understand," he said. The smile retreated. "Let's do this. You'll come out to my house this weekend, meet my wife, and we'll talk about it some more. Okay?"

"Sure."

Peter signed the chit for the drinks and we walked down the stairs.

"I'll have Ricardo drive you home."

"That's kind of out of your way, isn't it?" I said. I had a sudden need to be by myself where I could absorb these new facts and think things through.

"No, no. The weather's lousy. I can't fly home. I'm going to stay at my apartment in town tonight. I'll just drop you off at home."

As the car glided downtown on the wet streets, Peter hammered at his basic points.

"Look, we'll make a few million dollars so I can open my own firm. Then you'll leave the *Journal* and come to work for me." This intrigued me. The column was a great job but it didn't entirely satisfy my curiosity about how Wall Street really works. This was sounding like a painless way to find out. With a little luck, I thought Peter might give my career a major new direction.

He did, but I had no idea how dramatic that new direction would prove.

My apartment was on a crumbling block of six-story tenements on East 14th Street, about a quarter of which were, or should have been, boarded up. A small community of drug dealers sold five- and ten-dollar packets of marijuana and a half-dozen shopworn prostitutes worked the sidewalks at all hours of the day and night. The pot dealers were the most aggressive and at night, from my living-room window, I could see them working the pedestrian traffic and dealing to cab drivers, college students driving late-model family sedans, and an occasional limousine that pulled up to the curb. The dealers vigorously competed with each other, chasing and ganging up like harpies on any car that showed signs of slowing, shouting their sales pitches at the driver through the closed window.

Ricardo guided the limousine to a halt in front of my building, across from a porno theater. A half-dozen scruffy-looking dealers sprinted down the middle of the street shouting at the car. Ricardo, a thin wiry Puerto Rican, cast a worried look at me over his shoulder, his big eyes bulging. I laughed.

"It's okay. They think you're here to buy dope. Just ignore them." Ricardo got out to open the door and the disappointed dealers retreated, muttering obscenities.

"You want me to send Ricardo to pick you up when you come out this weekend?"

"Nah," I said backing away from the car. "I've got a car. I'll drive myself. I'll call you for directions. Talk to you then." They drove off and I turned, searching in my briefcase for my house keys. A disheveled sack of a man with filthy long hair, dressed in clothes so dirty I couldn't identify the original colors, was pissing on the wall next to my door. I shoved the key into the lock and went inside.

2

Main Street to Wall Street

At *The Wall Street Journal*, we believe that building
a dream takes more than luck and hard work. It
also takes knowledge, the knowledge of what tomorrow holds today.

—from a *Journal* television advertisement

A good reporter is instinctively curious. He has a compulsion to
uncover secrets. It's that way in the stock market, too. The ultimate
goal in either setting is to acquire knowledge ahead of the pack.
Such curiosity was a strong force in me.

But what got me to the *Journal* was a dream to be a famous
newsman, an instinct for what makes a good story, and a few lucky
breaks. I busted out of college after twice trying to finish my
freshman year. The closest I came to the New York Stock Exchange before I worked for Dow Jones was one day when I got lost
on Wall Street and noticed a dozen limousines parked at the curbs
at crazy angles—like jackstraws.

My parents struggled as dairy farmers until 1955. I was six
years old when milk prices collapsed under the weight of a glut and
my parents had to sell the cows and give up their dream. We moved
into a ranch house my mother and father designed and mostly built
with their own hands.

16

I am proud of my parents. They were survivors and they were modern, openhearted people. My father had kayaked and tramped all over the Adirondacks. He read philosophy and had consumed all the volumes of the Durant series, *The Story of Civilization*. My mother was just as comfortable with a saw and hammer as she was with a flour sifter. She took a career job as a bookkeeper when my brother and I were still in elementary school. Later my parents bought a small business that imported smoking pipes and smokers' accessories, and they ran it together for about fifteen years.

My first and only other brush with the law was the winter I was fourteen. I stole cars. Well, I didn't really steal them, I just borrowed them in the middle of the night—without asking. I was infatuated with driving cars. They were magic carpets I controlled and in which I could escape the feelings of isolation and alienation that bedeviled me. People still left their front doors unlocked and the keys in the ignitions in 1962. I'd sneak out my window in the middle of the night and find a car in someone's driveway. I borrowed about a half-dozen cars that winter, drove around for an hour or so each time and returned them exactly where I'd found them. The smell of a car made my blood quicken, as did the feel of the steering wheel. The next to last car I borrowed was a Ford Fairlane parked at a neighboring farm. I got bored after an hour or so tooling around the country roads and parked it on a side street in our little town two miles away. Then I borrowed a Corvair I'd had my eye on. It started to snow. I was ready to return the Corvair but as I approached the house where it belonged, I could see the porch light was on. Then I noticed a patrol car parked out front and two cops standing on the porch talking to someone through the door. I gunned the car and it fishtailed on the slippery road. I hit the brake and it swerved to the right, skidding to a halt at the curb. The cops spotted me, ran for their car, and gave chase. I bolted from the Corvair as soon as it stopped sliding and ran like hell up a hill to the train station. I huddled under a freight car most of the night, listening and watching the snow deepen. Finally I screwed up my courage and crawled the two miles home in the snow on my hands and knees. On the way I put the keys to the Ford in the owner's mailbox.

I read the local paper for weeks after looking for some mention of the mad car thief of Doylestown but the press was silent. I carried this secret around for sixteen years before I could tell anyone about it.

My dream of becoming a famous reporter began the day President Kennedy was shot. I was fifteen. With the rest of the world I stayed glued to the television and to my radio listening to the electrifying, authoritative voices of Walter Cronkite, Douglas Edwards, and Roger Mudd. These guys witnessed history in the making, firsthand and up close. I couldn't imagine anything more exciting. I borrowed a tape recorder and read *The New York Times* aloud to see how I sounded. I helped launch a newspaper at my high school and won a reputation for being a rabble-rouser.

College was a disaster, a year or so floundering around at McGill University in Montreal where I overslept, skipped classes, and socialized with a clutch of West Indian kids who played Ping-Pong or snooker in their spare time. When they were away at classes, I decamped to the college radio station where I occasionally wrote scripts with clumsy sexual innuendos imbedded in them.

I gave up on school in November of my second attempt to finish my freshman year, came back home to Pennsylvania, and started my news career at the hometown paper, the *Doylestown Daily Intelligencer*.

My first big story was a house fire. I was standing in front of the burning house when two volunteer firemen dragged a body out of the front door and dumped it at my feet. I jumped back. The skin was charred, the clothing burned, and little wisps of smoke rose from the corpse. This was my first face-to-face meeting with death, and I shook as I drove back to the office. But as spooky as the image was, an image that, to this day, is still fresh in my memory, this was why I wanted to be a reporter: to see and experience elements of life, and death, that most people only read about. I was being paid to do something I would have done for free.

I spent the first year or so of my news career covering fires as well as local school boards, sewer commissions, and planning boards. The work was usually dull, punctuated every so often by an hysterical group of taxpayers bearing petitions about leaf collection, sewer rates, dirty-book stores, American flags left out in the rain, traffic lights, Communists, trucks parked overnight on residential streets, and vandalism.

From the *Intelligencer*, I moved to another paper nearby—the

Courier Times in Levittown, Pennsylvania. Back then, reporting jobs were a cheap and abundant commodity, requiring little of applicants at most small-town newspapers—four years of gym and a set of car keys usually fit the bill. The editors sent me out about a half-dozen times to interview families whose sons and husbands had died in Vietnam. These actually were choice assignments but I approached them with pounding anxiety. Also, there was something singularly obnoxious about asking people how they felt upon learning their men were dead. But some of these people wanted to talk and I discovered that seeing their men memorialized in print helped give meaning and purpose to their grief.

A bout of oversleeping at my next newspaper job, in New Jersey at the *Trenton Times*, and an inaccuracy (I misquoted a public official) got me bounced to the graveyard shift, 7 P.M. to 3 A.M. I left and spent a couple of years bumming around the country, working here and there at odd jobs and on newspapers.

My parents had purchased their tobacco and smoking-pipe business by then, and in 1970 I accepted their invitation to join them as a salesman.

It wasn't until 1972, at the age of twenty-three, that I met someone who introduced me, practically overnight, to my true identity. I suddenly realized that I was gay and that's why I had been so clumsy around women. By 1974 I had set up house with David Carpenter, seventh son of fourteen children born to an Oregon logger and his wife. We met in Portland, Oregon, during a visit I made while I still worked for my parents. We lived together for 12 of the next 13 years.

I extricated myself from the family business in mid-1974 a very different person from the one who'd gone to work for his parents nearly four years earlier. By now, I had found the truth of my sexuality and was determined somehow to pick up the loose threads of my truncated writing career. I began half-heartedly to look for writing work. The job market for reporters had tightened up after Watergate and my prospects seemed dim. In the meantime, I took odd jobs: as a waiter, as a credit manager, and as a New York City cabdriver.

It took me more than three years to pull it off but finally, in the fall of 1977, I found myself in a newsroom. It was in Trenton again, only this time I was hired by the other newspaper in town, the

Trentonian. My first choice had been to work for my alma mater, but I didn't have the pedigree any longer for the *Trenton Times*. It had come to fancy itself as a small-town *New York Times* since its acquisition by the *Washington Post*, the paper credited with breaking the Watergate story and glamorizing the profession. The *Trentonian*, a spicy tabloid whose stories carried such screaming banner headlines as "Mom Knifed, Eaten," hired me to cover the Trenton school board.

The paper, like the town that it served, was as colorful and feisty as its headlines. I arrived at the end of the *Trentonian*'s golden age, a several-year period during which a dynamic and innovative managing editor, Gil Spencer, had elevated the quality of the staff and the paper and won for himself, and the *Trentonian*'s reputation, a Pulitzer Prize for editorial writing. I just missed working for Spencer, who went on to manage the *Philadelphia Daily News* and, some years later, the *New York Daily News*. But his handprint was everywhere: the news staff was young, enthusiastic, and irreverent. The writing was bright and inspired. The reporting was aggressive. The place had a real harmony to it. I attacked my first newspaper job in seven years with fanatic fervor, glad to be back in the action and determined to make up for the time I had lost.

The next three and a half years I spent covering mostly local news, a few statewide developments, and an occasional national story. My beats included the city schools, city government, county government, and the courts. I discovered how much I hated covering esoteric and speculative subjects like politics and how much I enjoyed writing about people in dramatic situations, particularly those involving crime and punishment. The reporters at both newspapers in town jostled each other for the best story or the best angle on a story. I learned I had good instincts for what makes news and sometimes could spot it before the next guy.

These skills served me well in Trenton, but after a couple of years my mind began to wander. The bright and talented people who formed the core of the newsroom when I arrived began to leave for other jobs. The new managing editor showed little interest in incisive, aggressive reporting and tight writing. He seemed to prefer hiring local people he knew, cronies and older reporters who had lost interest in changing the face of history and were content to lie back and coast the rest of their careers. The best and the brightest worked down the street at the *Post*'s satellite, the *Trenton Times*.

The *Trentonian* staff was gradually converted until all of the old professional camaraderie had been extinguished. The paper added just two major new features while I was there, and they symbolized its emasculation: a section of homemade photos of local residents on their vacation, called "Neighbors"; and a similar photo section for their furry friends, called "Pets on Parade." The *Trentonian* surrendered any pretension to greatness or to exerting influence outside its circulation area.

But not me. Instead of looking for a full-time job somewhere else, I wrote stories for other more prestigious publications in my spare time. A couple of *Trentonian* reporters were already doing this and I mainly copied them with one important difference: I aimed a little higher and eventually got my stuff printed regularly in the *New York Times*. I also earned extra money selling stories to other newspapers, including the *Philadelphia Daily News*. The extra money was great; my salary at the *Trentonian* was about $14,000 a year. But the recognition was more important than the dough. It gave me a big thrill on Sunday mornings to open the New Jersey section of the *New York Times* and see my byline printed there on the first page. These stories would carry a lot of weight in future job interviews and help balance the scandalous tone and subject matter of my *Trentonian* stories.

By the fall of 1980, my search for a new job was in full swing. There had been a dramatic change in my personal life: David had moved back to Oregon after his father's death, and I was single for the first time in years. The *Trentonian* had a new city editor whose idea of a hot story was to have me phone the state highway department to find out why the grassy strips in the middle of the interstate were chewed up with tire marks. He once sent me out to find out why his neighbor had removed an American flag from the front lawn. The essence of the news often depended as much on what he'd seen that morning through his windshield on the way to work as it did on developments of real interest to the community.

I was thirty-two years old. Some of my journalist friends had graduated to big incomes at metropolitan newspapers, national magazines, or wire-service bureaus in exotic places like Moscow. I felt like the class retard. My best journalist friend sent me a photograph of herself boozing it up; on the back she had written, "Remember, this is the 80s when our ships come in." It was beginning to look like mine had run aground and I'd have to swim out to meet it.

New York seemed to hold the solution. There a stagnant career could get moving again. It would be easy to meet interesting people, my lifestyle wouldn't be judged, and a cultural fix would always be just a subway token away, twenty-four hours a day.

New York also was the center of the news universe, home to *The New York Times*, the three major television networks, several international newswire services, and the publishing industry. I was sure I could find something in writing to support me. I even mentally prepared myself to quit the news business altogether and try public relations. I lacked the pedigree to get a job at the *Times* or the *New York Daily News*, the *New York Post* was just an overgrown *Trentonian*, and I had no credentials for broadcast journalism. Business journalism was a specialty I knew absolutely nothing about. But, on a whim, I contacted *The Wall Street Journal*. It was a big newspaper and it was in New York. That was enough for me.

My chief aim was to match, at least, the combined total of my weekly income at the *Trentonian* (about $340) and my freelance income ($50 to $100). The long hours seven days a week generating and executing freelance ideas were wearing me out. I pined for one good job I could enjoy that would pay me $450 or $500 a week, the amount I expected I'd need to survive in the city. Even at that I thought I'd have no choice but to live a bohemian lifestyle in a studio in a marginal neighborhood. That had been the story of my life all along anyway. I lived and spent modestly, ate at home most of the time, and bought clothes in army-navy and secondhand stores only when the old ones practically fell off me in threads.

My chances of landing a job with *The Wall Street Journal*, I knew, were puny to none. In November 1980 I mailed a copy of my resume with a couple of samples of my work from *The New York Times* to Stewart Pinkerton, manager of the *Journal*'s New York bureau. I followed it in December with a phone call and, to my shock, won an interview for January 7. The *Journal* had published a front-page feature the preceding April about the Trenton newspaper market. Both Trenton papers gained visibility from the piece, which described Trenton as one of ten fiercely competitive newspapers markets left in the country.

But the *Journal* piece also held the *Trentonian* up to riducule, especially for those new features with the homemade photos. I hoped my *Times* samples would balance out any prejudices Pinkerton might have as a result of the article.

There were no signs in the lobby at 22 Cortlandt Street to suggest that upstairs beat the heart of the largest and most respected daily newspaper in the United States. It took me ten or fifteen minutes just to find the door to the building. The street number was barely visible. The only businesses on the short block were a Woolworth's, a drug store, and a savings bank. Across the street stood a tall black tower, the national headquarters of Merrill Lynch. I'd heard of them.

Upstairs, Pinkerton kept me waiting in the reception area a few minutes, during which I studied the traffic: everyone in business suits, mostly white shirts and short hair, mostly male, mostly white, mostly young. They all looked . . . so intimidatingly together.

A secretary finally showed up to guide me into Pinkerton's office, which opened onto the newsroom. He was built like a bear and had wavy black hair. His face was pleasantly arranged except that the eyes were set a little too close together and, through his glasses, appeared slightly crossed. The skin between his brows would knit up when he spoke. His smile looked more like a grimace. Pinkerton was polite and cordial but distracted. I imagined he was busy as hell, a tough, big-time editor who filled three wastebaskets a day with resumes like mine. The session lasted just a few minutes.

"Your clips look good," he said, flipping through the sheaf of additional samples I'd brought along. "But I don't think you're quite qualified for the *Journal*, at least just yet. And openings are rare these days. But if you like, I'll pass your resume over to the Dow Jones News Service. They need people from time to time and it would be a good place to get some training in business news."

I read into this rejection only a glimmer of hope. This Dow Jones News Service thing sounded vaguely like something I didn't want to do, but my mind was open.

The following Saturday's mail brought a letter, dated the day after my interview with Pinkerton, from Everett Groseclose, managing editor of the Dow Jones News Service.

"I would be interested in chatting with you—although we

have no openings at the moment—about any possible interest on your part for the future." I had a couple of other irons in the fire at the time—a job as a television news researcher, junior public relations writer for the attorney general of New York State, reporter for Associated Press, reporter for a legal newspaper. But I was not a strong candidate for any of these jobs and I was growing impatient to move on.

I called Monday morning and set up an interview with Groseclose for February 2. He turned out to be Pinkerton's opposite. His hair was straight, short-cropped, and a gleaming blond color. His handsome face was distinctive and strong, set off by a square jaw and a warm smile. His deep, commanding voice had a slight drawl that hinted at his Texas upbringing. He smoked a pipe and tilted his chair back. He looked and sounded like a benevolent Dan Rather with blond hair, relaxing off-camera. While Pinkerton seemed too busy shredding resumes to spend more than a few minutes with me, Groseclose rambled at length about his experiences with Dow Jones like a Green Beret waxing sentimental. I asked him more questions than he asked me.

Like most Dow Jones news executives, including Pinkerton, Groseclose was a lifer who had risen through the ranks during his twenty or so years with the company. He hired on as a reporter and was plucked up like a chess piece and moved from time to time among the Journal's outlying bureaus, paying his dues and learning the business in towns like Dallas and Cleveland. He edited copy in New York for a while, including the *Journal's* "Heard on the Street" column when it was written by Dan Dorfman, before Dan defected to *New York* magazine and the *New York Daily News*. Groseclose had just finished a stint as the company's public relations officer. That made him something of an oddity in my eyes because newsmen and public relations people tend to be natural enemies. I wondered how a person could switch between these two careers without being dishonest in one of them. He returned to the news side a few months before I met him by assuming the throne at the news service—known at Dow Jones and around Wall Street as "the ticker" or, among grayer heads on the Street, as the "broadtape" or "news ticker" to distinguish it from the ticker tape on which brokers used to get stock prices. Groseclose said he liked my *New York Times* clippings and we agreed I'd come in for a one-week tryout a month later. I was unsure whether I would keep this appointment. I figured something better would probably come up in the meantime. Also, I would have to use a week's vacation from the *Trentonian*. But he promised to pay me fifty dollars a day, which, when added to my vacation-week check, helped console me. I would have spent that vacation week doing freelance work anyway. And if something did pan out at the ticker, I'd at least get an education in a hot specialty—business news. I'd be more market-able after a spell on the ticker.

After I left my interview with Groseclose, he jotted a private note down on my resume which I saw several years later: "Looks good. Invited him in for tryout. Asked about $. Cited entry level 'A' [from the union contract pay scale]. Hours important to this chap. Is industrious. Will confirm by mail."

The ticker salary scale was a kick in the pants. Entry level "A" provided that I would be paid no more than $379 a week to start, less than the $450 to $500 I thought I would need to survive in New York. It looked as though I'd have to keep on freelancing.

Friends put me up in the city during the tryout week. The pace was frenzied, and I was completely befuddled by the language and the definitions of Wall Street. The ticker looked like a dictation pool, not a news organization. Five or six editors sat around a large doughnut-shaped table called the rim. An impatient, demanding, white-haired editor named Harry, who was built like a fire plug and smoked vile-smelling cigars, sat in the hole of the doughnut—the slot. The rim editors fed him little strips of paper with edges ragged from being torn off the sheet of paper in their typewriters. The strips contained phrases or sentences of stories that were being dictated to them over the phone. Harry sorted the pieces by urgency, performed some last-minute surgery on the headlines, and handed them to a teletype operator for transmission over the wire to subscribers. The lights on some three dozen phone lines pulsed all day long and the bells rarely stopped ringing. The noise was constant. If the phones weren't ringing, the room was domi-nated by the steady grinding sounds of about a dozen teleprinters. Rim editors answered the phones and, on their decrepit manual typewriters, pounded out headlines and stories on plain white three-part carbon sets. (This system has since been replaced by computers.) The phone calls fell into three main categories: stories called in by *Wall Street Journal* reporters; press releases submitted by companies whose stocks traded in the market; and stock ex-change employees reporting market statistics.

Most *Journal* reporters were trained to read their stories to us the way they were supposed to appear on the ticker: headline first, the city of origin (the dateline), and the essential news in the first paragraph. Most items ran four paragraphs or less. The ticker, I quickly learned, is the brainstem of Wall Street through which all of the vital signals pass. Its teleprinters and computer billboards are installed in nearly every brokerage office, stock exchange, and money management firm in this country and in many offices abroad as well. Even the corporate public relations departments at major U.S. companies have a ticker printer grinding away in a corner of their offices.

The ticker's greatest value is in stock trading. Active traders keep one eye on stock prices and the other on the ticker. As soon as the teleprinters type out the first words of a major news headline, decisions are made to buy or sell hundreds of thousands and even millions of dollars of securities. When the ticker prints out "FED CUTS D. . ." stock traders don't wait for the full headline. They already know that the full headline could only be "FED CUTS DISCOUNT RATE." They know it means lower interest rates, and by the time the full headline is printed they are on the phone barking buy and sell orders like field marshals in battle.

Headlines always moved first. Transmission of the balance of the story might be delayed for up to thirty minutes by other breaking news. Speed was essential. Accuracy was holy. An editor at the ticker once observed that there were four qualities to the successful news service editor: Accuracy, Accuracy, Speed, and Accuracy. Investors could, and sometimes did, lose money when a headline was backward, garbled, or inaccurate. Bloopers could be corrected within minutes because the ticker continued to print all day, from 8 A.M. to 6 P.M. But stock prices could gyrate wildly in the space of minutes, even seconds, in response to news.

It was a confusing week. The terminology was foreign, the atmosphere corporate, and the subject matter a big ball of fuzz. Friday of my tryout week I met briefly with Groseclose. He said my work had been up to par and, happily, one of his editors had just decided to quit. He made me an offer.

Groseclose later wrote himself a note:

"Talked to Winans about $379. Said he'd have to look at other salaries and see how it compared. Freelance & Mag. Also, a week's vacation pay unpaid. Call him Monday about offer."

That weekend I debated. I'd been with the *Trentonian* for three and a half years and I wanted my next move to be the right one. I started out wanting to reject the job offer and sought counsel from a few friends. This was the only thing I had going and it wasn't quite what I had in mind. It lacked creativity, it meant a lot of pressure, it paid poorly, and the subject matter promised to be dull. But as the hours passed, it looked pretty good compared with the *Trentonian*. The only interesting story I'd worked on in months was about some clown who claimed he was the Lindbergh baby. It was better than the chewed-up median strip on the interstate—but not by much.

I took the job but without much confidence that it would sustain my interest. I expected that in six months I'd go get a job paying twice as much—writing press releases about venetian blinds or shampoo or some such thing. I took a year's leave of absence from the *Trentonian* just in case New York turned out to be a bomb. One of the editors I knew at *The New York Times* made a gagging sound into the phone when I told him about my new job. "Business," he said, pronouncing the word as though doing so hurt his tongue. "Why the hell do you want to do something boring like that?"

For the first nine months I lived with a friend and his arthritic Great Dane in a semi-demolished apartment he claimed he'd been renovating for ten years or so on the Upper East Side. The plaster walls were riddled with gaping holes that were waiting for light fixtures. The kitchen looked like a men's room in a real busy gas station. Very fine plaster dust of near-archaeological significance gently filtered from the ceilings twenty-four hours a day. He'd lived there like that for years.

Because of New York City's tough housing laws, the rent was artificially cheap. My half came to $120 a month. The landlord had just rented an empty apartment across the hall for $1,500. The bargain housing gave me a breathing spell to get settled, close my apartment in Trenton, and find my own space in New York.

The ticker newsroom was tiny. The doughnut-shaped desk took up most of the space. The rest of the area was devoted to teletype machinery, three or four desks, and a bank of wire machines grinding out mounds of paper—stories scheduled for the *Journal's* next edition, interoffice teletypes, news wires, and tele-printers receiving press releases directly from companies. The whole thing would have fit into a corner of the *Trentonian* newsroom. And it did fit into a tiny alcove of the same floor as *The Wall Street Journal*'s offices. In the company's early days, the roles were reversed.

Two newspapermen, Charles Dow and Edward Jones, started the company in 1882 on Wall Street when they began their service—reporting and composing handwritten stock market news-letters. These "flimsies," as they were called, were hand delivered to subscribers by messenger boys. Later, the newsletters were printed on a hand-cranked press and, in 1897, the company began operating the first news ticker service. Eighty-four years later, the tall branches of *The Wall Street Journal* had long since blocked out the sunlight that used to fall exclusively on the ticker. Yet the news service, in its mundane way, remained a powerful force. It claimed 95 percent of the market for business- and market-news wire services. Reuters, the London-based news agency, was a mere speck in the distance with most of the remaining market share. Reuters was aggressive and the ticker tried hard not to get beaten to the punch on major stories. Nowhere as much as on Wall Street are seconds and minutes so valuable. The trader who gets the latest news a few seconds ahead of the next guy has a potential advantage. The fastest news service was the most valuable one, and Dow Jones jealously guarded its reputation for speed and accuracy. But Reu-ters was nipping at the ticker's heels and even getting there first with some major stories. So Dow Jones indulged in some low-level industrial espionage.

"This is Bill with a bell," the male voice at the other end of the phone said when I picked it up one day.

"What?"

"This is Bill. I've got a bell. Just tell Harry."

"Bill with a bell? What is this, a joke or something?" I muttered. "Harry, some guy here says it's Bill with a bell, what-ever that means."

"That's Bill," Harry said, laconic as always. He liked to make young punks squirm and ask stupid questions. His raised eyebrow said, So, what's the problem?

"Well, um, what is it?" I asked.

"Bill's our spy," Harry said proudly. "He sits in a brokerage office in the neighborhood here and calls us whenever Reuters has a story we didn't."

"What does it mean, 'with a bell'?"

"Oh, that's just when they run a hot story," he said. The ticker also did this. When a major story was being transmitted, the teletype operator would press a button that rang a bell inside all the ticker teleprinters all over the world to let people know that something big was up. One bell meant hot news. The urgency graduated to four bells, which was reserved for presidential assassinations and nuclear war.

"Why don't we just call up Reuters and get a machine put in here?" I asked.

"They won't give it to us," Harry said. "And we won't give one to them either."

That was the easy stuff. I started at the ticker in April 1981 at the beginning of one of the four frenzied periods during the year when most companies report their quarterly earnings. We were deluged with profit reports that appeared on the ticker machines with cryptic headlines that made no sense unless you knew the language of Wall Street.

> *In'tl Armbuster 1st Qtr Net*
> *Cont Ops 36c a shr v 43c*

Translation: International Armbuster Co. says that in the first three months of the year it earned a profit after all its expenses of thirty-six cents multiplied by the total number of shares outstanding (usually in the millions), not including some money it got from the sale of that Florida swampland it was so excited about last year. Last year, in the same three-month period, the company earned a profit of forty-three cents times the total number of shares outstanding.

I turned out to be a quick learner, although I needed hand-holding every step of the way. An error not only was embarrassing but raised the possibility of lawsuits by investors who may have bet the wrong way based on our sloppy editing. I spent weeks working side by side with Jack Hennessy, a patient veteran of the ticker and an irrepressible jokester.

"Give it time," he said when I got frustrated. "After you've been here ten or fifteen years you'll get the nuances of the business. That's what you need. The nuances."

The ticker was the slave galley of the Dow Jones fleet, which included the *Journal*, *Barron's*, *The Asian Wall Street Journal*, and a chain of community dailies. The job required basic secretarial skills: fast typing, good spelling, accuracy—and an ability to take incredible pressure without cracking up. The *Journal* people never really considered it a news operation because of the mechanical nature of what we did: running stories and editing press releases. Most of the ticker editors had little, if any, other news experience and one of them had been the boss's secretary. (She turned out to be the best of the bunch.) That the ticker was no springboard to the *Journal* was made clear to me from the start. It must have been a common frustrated fantasy of ticker employees to dream that they might get to the *Journal* through the servants' entrance. Only one person in recent memory, according to ticker lore, had ever escaped through the invisible iron wall that seemed to separate the ticker from the *Journal*. And he didn't count because he was hired as a consultant, not an editor.

The pressure to transform the confetti we pulled from our typewriters into printed items on the subscribers' teleprinters was intense and manifested itself in every aspect of the operation. We answered the phone, "Ticker!" instead of the longer form, Dow Jones News Service. Relaxing moments between calls were rare— the phone consoles kept winking. This was the first place I'd worked where coworkers rarely spoke to each other. I knew more about some of the *Journal* reporters I talked to on the phone than I did about some of the people with whom I worked shoulder to shoulder.

Harry, who had been with the ticker as long as anyone could remember, was a portrait in tension. If I had an urgent item that needed to run on the wire even as I took it over the phone, Harry would sit across from my station on the rim, his teeth clenched on a cigar, holding out his hand and rubbing his fingers together until I'd fed him the next piece of paper. I remember Harry actually shouting only once or twice. But if I handed him a headline that didn't make sense, he'd gravely shake his head and say very deliberately and very loudly, *"No! No! No!"* Sometimes he'd make some sarcastic inquiry through me of the flustered reporter on the other end of the phone. "This is very nice. Does she *mind* telling us *which* company is going to be acquired?"

Harry gave the ticker its only real color, and even that had a brown or gray feeling to it. At first I found him irritating. But he was almost always right, and I came to appreciate him for his eccentricities. Every payday, for instance, he'd come back from cashing his check (who cashes paychecks anymore?) and methodically count out his money in the middle of the slot, for all of us to see, like a croupier balancing his table receipts at closing time. He'd been doing it at Dow Jones for more years than I'd been alive.

I developed a reputation among those who worked for the ticker for knowing, and inflicting on anyone within earshot, a seamless string of tasteless jokes. They helped break the tension. The sicker they were, the more tension they broke. I heard them over the phone from *Journal* reporters and retold them all day. After a few months I'd built a network of reporters I could always count on for a new gag. An eavesdropper on my phone line would have believed that the Dow Jones News Service had merged with Dial-A-Joke.

Working at the ticker is to business news what living in France is to the French language—a crash course, an immersion program. Pinkerton had been right. It was a great place to learn the nuts and bolts. Before long I'd learned to scan an earnings statement and uncover the bad news hiding in a footnote, where companies hoped reporters and shareholders wouldn't look. I learned to sift through ten pages of public-relations fluff in a minute or two and find the meat of the story. A thousand new bits of information I hadn't cared about acquired dimension, shape, and weight. To varying degrees, individually or in groups, or in combinations, these bits had the power to move stock prices. My curiosity was stoked.

New York, meanwhile, was living up to its promise. Some of the money I saved on rent went toward overhauling my wardrobe. I finally retired the orphaned socks, holey underwear, and dress shirts with frayed collars and missing buttons. I bought the first new pair of dress slacks I'd owned in seven years. I didn't socialize much, but I spent hours riding my bicycle around the city, scouting neighborhoods I thought I could afford. When I had to get out I went to the Village, usually someplace where there was music. But this was all a bonus from the real everyday theater of New York: the sidewalks. I would have been content with the bag people, the vendors, the gorgeous men and women, the sidewalk musicians and the comics. Surrounded by seven million people, not just a few of them off their rockers, I felt more secure than I'd ever felt before.

I had been working on the rim about three months, rapidly

gaining confidence and knowledge and idly musing on what lay in the future, when Groseclose hit me with the answer. The ticker ran general market commentary, written by a senior editor, at the opening and closing bells with an update at midday. Groseclose called me into his office one day and, out of the blue, asked me if I wanted to cover specific market developments and stocks, like the *Journal*'s "Heard on the Street" column.

"I confess I had this in mind when I hired you, Foster," he explained. "But first I wanted to make sure you could handle the basic work. You haven't let me down."

Me? Go head-to-head with the "Heard"? To me those reporters were the gods of the business. One of my jobs each night before I left was to put a headline on the "Heard" and mark it up to run on the ticker first thing the next morning, for our subscribers in the boondocks who couldn't get their copy of the *Journal* until after the stock market opened.

The offer was exactly the kind of challenge I had accepted and learned to relish in Trenton. Competition made my juices flow.

The rim, with its more mundane duties, was still my main obligation. But I spent increasing time on the phone prying investment opinions out of stock analysts at major brokerage firms and writing up their explanations for why the price of International Armbuster shares had just soared five points.

"Well, it looks to me like the P-E was undervalued and the market's just beginning to realize that," an analyst said to me one day.

"Um, okay," I said, pausing. "Uh, look, I hate to sound stupid but . . . what the hell's a P-E?"

This was journalism at its best, learned on the job. Sometimes the less I knew about a subject, and the dumber my questions were, the better my stories turned out. I was never afraid to sound stupid. I was surprised how quickly the pieces of the stock market puzzle fell into place. I only bought two books and neither of them helped me much. One was on the bond market and the other was about stock options. The market, however, was more about instincts, common sense, and psychology. On these levels, it was all starting to make sense to me. Stock prices were all about news and expectations. People bought and sold based on their perceptions of the world around them: interest rates, profits, war, astrology, disasters, elections, weather . . . You name it. News that before had seemed to me static and one-dimensional now could be measured in finite units—dollars and cents. I began to wonder what I had ever found so exciting about covering a fire or a murder.

As part of my education, Groseclose introduced me to Charles Elia, a former *Journal* reporter who wrote the "Heard on the Street" column for many years and, about the time I came to work for the ticker, quit to join a small money management firm in Manhattan. I talked to Charlie first thing nearly every morning. He was kind of a guru to me although it never developed into a real friendship. He was good at pointing out the kinds of developments in the market, and the hidden gossip, that made for good reading each day on the ticker or, for that matter, in the "Heard."

Changes in analysts' profit forecasts or changes in their stock recommendations were the most common kinds of developments I wrote about. An analyst at XYZ Securities would wake up one night in a cold sweat, worried that Armbuster's sales of manure shovels were about to be buried by a wave of cheap Japanese imports. He'd rush to work at 5 A.M., run a few numbers through his computer to back up his thesis, and by 9 A.M. phone his clients—usually banks, pension funds, and insurance companies— to tell them that he thought Armbuster's profits for the year would be lower than he originally forecast. At 10 A.M. with the opening bell on the exchanges, some of his clients and other investors who had heard through the grapevine of the new forecast would be inspired to sell the Armbuster shares they owned, thereby driving down the price of the stock.

Soon after the opening bell on the exchanges, I would notice on my computerized stock-quote machine that Armbuster shares were trading off a point or two in the absence of any news. My job was to canvass analysts who covered the manure-shovel industry, and money managers who invested in it, until I had either hunted down the guilty party or learned another more logical explanation for why the stock was falling. In this example, I would quiz the analyst about his reasons for dropping his profit forecast, interview other analysts expressing the same or contrary opinions, and report what I heard to the ticker's subscribers.

Takeover rumors were the most lively because they involved corporate secrets that had escaped their natural habitat. When Pixelated Semicomputers jumped three points on heavy volume and the market was wild with rumors that Behemoth Corp. was prepared to launch a takeover of Pixelated, I interviewed analysts who followed both companies and reported the rumor, along with their assessment of its probability. Even I was shocked at how accurate these stories sometimes proved to be.

My story reporting speculation that Motorola would acquire Four Phase Systems ran on the ticker several hours before Motorola offered $45 a share for Four Phase and several days after I'd reported that someone had tacked a bullseye on the company.

After eight months working at the ticker I got another lucky break. Each *Journal* bureau has a section called spot news. Working in two-week rotations, spot news reporters were responsible for reporting, checking, and writing the many short items that appear in the *Journal* each day and for phoning stories to the ticker. The *Journal* occasionally invited employees of its other news operations to spend a two-week stint on spot news. It gave the paper a chance to forage on its own estate for fresh talent. Groseclose offered my name, and I spent two weeks on the spot news desk in New York working on the unending stream of boilerplate financial stories that gives the *Journal* its texture. I also wrote a short feature on the discovery of a forgotten nursery full of rare and exotic trees on Long Island. It felt great to be writing for a daily newspaper again.

Spot news introduced me to the dragon lady of the *Journal* newsroom: Georgette Jasen, a short, crisp woman who had the clipped speech and robotic movements of a humorless schoolmarm. She was the kind of editor who nitpicked every line of every story until it fell apart in your hands. She'd stand in front of my typewriter with one hand on her hip and the other clutching the pages of the offending story.

"Foster," she'd say deliberately but without malice, "is it Johnson & Johnson Company, or Johnson & Johnson Corporation, or Johnson & Johnson, Inc.?"

"Foster, this doesn't make *any* sense at all. If you don't understand it, neither will the reader. So call the company back."

She always said it out loud, so everyone within twenty feet of the spot news desk could hear every modulation of her voice. Georgette drove plenty of veteran *Journal* reporters (she was one herself) to the limits of their good humor with her microscopic editing and prissy manners. The real problem with Georgette was that she was so often right. It made her impossible to dismiss or trivialize. She'd have been hard pressed to find a single reporter who ever worked for her whose neck she hadn't saved at least once by catching some stupid error before it got into print. She was perhaps the truest symbol in my mind of what set the *Journal* apart and above all other newspapers. The *Journal* tended to hire, and give on-the-job training to, young and inexperienced reporters, some of them freshly-minted college grads. What saved the *Journal* and these greenhorns from themselves was this army of Georgettes, ex-*Journal* reporters with years of experience and strong memories of their own mistakes. They kept the paper, and everybody in it, alert and out of trouble. When the system worked the way it was supposed to, the *Journal* proved itself to be a model of the right way to report the news, as it did during a railway workers' strike in the upper Midwest some years ago. According to *Journal* lore, a business lobbying group held a press conference at which it claimed that ten thousand employees at businesses served by the railroad were about to be idled by the work stoppage.

While the rest of the news media rushed to press with big headlines reporting the supposed secondary-unemployment effect of the strike, the *Journal* reporter got on the phone and started calling the companies where the pink slips were supposed to be flying. "No layoffs here," he heard over and over. The *Journal* made its competitors look like fools.

After two months of getting up at 6 A.M. every Wednesday to get an early shot at the rental ads in the *Village Voice*, I finally found my own place, a clean, one-bedroom apartment. It was in a safe, well-kept building just fifteen minutes from work. But it was on a slummy-looking block of East 14th Street. The rent was a joke, $700 a month. I had paid $300 a month in Trenton for twice the space. But I was grateful to pay it. David was about to return from Oregon and we planned to live together again. Before he arrived, I put him in touch with the supervisor of the *Journal*'s New York communications center about a job. Between the two of us I thought we could earn enough to carry the rent. David moved back in mid-December and went to work a day or two later as a news clerk in the *Journal*'s New York wire room.

Things were looking up. My ship was easing into the dock.

The landlord gave me a sublease for just six months. It had taken me so long to find the place, I dreaded the prospect of having to repeat the process again in a few months. Two weeks before Christmas, tenants of the building hired a lawyer to negotiate with the landlord the terms of a co-op plan he'd proposed for the building. There was talk that some of the leases were illegal and the rents inflated.

The next day my landlord was knocking on my door. By the time he left, he had voluntarily reduced our rent to $450 a month and had given us a full lease that automatically placed us under the umbrella of New York's extensive tenant protection laws: Rent increases were controlled and held down by the government; eviction was time-consuming, costly and the process favored the tenant. We knew we could stay where we were as long as we wanted. Just about everyone in the building received a rent reduction and huge cash rent rebates totaling thousands of dollars. David and I had hit a lucky streak. Between us we were taking home in one week enough to pay a month's rent. We now knew we wouldn't have to move. What more could we have wanted?

The luck held over into the new year. A growing number of my ticker stories were home runs. Stock market news and gossip seemed to suit me and held my attention. The *Journal* editors and "Heard" columnists, most of whom read the ticker every day, couldn't help notice my work, in part because I was picking up items that would have made good "Heard" columns. And I was getting them first, although that had something to do with an unfair advantage: my stories were published as soon as they were written, the same day, and transmitted to all of the ticker's subscribers, including some daily newspapers which competed with the *Journal*. I started kibitzing with the two "Heard" writers and became friendly with one of them, George Anders.

George was the closest living thing I ever encountered to a composite profile of the average *Journal* news person. He came to the *Journal*'s main editing desk in New York fresh from Stanford University. He started as a copy editor and rapidly graduated to writing and editing one of the front-page news summary features, called "World Wide." When I met him in early 1982 he had been writing the "Heard" column with another reporter, Gary Putka, for more than a year.

George once remarked that the *Journal* was staffed by an army of introverted egomaniacs. I knew what he meant, and there was no doubt that he included himself in that description. *Journal* reporters were achievers as a rule, self-confident and self-motivated. Yet they harbored deep-seated fears that they might stumble and cause a monumental mistake that would embarrass themselves and, especially, the paper. It was a fear the *Journal* nurtured. This collective sense of vulnerability helped give the paper a feeling of community and a kind of classlessness. There was no star system that I could see. And even those who rightfully could have been stars neither sought nor received any extraordinary treatment.

I always enjoyed running into George, even if it was only a chance meeting in the hallway. He was a water-cooler philosopher and pundit on the eccentricities of the paper. He was bright, always eager to debate the merits of a possible story idea, and, most importantly, he laughed at my jokes. He had a comically deliberate way about everything he did. George's stiff arms mechanically swung, and he bounced, when he walked down the aisles. He had an excessively formal and polite way of speaking. Instead of saying, "Foster, that's a bunch of cow chips and you know it," he'd say, "I suppose that has merit. But you don't think . . ." You could hear Mrs. Anders telling little George, "If you don't have something nice to say, don't say anything at all." The *Journal* editors were more pointed. They nicknamed him Mr. Spock.

He invited me out for a beer one night after work.

"I suppose you've heard the rumors around here that the company plans to launch a European edition," he said. The gossip had been around but I ignored it. I knew the *Journal* flew domestic copies of the paper to Europe every day. Now the company wanted to publish an edition on European soil with more local news, or so the jungle drums had been saying.

"Well, I've put in my bid for reassignment to Europe, if that should ever prove possible," George said. "Which would mean, of course, that there might be a vacancy on the 'Heard.' Your work on the ticker has been noticed upstairs and I think they could be persuaded that you'd make a good 'Heard' writer."

This was a fantasy too wild even for my imagination. The "Heard" was the premier stock-market gossip column in the world and I had been covering the market in an unsophisticated way for only a year. Yet there was a certain logic to what he was saying. George, after all, had had less reporting experience than I did when he became a "Heard" writer. George carried some clout, or so I thought, with the moguls at the *Journal*. He seemed to have the inside track on most of the major rumors and appeared to be on friendly terms with Norman Pearlstine, the paper's favorite son who was then running the Asian edition.

Pearlstine was marked to launch the European edition and to

become the next managing editor. He was the only *Journal* news employee with real star status. George seemed too cautious a person, too much in touch with office politics, to speculate out loud about his future or mine without some solid inside information.

I pushed myself even harder at the ticker to come up with winning stories. In the spring of 1982, the *Journal* formally announced plans to launch the European edition at the end of the year with Pearlstine at the helm. Norm temporarily was bivouacked in New York plotting his assault, assembling an entourage, and tying up loose ends. I stopped to see him one day to test the water. Norm's office was in a corner off the news desk, his credenza piled with memorabilia of his time in Asia. He was always busy, so I drove right in.

"I've been talking to George about my interest in someday writing the 'Heard' column. I thought I'd check with you to see what your thoughts were on the subject, and whether there was anything I could do to enhance my chances."

"Well," he said, "I've been hearing good things about your work from people I know on the Street. The only advice I can give you is to keep up the good work." The water was warm.

George gave me periodic updates on the European edition schedule and his role in the project. It was looking more and more as though he would be going to London as an editor. Finally, I had to come clean with Groseclose. By now a handful of editors at the *Journal* knew I had designs on George's chair.

"You know I feel kind of funny about all this," I said to Groseclose in his office one day. "You've been good to me. You gave me an opportunity here I had not thought possible, you encouraged me, and now I feel a little like, well, like I might soon be biting the hand that fed me."

"Absolutely not," he said. "I want the ticker to have a reputation as a training ground for the *Journal*. It hasn't had that and it's been hard to get good people to do this kind of work as a result. The impression that people might be able to move ahead in the company helps me attract good editors. Besides, you did the great work, not me."

Groseclose could have sunk my chances by invoking an unwritten Dow Jones rule that divisions don't raid each other's staffs without permission. Instead he treated me like a son—honest yet gentle with criticism, quick to praise when praise was appropriate—and knew when to let me move on.

Events came to a climax in July. The stock market was weak, there was talk of a worldwide depression, and Wall Street was transfixed by the continuing takeover wars among the behemoth oil companies. On the 12th I had lunch with Larry O'Donnell, the *Journal*'s managing editor and a thoroughly inscrutable man who was a ghostly and fleeting presence in the newsroom. I rarely saw him and never quite understood how he occupied himself. It wasn't much of a lunch. He said he'd noticed my work and thought I was doing a good job. I understood from Groseclose and others that this was to be my interview before I could be hired at the *Journal*.

Thursday morning, July 22, ten days after my lunch with O'Donnell, I stepped away from my desk for a few moments. When I came back, I found a note written on a Dow Jones memo pad. The note read:

> Foster—
>   Pls see me.
>   —Stew Pinkerton

The skin on the back of my neck started to tingle. I looked for my jacket and it hit me that I had decided against wearing a tie that morning because of the summer heat.

"Hey, Tom," I said to another editor. "I've got a meeting at the *Journal* and I can't go looking like this. Lend me your tie for a couple of minutes. I'll bring it right back."

He yanked it loose and I sprinted to the bathroom where it took me three tries to match up the ends. I washed my face, took a deep breath, and presented myself at Pinkerton's office door.

He fought back a broad smile, extended his hand, and said, "Welcome to *The Wall Street Journal*."

3

Wild Man of Borneo

So he invented just the sort of Jay Gatsby that a
seventeen-year-old boy would be likely to invent,
and to this conception he was faithful to the end.

—*The Great Gatsby*

He showed an early interest in horses. At the same time that his little pals began to explore new worlds of fast cars, rock music, and drugs, Peter Bornstein was learning about horses—how to ride them, how to care for them, how to bet money on them. As early as his thirteenth summer, he'd tell his mother he was going to the beach. He'd walk down to Main Street instead and catch the bus to Fort Erie Park, a parimutuel track across the Niagara River in Canada. Sometimes he'd talk his friends into going with him and get an older brother to drive them. Once there he'd watch the races and wager his allowance.

He grew up in a dense residential neighborhood of North Buffalo which was populated in the 1950s and 1960s by middle-class Jewish and Italian families whose husbands and fathers were merchants and professional men. The fronts of the houses lined up in neat rows, like boats at a dock, with just enough side yard to squeeze in a driveway and just enough front yard for a small patch of grass and a bush or two.

40

From the outside the house offered little to recommend itself. A small peaked roof over a plain front door served as the sole adornment. Compared with the houses on either side, which sported details like columned porticos and window shutters, the building looked like a cardboard box.

Peter's father, Morton, was an insurance agent in his early twenties when he and his wife Marcia started their family. The first child, Charles Zachary or Chuckie, showed strong artistic inclinations early on. The Bornsteins bought him a baby grand piano on which he became an accomplished pianist and a local celebrity. He had a wild temper that gave way at times to screaming matches with his father.

Peter was the second child and an opposite personality. He seemed to have innate social skills and a passion for nice clothes which he may have inherited from his grandfather, a tailor and Jewish immigrant from Russia. He also had a passion for money.

In addition to his racetrack forays, Peter played poker, although he lost more often than he won. His social group consisted of a half dozen or so Jewish kids, all the same age, who'd grown up together from kindergarten and remained loyal to each other through high school. He was the undisputed risk taker in the group, whether it was stealing candy bars, ringing doorbells and running like hell, or cheating on tests.

From junior high on, when his schoolmates were wearing bell-bottom jeans and knit tops, Peter showed up for school in gray flannel slacks, alligator belt, penny loafers without socks, and button-down Brooks Brothers shirts, bought mail-order, with his monogram—PNB—sewn on the pocket. He kept the top three buttons of his shirt open, a fashion statement his friends used to tease him about. He seemed to always have a wad of cash in his pocket. Once, in junior high, Peter pulled out a roll that contained as much as two hundred dollars. In high school he bought and drove an aging Rolls Royce Silver Cloud with right-hand drive. His Bar Mitzvah was held at one of the better restaurants and was the first Bar Mitzvah in his group with a live band.

"I think none of our group ever doubted that Peter was going to go places," a boyhood friend recalled. "Peter always projected an image of success. Even in third and fourth grades he carried twenty or thirty dollars with him all the time. We never knew where it came from but he always had it. He was a go-getter. Peter always had a plan, a scheme."

He was well liked within the small group, especially for his ready sense of humor and his penchant for clowning. Peter was the kid giving the finger behind the back of the head of someone having his picture taken. He was thought of as a generous and loyal friend. "If you called him at three o'clock in the morning and needed help, he'd be there by the time you hung up," said one.

Peter was bright, his I.Q. well above average. But he was uninterested in school. Friends sometimes helped him cheat on tests he hadn't prepared for. Peter was bold. He'd call out to one of his friends to help him with the answers as soon as the teacher had left the room.

His four years at Bennett High School—a period leading up to his parents' divorce—saw his grades, his attendance, and his teachers' assessment of his motivation track a steady decline. Bennett recorded 64 days absent out of a possible 180 days in his senior year. By the second half of his last year at Bennett in 1970, his grades had sunk to an average of D+, he failed chemistry, and the personality ratings submitted by his teachers painted a picture of a troubled boy with particular problems in his "seriousness of purpose" and "industry." But this was not the Peter Bornstein his friends knew.

Out of school, he was a blur of motion and ambition. He worked after hours during high school in a clothing store in downtown Buffalo and spent long hours working in a stable, exercising horses and teaching himself how to ride. With a friend, he sold leather goods at fairs and flea markets.

For all the time the group spent together, Peter left his friends with the impression he was a loner. He never got close to any of them. Peter moved on his own, way ahead of his peers in every-thing from fashion to his big plans for life, which, by graduation, were somewhat unsettled.

Peter applied to several Eastern colleges in December of his senior year, but ended up at a garment-industry business school in New York called the Tobe-Coburn School for Fashion Careers. His father helped pay for the move to New York, where Peter shared an apartment on the Upper East Side. As part of his retail training, he told his friends, he worked as a clerk at Bloomingdale's.

But the experience was unsatisfying. By the time his parents separated in 1971, Peter was back in Buffalo, working at odd jobs. In February he sent an application to the University of Pennsylvania. That summer he wrecked a friend's car in a late-night crash at an intersection near home. His face hit the steering wheel and his teeth cut through his lip, leaving a small scar.

In November 1971 he applied to Babson College in Wellesley, Massachusetts. In the fall of the following year he loaded his monogrammed Brooks Brothers shirts into his yellow Volkswagen and left his mother's home to start a new life. He would return infrequently, and mainly to take care of small items of personal business.

Peter had barely moved into his room at Babson College in the fall of 1972 when he stumbled onto a game of quarter-stakes poker in the basement of his dormitory. The players were mostly sophomores and were dressed like college kids—painter's pants or jeans, T-shirts, sneakers or bare feet, and long hair. Ken Felis looked up from his cards to inspect the newcomer.

"In walked this guy with not a hair out of place, wearing a monogrammed dress shirt, dress slacks, and Gucci loafers with the little metal buckles," he recalls. "A real slick article. He asked if he could play and he sat down and started betting up a storm. He was winning and we were talking. The guy was funny but he was kind of intense. He went to the bathroom or something and while he was out of the room, some of the other guys started talking like they wanted to skin him. Instead of playing against each other they wanted to all play against him. I said that's bullshit and when Peter came back, the game went on and he and I ended up being the only winners."

Thus began a devoted friendship based on contrast that would last nearly twelve years. Ken was an outdoorsman, one of the boys. He preferred to spend his time shooting a few baskets, skiing, hunting, or tossing around a football. He grew up in the woods, but not the sticks. His family lived in southwestern Connecticut in Fairfield County, a prosperous and heavily-wooded commuting suburb of New York City. His family was descended from Italian immigrants. His father was a professional man, an accountant, and a grandfather was a state judge. To his parents' mild consternation, Ken preferred to work, and play, with his hands. He was a jock, a determined and accomplished athlete with a cherubic face, long dark eyelashes, and facile hands. An ample mop of shiny, jet-black hair framed his round face, full lips, and slightly limpid eyes. He was headstrong and independent but he had common sense. He was popular with the boys, a social leader, and dated the prettiest girl in high school.

Ken also had a soft spot for people in need, a compassion—or a need to be needed—that he sometimes indulged. He was popular and socially secure. He could afford to adopt an occasional outsider he felt sorry for. There was something about Peter that was needy and inspired Ken to run interference for this stranger when his dormmates proposed to rip him off. Ken saw that Peter was out of step and that he wanted to belong.

For his part, Peter couldn't help but recognize that Ken was the leader of this pack. Peter was the new boy in the dorm, and Ken offered friendship and instant access to a social group. Ken would prove a valuable friend and help protect Peter from the more subtle social cruelties, like ganging up on the kid in the weird clothes in a poker game. The interplay of their introduction—Ken's compassion and Peter's neediness—would periodically resurface in their friendship.

When the two players had gathered up their winnings, they headed for the student lounge where they got further acquainted over beers. They discovered that they both had roommates they couldn't tolerate. Peter's was a cowboy type from Texas named Duane. Within three days, Ken had kicked his roommate out and Peter had moved in.

Ken didn't own a suit and had little interest in clothes, other than sweatshirts and jeans. He'd never hung out in New York City, though it was only fifty miles away from home. Peter, who had lived most of his life in Buffalo, appeared to Ken for all the world as though he had been born and raised on Fifth Avenue in Manhattan.

"He moved in and started unpacking all this incredible stuff. He had field glasses because he went to the racetrack all the time. I had never been to a racetrack. He had a money belt that he wore like a shoulder holster. A picture of himself leaning against a Rolls Royce. Alligator wallet. And clothes. A closetful of expensive clothes. It was stuff I and most of my friends had never seen before. And he had wheels, which most of us didn't."

Ken was mesmerized and the friendship blossomed. Peter gave life and breath to a make-believe world Ken had only seen in movies. In return, Ken gave Peter a sense of family and home.

"He was very entertaining to be around," Ken said. "It was a real learning experience. I hadn't even heard of Brooks Brothers before and all of a sudden, Peter had arranged for me to have a Brooks charge account at their store in Boston. I had never had a credit card before and all of a sudden I had charge cards. It wasn't these things that I wanted so much. I wanted the experience of learning about how the other half lived and playing at it myself. It was a game of grown-up."

Ken found that Peter was susceptible to bouts of arrogance that were just shy of being obnoxious. The other students in the clique endured Peter's high-toned ways by making fun of him. They teased him about his clothes and made fun of his name. Ken, however, remained tolerant. What saved Peter in his eyes, and made him entertaining to be around, was Peter's ready sense of humor about his pretensions, a sense of humor he rarely shared with the other students. The arrogance, Ken discovered, was part of an act. It was a preparation for the real world, where posturing and blustering would prove valuable and even necessary if Peter was to fulfill the ambition he then expressed in his clothing, his manners, and his airs.

There was the time they went out to dinner and Peter ordered a bottle of wine.

The two of them drove to Dartmouth for a rare double date—Ken with his high-school sweetheart, Peter with her roommate. Since Ken didn't yet own a suit, Peter had dressed him up in clothes of his own, and they hit the town all decked out and ready for mischief. They ended up in a French restaurant, complete with a maître d' and big prices. All they had with them was Peter's checkbook, and not enough money in the account to pay for one meal let alone four. Peter, with almost reckless perversity, ordered a hideously expensive bottle of wine with dinner. A waiter with a French accent presented the bottle, opened it, and placed the cork in front of him. Peter knew little about wine but he picked up the cork, broke it in two and sniffed it with a look of omniscience on his young face. Ken was uneasy. Peter had a twinkle in his eye that looked like trouble.

Without even tasting the wine the waiter had poured into his glass, Peter announced, "This is no good. Take it back."

"What do you mean, 'this is no good'?" the waiter snorted, regarding this table of teenagers with disdain. Peter repeated himself. "This is no good."

The waiter grabbed Peter's glass, swirled the wine around inside, and took a sip.

"You're out of your mind," he said.

Peter demanded to see the maître d', who poured some of the wine into another glass and tasted it.

"This wine is fine," he declared.

"No, it is not fine," Peter insisted, tilting his head back in a gesture of defiance.

The other diners by now had paused in their meals and were watching the scene unravel. Ken was flushed with embarrassment at what his pal was doing. Peter was demanding a top-notch bottle of wine, about which he knew next to nothing, they were broke, and Peter was making a scene in front of the whole place. Ken slid progressively lower in his chair as the drama mounted.

The maître d' fetched the owner, a woman, who flashed a broad, polite smile and said, "I think it's just a wonderful thing for young people to be interested in wine and have such fine taste." Behind her stood the chagrined waiter, clutching a fresh bottle of wine which he presented to Peter saying, "This is on the house."

"All of a sudden he went from being the bad guy to where everybody in the place was practically rooting for him," Ken said. "You could see the smiles on the faces of the other diners. We paid with the rubber check and somehow figured how to cover it later. That's Peter. That's how he got what he wanted all the years I've known him."

Peter dated infrequently. He seemed awkward around girls and compensated by making fun of them. The Babson men spent most of their social time chasing the rich girls at Pine Manor, a tony women's school near Boston which they nicknamed Pine Mattress. Peter rarely participated in these outings. Instead, he was off by himself, sitting in his room or out with his Wellesley friends, an older group he'd fallen in with. Peter talked about sex a lot but that seemed to be about as far as it got.

Ken liked to party, and he organized a few dances with the girls from Pine Manor at a boat club in Cambridge. Peter again provided Ken with sartorial assistance. When he'd finished, Peter had outfitted Ken with a new wardrobe including two tuxedos and a dinner jacket. The first time Peter attended one of these dances, he went out and bought himself a custom-made double-breasted tuxedo with peaked lapels, shirt, gold studs and cufflinks, which cost $300 or $400, an unthinkable extravagance in Ken's crowd.

Yet the whole time he was at the party Peter stood by himself off to the side, his arms folded in front of him and his head tilted back, talking to no one. He told Ken, "Ah, they're just a bunch of stupid little girls, mongrels." His face was pinched and distorted in an expression of exaggerated or mock disgust that was so comical to look at that Ken burst out laughing which, in turn, set Peter to laughing at himself.

Peter went to few of these events. He often hibernated in his room in a bathrobe and slippers, smoking a pipe and occasionally sipping a glass of Chivas Regal from a bottle he kept on the dresser. He rarely got drunk or shared in the joints or bowls of grass that often made the rounds. A schoolmate with whom he occasionally played squash once encountered him in the local greasy spoon reading *The Wall Street Journal* and gobbling vitamin pills.

"I don't take them for how I feel now," Peter explained. "But I think maybe they'll help me live longer."

His screen hero was Cary Grant, and Peter was convinced that he bore a resemblance to the actor.

In Peter's first year at Babson, he found a chance to profit from his knowledge of race horses. One of his dorm mates, John Gerweck, had an uncle who owned a thoroughbred farm in New Jersey. John was short of cash and talked his uncle into putting him in touch with a horse tipster in New York who called himself Tony Russo. Peter quickly found out about John's connection and demanded that he share Russo's tips. "What's the next race? Who's gonna win?" Peter hammered John until he got the details.

Peter and Ken next organized a pool collected from students in the dorm, and the two of them flew on the shuttle the next Saturday from Boston to LaGuardia Airport in New York and hopped a cab to Belmont. Sure enough, the Russo horse finished in the money and they returned triumphant to Babson, driving down the main street on campus, hanging out the window, waving fistfuls of cash and hooting with joy.

The same thing happened the next Saturday.

By the start of the third week, the skeptics had been converted and were jostling to get in on the free-money caper they'd been passing up. The first two tips had made the group a couple of thousand dollars, and now everyone was throwing cash at Ken and Peter for the next race. But this time when they got down to Belmont, the horse stumbled in the gate and finished far back in the pack.

Peter had bet to win and lost. When he and Ken got back to Babson, Peter hunted John down and proceeded to razz him unmercifully, as though it was on account of his stupidity that the horse didn't win. Some hot tip, he told Gerweck. A couple of nights later, the group was hanging out in the parking lot and Peter was still tormenting John.

"You stupid Polack. You and your stupid, dumb horse tips," Peter sneered, over and over again, his face screwed up in mock disgust.

John, who had been drinking and was feeling a little unsteady, finally snapped.

"I'd just done two great deeds for the guy," John said, "and I wasn't going to take shit from that arrogant bastard anymore." He exploded in a murderous rage, chasing Peter—dressed in his button-down shirt, white pants, and Gucci shoes with metal buckles—around a car in the parking lot. Peter shrank from any sort of violence, and Gerweck looked pretty threatening all flushed with rage. Peter jumped in a car and locked the passenger door. But John got to the driver's door before Peter realized it was unlocked. He shoved his way inside, madly flailing and grabbing at Peter, who escaped. With John huffing and swearing after him, Peter sprinted into the darkness until the only sound was the rhythmic clinking of buckles slapping on a pair of Gucci loafers.

Peter and Ken had their best times together playing a kind of dress-up game. This playacting was part of Peter's self-training program, a willing apprenticeship to success and respectability. Ken treated it like a goof, something he'd never done before. Peter made it fun.

The two of them put on their best clothes, sometimes tuxedos, and on Friday nights drove into Boston where they claimed a couple of seats at the bar of one of Boston's popular restaurants. They were underage but so overdressed that no one questioned them. For good measure, Peter usually slipped the maître d' five bucks.

They'd sit at the bar making up fantastic stories about themselves. They were multimillionaires waiting for some lonely thirty-five-year-old divorcee to show up so they could try to impress her with their stories. She never did but they put on a show anyway for the junior executive crowd that stopped in to unwind at the end of the week.

"We'd be sitting next to these working saps with their collars unbuttoned and their ties loosened and we were all tuned up and ready for action," Ken recalled. "We'd rank on these guys, goof on them like we were above them and talking down to them. Then we'd break up laughing at ourselves and nobody could figure out why we were laughing."

Peter shopped at Brooks Brothers' Boston store and at Paul Stuart, another exclusive men's store. He bought several more pairs of Gucci shoes and amassed an even bigger collection of clothes.

Sometimes, after a credit-card shopping spree and when he was low on cash, he'd have a sale in his room. "I bought a Southwick sports coat from him for $15 that he must have spent $150 for," said a dorm mate. "He lived like a millionaire."

He frequently ate out, rejecting the "garbage" served in the Babson cafeteria. While the rest of the dorm slaved over coin-operated washers and dryers, he sent his laundry out, including his underwear.

He was uninterested in his classes, and a little dense at times about more complex subjects like economics. Babson is a business school with heavy emphasis on entrepreneurial skills. Ken helped Peter with his work sometimes and grew frustrated with Peter's inability to grasp the more esoteric material.

Ken's parents had adopted Peter and he spent most of his holidays and summers with them instead of his own family, which he usually spoke of with derision. The summer between his sophomore and junior year, however, the two men decided to stay in Wellesley. They shared a rented room in the basement of one of the dormitories at Babson and got themselves jobs working at Charlie's Saloon.

Peter worked there first as a busboy and somehow got himself promoted to waiter. He got Ken a job as a busboy so that they could work together. But one day at work, after four or five days of lugging around trays of dirty dishes, Ken went to Peter and said, "This is bullshit. I quit." So they both walked out.

The college employment office immediately found them jobs at Bowmar Instruments, the company that made it big and then flopped in the hand-held calculator business—the Bowmar Brain people. Bowmar wanted a team of accounting students to document its accounts receivable. The company had grown too quickly and one day found itself with $5 million to $7 million of aging receivables. Ken and Peter felt like they'd gone from being busboys to executives overnight.

Ken, the social leader at Babson, also emerged as the leader of the six or so Harvard and Babson students Bowmar hired. They discovered that Bowmar had no system for issuing credits to customers for defective or returned merchandise and that was what most of the accounts receivable represented. The group spent the summer documenting and issuing credit memos.

Peter wasn't all that interested. He collected his paycheck, about $200 a week, but he didn't do much else, comfortable letting Ken cover for him. He'd gone out and bought a couple of Brooks Brothers suits for the job. He showed up for work all decked out like a successful businessman, right down to the gold cufflinks and the Rolex watch, driving his shiny new Buick convertible and looking down his nose at career employees making $20,000 a year, wearing double knits, and trying to raise a family with two or three kids. Peter arrived at work at 10 o'clock instead of 8:30 like the rest of the crew and spent the day reading *The Wall Street Journal*. At lunch he'd lie on a wall in front of the building, still in his suit, sharpening his tan with a reflector tucked under his chin and his face lifted to the sun.

Ken wasn't about to turn in his best friend. Besides, he was mesmerized by Peter's act and the bold contempt he showed for the rest of the working world. Ken saw Peter's goldbricking as just another mannerism that made him interesting.

At the end of their summer assignment, when Bowmar called each student in for an evaluation interview, Peter panicked. "How do you issue a credit?" he asked Ken. Ken covered for him again.

Peter took riding lessons while he was in college at Dana Hall, a private girls' preparatory school about a mile down the road from Babson. Through his brother, Chuckie, who had gone on to distinguish himself at Juilliard and in the music world, Peter met Van Cliburn, the pianist. Peter spent a summer as Van's valet, crisscrossing the country on tour, staying up all night, attending black-tie receptions and dinners, and sleeping during the day. Van later bought him a pair of Gucci riding boots for $1,200 and Peter once showed Ken a check from Van for $10,000 toward his education. He bought a new saddle on which he had installed a brass nameplate with his monogram on it—PNB.

Ken couldn't identify with Peter's hobby but he knew Peter was proud of it. So when Peter begged him to come watch the graduation program at the riding rink, Ken gave in. He watched from the grandstand, sitting among the proud mothers and fathers. The riding students, all of them young girls fourteen or fifteen years old in formal riding gear, paraded around the rink, jumping their mounts over tiny little barriers no more than eighteen inches high.

Then it was Peter's turn, and out of the wings came a tall, strapping college man dressed in a tweed jacket, riding pants, and massive Gucci riding boots, seated on a brand-new top-of-the-line saddle.

"I think he won a ribbon," Ken said, "and was just as proud as he could be. I was laughing but tried not to show it. He was blind to how ridiculous he looked."

Peter was the only one in Ken's crowd who embraced and cultivated a millionaire image. It was the fulcrum of his master plan. Rich people rode horses, played polo, played squash, and wore expensive traditional clothes. He wanted to infiltrate society and this was his way of doing it. He told Ken: "It's fake it till you make it."

Peter never excelled at any of the sports he pursued, which would later include fly-fishing and bird shooting as well as an enduring interest in polo. But he pursued them with driving intensity. As an athlete he was frustrated. He threw wild tantrums, smashing a brand-new racket up against the wall, all red in the face and furious over one point in a squash game with Ken. Then, a minute later, he'd be laughing. He never showed his anger this way with other players. He trusted only Ken.

When Peter ran into a credit squeeze he couldn't solve with a room sale, he invoked his charm, including that seductive and conspiratorial half-smile. He convinced the loan officer at a local bank to lend him the $4,000 or so he needed to buy the Buick convertible he drove to Bowmar. Ken was flabbergasted. Peter talked the credit department at Brooks Brothers into letting him take delivery of three new suits on credit. He convinced the credit manager that he was destined for success and promised that by the time he was a success he would be spending thousands of dollars at Brooks Brothers every year. And he did exactly that.

Peter was bold in just about everything he did. He'd often

catch people off guard with his bluntness and charisma, qualities he had long ago learned could be used to pry what he wanted out of life. He was an earnest and mature young man on the come, a precocious child who had the ability to coax people into doing things for him. He made it personal, as though you were delaying his inevitable success if you didn't help him out and would benefit along with him if you did. He could stimulate an element of compassion in other people, just as he had in Ken.

Peter Bornstein could take his share of ribbing from his dormmates and got it—for his clothes, his arrogance, and his airs. He was able to roll with these punches, especially because he was friends with the leader of the pack, Ken, who never needled him with malice. But Peter had one wound in his psyche that wouldn't heal. His dorm mates discovered it by accident and repeatedly pecked at it when they wanted to torment him.

They made up variations on his name.

First they called him the Wild Man of Borneo, which seemed to bug him a little and gave them the scent of blood. They tried other nicknames until somebody finally hit the jackpot with the one permutation that he couldn't laugh off. They used it repeatedly until Peter Bornstein either lost his composure and started swearing at them or retreated to sulk.

They called him BornJew.

Peter dressed, played, and acted like a wealthy Wasp. The last thing he wanted to be reminded of was his heritage.

In his junior year, which was Ken's last year at Babson, Peter decided to change his name.

When he first mentioned it, Ken knew right away where he got his inspiration. Peter wanted to change it to Brant. Ken recognized the takeoff on the name of Cary Grant, but Peter denied the link. Ken at first thought it was disgraceful for Peter to turn his back on his heritage like that. Ken's great-grandfather left his parents in Italy and emigrated to America during the Industrial Revolution, working in sweat shops. Later he founded a metal plating and polishing operation that prospered well enough to support his family and three more generations after him. Ken was proud of that heritage and couldn't understand Peter's attitude.

"Yeah, *you* can say that," Peter defended himself. "But I'll never get anywhere with this fuckin' name."

They talked about it off and on for weeks until Peter finally convinced Ken that he would never be happy or successful unless he changed his name. Considering where Peter wanted to go—to infiltrate high society and make a lot of money—Ken decided the name change was a good idea after all. Eventually, Peter even had minor flaws on his face repaired by cosmetic surgery—the cut on his lip from the auto accident and a few moles.

By the time Ken graduated in 1975, the end of Peter's junior year, Peter was fast approaching the final stages of his metamorphosis. He had established himself as a young horseman, he had the wardrobe, the car, and the habits he would need to pass undetected among the gentile elite.

The beginning of Peter's senior year saw the start of the separation from his father that still hadn't healed in 1986, more than a decade later. Peter asked Morton, who had gone back to school and become a lawyer, to file the necessary papers to change his last name. In the middle of October 1975, Morton drove downtown to the Erie County Courthouse in Buffalo and filed a petition for Peter to change his name to Brant from Bornstein.

The petition claimed:

> The name is constantly being mispronounced and [Peter] is constantly being asked to spell it, which is annoying; the name is constantly being misspelled and it is a necessity . . . to have a short usable name for the reason that [he] will most likely enter into an executive position in business after completing this last year of college.

On one of the forms, someone accidentally wrote the new name down as Grant (as in Cary), then crossed out the *G* and wrote in a *B* instead. His last name had to start with a *B* since all his clothing and riding gear was already monogrammed PNB.

Morton didn't ask why. He didn't fuss. He just assumed Peter wanted to remove the disability of having a Jewish name. It was a whimpering end to a tenuous relationship. Peter had been so vocal about his hatred for his father that some of his friends wondered if perhaps he had changed his name just to stab Morton in the heart, to hit him where it hurt most.

But Peter told a Babson alumnus that he'd been turned down for membership at an exclusive polo club near Boston because of his Jewish-sounding name and swore, "I'll never let that happen to me again."

Peter N. Brant was accepted in his senior year as a member at the Myopia Hunt Club, a private polo enclave north of Boston where he frequently played on a pony appropriately named Myopia—but not after the club. The horse had been injured in a game and lost the use of one eye. Peter bought it on the cheap from a player who had a stable of prize ponies. The animal, which with full eyesight might have fetched $5,000, Peter was able to buy for under $1,000.

That year he invited his former Boston dorm mates, most of them graduated and out working on their careers, to the Myopia one weekend to see a match. A group of them showed up in high spirits with the makings of a tailgate party. They were cutting up on the sidelines during the match, making jokes about Peter's play ("Look at BornJew!").

When the play brought Peter near his guests in the stands, he craned his neck to see if they were watching. During a break in the game, Peter rode up on his horse and jumped off. His scowling face was flushed.

"Try to behave," he said. "You're embarrassing me. Go home unless you want to just sit there and watch and not say anything. There are a lot of important people here!"

If he hadn't realized it before, it hit like a ton of bricks that day on the polo field: he would have to sever his social ties with Babson—except Ken of course—or risk the constant threat of exposure through an ill-timed slip of the tongue. He had vowed not to let his name stand in his way again. He had worked too hard to polish his new image to allow some wiseguy from Babson to blow it all.

As graduation day approached, Peter abandoned a plan to go into the garment business with a dress manufacturer he'd met through Van Cliburn. At Myopia he was introduced to an executive with the Boston office of Kidder, Peabody & Co., a stodgy old-fashioned Wall Street brokerage firm. He interviewed in the spring and in July 1976 was hired as a sales trainee in the bond department.

The men at Babson, except perhaps Ken, thought Peter would be in for quite a shock when he got out of college. He had no family business to go into. They were pretty sure he'd been living the life of a millionaire on credit and probably was broke.

Where the hell, they thought, does a guy get a job right out of college paying $100,000 a year, which was what they guessed he'd need to pay back his debts and live as well as he had at school.

His dorm mates ended up the ones in shock, though. Inside of three years Peter had passed the $100,000 mark and was on his way to nearly twenty times that.

When he left Babson in 1976, Peter Noel Brant had completely severed his ties with his father, after Morton rejected his request for a temporary allowance of $25 a week.

Peter had few social contacts with women until he finally met one who suited him. Through his part-time work in Wellesley as a salesman in a men's clothing store, he met Lynn Johnson. She was very different from the little girls with cotton-candy brains that Peter had rejected at Pine Manor. She was ten years his senior, in her early thirties, separated from her husband and living on a meager income with her two young children in a tiny cottage in town. Lynn had the understated sensitivities and artistic tastes that Peter associated with old money. She had grown up in an upper-middle-class family in Worcester, Massachusetts, and socially was at ease with the lifestyle to which Peter aspired.

Lynn offered an instant family that, in spite of her unresolved marital problems, might have looked attractive to someone like Peter who was alienated from his real family.

And unlike the young girls his dorm mates knocked themselves out like peacocks to impress, Peter didn't have to strut for Lynn. She was mature and more appreciative of his maturity and youthful charisma. He told Ken she was the most beautiful creature on earth. Her face was plain in some ways: wide-set eyes and a dopey smile. But she had a model's high cheekbones and strong chin. Her wide, well-formed mouth and thick, wavy brown hair gave her a slight resemblance to Jacqueline Onassis.

Peter left Lynn temporarily behind when he graduated from Babson until he could get himself set up at Kidder, Peabody. His starting annual draw against commissions was $11,000.

Peter lived in New York the first few months on the job while he worked his way through the company's orientation program and studied for his broker's license. He also lived for a time in Connecticut with Ken's parents.

Ken, meanwhile, joined his father's accounting firm right after he graduated. After about a year of crunching numbers, Ken decided he wanted more action. He had a client who was in the business of printing pressure-sensitive labels. Ken saw the books and decided he could run a business like that and make more money doing it. After trying to talk Ken out of it, his father staked him to a start-up loan. With additional money he raised elsewhere, Ken opened for business in a rented garage in a neighboring town, much as his great-grandfather had done nearly a century earlier. He slept on a cot in the garage and showered and shaved at a nearby golf club.

He designed his own printing and die-cutting machines and called on customers, taking orders from drug companies and video-game makers for product and identification labels. The business grew and flourished. Ken enjoyed most of all rolling up his sleeves and tinkering with and inventing machines. He retired the tuxedos and suits Peter had helped him buy and dressed instead in jeans and sweatshirts. Even years later, when most of his time was consumed with administrative details, he still visited the press room each morning. He compromised in his dress only when calling on customers—he'd wear a tie and sports jacket.

Ken married his high school sweetheart, Vicki. They bought a house near where they'd grown up, and started filling it with their children.

Peter and Lynn had their hands full. They couldn't marry until Lynn's divorce was final. They wanted to live together but couldn't afford to have the kids with them. Lynn was torn between sending her son and daughter to live in Boson with their father so she could be with Peter or staying put until Peter had established himself and could afford to support them all. They finally lived together with the children in a rented house in Southport, Connecticut, a speck of a New England village on the coast. Peter commuted by train each day with thousands of other working stiffs in a seamless crush of gray suits clutching copies of *The Wall Street Journal*. He hated it, and within a few months they sent the kids back to Boston and moved to New York where they rented a small apartment on the Upper East Side. Later, when Peter was making more money, Lynn was reunited with her children.

Peter hit the ground running at Kidder, Peabody. He already had some solid contacts, wealthy or influential people he'd met at the polo club and through Van Cliburn. But these contacts would take years to cultivate. Peter, for all his charisma, was still just a hot dog fresh out of college. So he worked the phones. In later years, he'd brag about how he sold power company bonds to people he'd never met in places he'd never been nor wanted to go.

Peter widened his leisure interests to include pheasant hunting, another sport of the rich. Ken had hunted most of his life in Connecticut and owned a small collection of shotguns. Peter learned of a private hunting preserve out on Long Island and they made plans to hire a guide for a day of shooting. It was to be Peter's first experience hunting and Ken was going to show him the ropes.

Ken told Peter to go buy himself a shotgun, figuring he'd go to Sears and get himself a sturdy, simple model suitable for a beginner. That would have been too simple for Peter. He had to have the best of everything. Instead he bought an expensive antique shotgun from England. He didn't take into account the fact that the gun was designed and built when people were a little smaller than they are today. The gun was so short that Peter had to tuck his elbows against his rib cage just to aim it.

They met up with the guide on the preserve and, with a bird dog, started tramping through the snow-covered woods. Peter showed up for the hunt dressed like an English lord out for a day of hunting quail on his estate. The dog was leading the three of them down a path in the snow when it suddenly froze, its nose pointed at a bush. Huddled down in the snow beneath it the hunters spotted a pheasant. They trisected a circle surrounding the dog, which was just a couple of feet from the bird.

For the longest moment, nothing moved as they waited for the bird to break cover and fly, which is the only time you're supposed to fire. The only sound was the wind in the trees. Then the bird stood up and looked around. A tremendous roar split the air and the bird blew up in a cloud of feathers. The dog yelped and jumped straight into the air. The guide's eyes were so big they looked like they were about to come shooting out of his head. He looked around wildly, shouting, "What the fuck! What the fuck!"

He and Ken looked at each other and then at each other's guns and then at Peter's gun. A small trail of smoke trickled from the barrel. Ken calmed the guide down and turned to Peter. "What the hell were you doin'?"

Peter lowered his head, shrugged his shoulders, and fought a sheepish grin. "It looked like it was going to run away," he said.

In the post-Babson years, their friendship was altered by family and business life. They only saw each other every few months or so, though they talked frequently on the phone. Peter sought Ken's advice, as he had at Babson, and sometimes Ken volunteered it when he thought Peter had strayed from doing the right thing. Ken repeatedly lectured Peter about the way he treated Lynn and her kids. He was as clumsy a family man as he was a hunter. He rode Lynn's children hard, ragging them unmercifully, especially Todd, the son, for minor infractions. He swore in front of them, a practice Ken condemned with particular passion. "He seemed perfectly oblivious to their needs," Ken said. "He cared but he just didn't know how to show it in a warm, loving way." Ken had a couple of kids of his own by now and he had taken the opposite tack: he had trouble disciplining them at all.

When Ken and Peter did meet, they'd talk for hours about nothing, like a couple of old cronies. They'd spend the day on Ken's boat on Long Island Sound or go golfing and never grow bored with each other's company and complain that the day had ended too soon.

Peter, meanwhile, was taking Kidder, Peabody by storm. After the first year or so his income soared spectacularly. He suffered as other brokers did in market downturns but his commissions consistently put him well above most and sometimes all the rest of the brokers at Kidder. He bought a condominium in Florida, near Palm Beach in polo country. He dabbled in the market himself, but months would go by without his making a single trade in his account. His Rolodex grew fat and he was accepted to membership in New York's exclusive Racquet and Tennis Club.

But even an above-average broker making in the neighborhood of $100,000 a year in good years, paying rents in New York's swankier neighborhoods, indulging himself in horses and horse upkeep, fancy clubs, black-tie socials, Florida real estate, and a family could be described as overextending himself. His future looked bright but he was no millionaire.

His real breakthrough came in mid-1980. In his travels around the polo circuit he played the game at a number of different clubs. At one of these, the Fairfield Hunt Club in Connecticut, he met a young lawyer from New York, David W. C. Clark, who had earned a law degree from Fordham University and passed the New York bar in 1975. The *W* stood for Windsor, a family name, and the *C* for Conger. Clark's pedigree was as blue-blooded as any in the crowd with which Peter mingled. Clark had inherited wealth.

He attended Deerfield Academy, a very private boarding school in Massachusetts, and Columbia University. He traveled in a social group oriented to the New York-Palm Beach axis with strong connections to England and France. His two brothers lived on Florida's Gold Coast, as did his mother, and in 1979 he was admitted to the Florida bar as well. He married a Connecticut debutante named Natalie White, with whom he had two children. He, and members of his family, were listed in *Who's Who*.

Clark and Peter struck up a friendship that grew into a business relationship. By 1978, Clark had introduced Peter to some of his law-firm clients as his "close friend." One of those, a young college student at New York University in his early twenties named Roger Wilson, opened a brokerage account with Peter that year. Wilson's late father, an oil company executive, left Roger a couple of trusts he could draw against, one of them when he reached twenty-one in 1977, and the other at age twenty-five in 1981. Clark handled Roger's legal and trust affairs and, in 1978, suggested he open a trading account with Peter.

The relationship between Peter and Clark continued to grow and took firm root in 1980 when, in February, Clark himself opened an account at Kidder, Peabody. Clark offered Peter a deal: he could have half of any profits the account showed. This violated the rules brokers were supposed to abide by, but they were friends and who was to know? Four months later, in June, Peter's moribund stock account, which had showed no activity through most of the spring of 1980, suddenly looked like an ant hill in a molasses refinery. The account was capitalized with a deposit into it of a check for $25,000. Another $5,000 was added four days later. Still another $25,000 credit appeared on June 18. Oil stocks were hot and he was trading them fast and furious. The pace of trading quickened over the next months with many same-day trades—buying in the morning and selling in the afternoon for a profit of from twenty-five cents to a dollar a share on trades of 500 to 3,000 shares a crack. By June of the following year, the worth of Peter's stock account had swelled to about $700,000 and he was making trades each month of a total value of several million dollars. The same pattern showed up in Clark's account, and the commission revenue Peter was bringing into the firm started to swell.

By mid-1981, the bloom was off the oil business. The shortages that had sent oil prices and oil stocks higher in the 1970s turned into a glut. Peter, who had been on the right side of the action on the way up, got whipsawed on the way down. The value of his account plunged to $380,000. By November 1981 he had pulled more than $100,000 in cash out of the account but the balance had withered to under $190,000.

Simultaneously, something screwy was going on in the trust account Roger Wilson had with Peter. More than a million dollars—about half of his original $2.3 million—was transferred into two of David Clark's accounts. Roger's account statements were automatically sent to Clark, trustee of Roger's estate. Clark now claims he threw his unopened brokerage mail into a drawer and forgot about it. Roger's attention was fixed on his nascent film career, including parts in teen-lust films like *Porky's* and *Porky's II: The Next Day*, and not on his estate. In a lawsuit he filed in 1984, Roger accused Peter and Clark of stealing his inheritance—except for $1.23 that remained in his Kidder account in June, 1983. In that lawsuit Peter claims that Clark, as trustee of the account, authorized these transfers. Clark, in turn, claims Roger okayed them. The lawsuit, which seeks $12 million in damages, remained untried by mid-1986.

In his phone chats with Ken, Peter began bragging that he was making $30,000 to $50,000 a month.

"How the hell can you do that?" Ken asked.

"I've got this client, a lawyer, who told me that if I make money in his account, we would split the profits," Peter said. "We've been making profits."

Peter's name began popping up with increasing frequency in the halls and executive suites at Kidder, Peabody. His commission revenue had grown and he was consistently Kidder's top broker.

The firm's executives began holding Peter up to the troops as an example of the type of broker the firm wanted. Kidder was a creaky old-money firm that catered, in large measure, to the conservative investment goals of the retail carriage trade. Which is another way of saying the firm preferred to choose its clients instead of the other way around. The onset of commission discounting in the mid-1970s caught Kidder poorly prepared and in a state of competitive decline. Peter had all the markings of a messiah. Big-producing brokers like Peter proliferated at more aggressive firms such as E. F. Hutton. Kidder brokers were plodders, accustomed to servicing the stagnant accounts of undemanding and loyal clients like Roger Wilson.

"Peter was held out to us as a star example of what a broker should be," a former salesman in Kidder's Boston office said. "This came from the national sales executives, from the top. But our bosses in Boston didn't agree. It wasn't anything they said but just a feeling that they didn't agree with the glowing characterization of him that was coming out of the firm's New York office."

Reports of Peter's success also filtered back to Babson's alumni office, which occasionally sent Babson seniors who were interested in the investment business to visit Peter in New York. He was usually receptive to these visits, some of which left a strong impression on his young visitors. A former Babson alumni director recalled that one of these visitors reported sitting in Peter's office during a horrendous screaming argument between Peter and his boss, the office manager, over expense vouchers for his car and driver. The office manager was complaining about the cost of it all. And when it was over, the kid said the office manager not only backed down but ended up agreeing the company would pick up the tab.

Peter and Lynn finally married but they did it surreptitiously, slipping off to a justice of the peace one day and then phoning everyone with the news the next morning. In the early 1980s, they moved with her children to Locust Valley on Long Island's North Shore. They rented a small house on the estate of a garment-industry executive. It was a neighborhood steeped in Wall Street history as well as the prestige and mystique of enormous Yankee wealth. Just a few miles away in Glen Cove in 1915, J. P. Morgan, son of the elder Pierpont Morgan, fought off an assassination attempt inside his mansion. The sprawling Woolworth estate, with its maze garden of fragrant boxwood bushes, was being renovated into a corporate headquarters nearby. The lush, rolling terrain was punctuated by monuments to the kings, princes, and robber barons of industry and finance.

"He struck me very much as a young man on the way up, a go-getter, a *quality*-type guy. Lynn was a real charmer," said Robert J. Turner, on whose property Peter and his family lived for about a year. "He had a kind of energy that was impressive. He seemed to be accomplishing what he set out to do. A real eye-opener."

Peter confessed to Turner his ultimate goal—that one day he would become president of Kidder, Peabody. Turner didn't doubt that he could accomplish it.

The Turners collected eighteenth-century sporting art and English furniture, which captured Peter's interest. He continued to play polo and purchased a couple of breeding mares. For all the experience on the field, and all the accoutrements, the word around Locust Valley was that he was "just a horrible player."

He tried to get into the local Piping Rock Club, among the oldest and Waspiest, and perhaps the most exclusive, country club in the nation. He was blackballed, possibly by another Kidder broker with whom Peter had had an argument.

Peter so impressed Turner that Turner opened an account with him in 1982, against the advice of some of his friends in the financial industry who had either met the whiz-kid from Kidder or had heard of him. "My friends felt like he was someone they'd run across before. That he was heading for a fall," Turner said.

Anyone who'd been in the brokerage business for more than fifteen years had run across a Peter Brant before. He was quickly becoming, almost overnight, one of a rare breed called the superbroker—roughly defined as a retail stockbroker generating more than $1 million a year in commissions. A broker doing that kind of business isn't on the phone all day begging his clients to buy or sell stocks. A superbroker almost never takes a nondiscretionary account. Every client must sign a form that, in effect, gives the broker complete discretion over what to buy and sell. To make a lot of money, the superbroker needs a lot of capital, his and his clients. And he needs just one great stock that will make his clients, and himself, rich and establish his reputation as a man with profitable ideas.

Peter found such a stock in early 1982—Digital Switch. He probably heard about it at a cocktail party, or even from one of his secretaries (by now he had two). He told some of his clients, "This stock will change your lifestyle." And it did. He bought huge blocks of Digital Switch and put it in clients' accounts beginning in April 1982. He continued to buy until one day, at his peak, he controlled a huge chunk of the company. The stock soared in a little over a year's time from about $11 a share to a high price of $147, giving a peak value to the stake Peter and his clients owned of more than $50 million.

His good fortune allowed him to buy a house for about $700,000 around the corner from where he was renting in Locust Valley. The two-story Georgian-style frame building sat on a few heavily wooded acres about fifty yards back from a small one-lane road that once was an entrance to an estate. Peter hired a decorator and a contractor—the same ones used by some of the North Shore cognoscenti he now traveled with—to spruce up the place. He spent about $400,000 on the house and had an architect duplicate an old carriage house he'd seen on another estate for use as a garage.

Peter was a huge success at Kidder and he was busy with the New York social life. But he hadn't found a friend in whom he felt he could place the kind of trust he had in Ken. They had remained best pals, in spite of the gaps created by family life and their respective businesses.

Peter made fun of Ken's little business, even though it was generating a big income, and joked that he should pack it in and come to work at Kidder as a stockbroker. He pursued this idea relentlessly but Ken resisted. Peter was convinced that together they could make much more on Wall Street than they could apart. Ken had valuable contacts in Connecticut, people whose accounts he could bring into Kidder. But he wasn't interested. He enjoyed living out in the country, his business was booming, and he knew absolutely nothing about Wall Street.

But as summer approached, Peter grew insistent.

"I really need the help," he said. Peter argued that Ken's presence in the office would free him to prospect for new clients. The market was in the tank but Peter was convinced that it was cocked for a bull market like a loaded gun just waiting for someone to pull the trigger.

"When it goes off," he told Ken, "we'll make millions over-night." He promised Ken 10 percent of his commission revenue until Ken got on his feet. It would be just like the Babson days, only they'd become millionaires and have fun doing it.

Ken thought Peter was exaggerating: maybe $50,000 over-night, which isn't bad work if you can get it. Ken did sort of miss the fun they'd had in school, Peter's restless driving energy and his sense of humor. He also was curious about Wall Street. He'd become a little bored with his business; it was almost running itself and he was making a fantastic living, a few hundred thousand a year. He had a partner now whom he could leave in charge, and Ken could monitor the label business by telephone from New York.

Ken was also just a little curious about what it would be like to wear a suit every day, like his father and grandfather, and to work in a professional environment. He was the oddball of the family, working with his sleeves rolled up. His family had wanted him to be a lawyer or at least an accountant. Yet, when Ken mentioned he was thinking about taking the plunge with Peter, his father tried to talk him out of it.

"I've been doing people's tax returns for twenty years," he said, "and every year I add up the trading losses for them. I've yet to see anybody make money in the market."

On July 19, 1982—exactly six years to the day after Peter went to work for Kidder, Peabody; less than four weeks before the start of one of the most powerful bull markets in history; and two days before Stewart Pinkerton welcomed me to *The Wall Street Journal*—Ken Felis and Peter Brant become roommates again. Only this time they shared a posh office on Park Avenue and the dress-up was for real.

4

Big Time

Reporters know the earnings capacities of the
people they cover. A young bond trader, barely
out of graduate school, receives as much as a
veteran reporter. Some analysts, whom the reporters consider dull-witted, though capable of
providing quotes on the market's action, may be in
the $70,000 class, while hotshot brokers possess-
ing the glibness of sideshow barkers take home
$100,000 and more. In one deal, Felix Rohatyn
can earn more than a reporter does in a few years.
                                   —Robert Sobel, *Inside Wall Street*

Partway through my tour of duty on the ticker, I gave a friend an
idea for an investment—call options on stock of G. D. Searle,
which had just gotten approval from the government to market
Nutrasweet, its patented artificial sweetener. He pocketed a $6,000
profit on a $1,000 stake in just four months. His good fortune was
the first time I'd rubbed shoulders with a real plunge in the market,
as opposed to my experience as an observer.

My friend never offered thanks for this nugget—not even a
bottle of wine. I couldn't believe it but I also couldn't think of a
graceful way to tell him. Watching his investment grow as it did,
knowing I had spotted the opportunity myself and could have
made the same $6,000, started some wheels turning in my head.

*   *   *

It occurred to me as Pinkerton welcomed me to *The Wall Street Journal* that I had never really applied for a job writing the "Heard." George Anders had started the ball rolling, and somehow it all just happened without my having to agitate, beg, or cajole.

I mumbled a thank you to Pinkerton the day he made it official. I grinned broadly but I was disappointed with the size of my raise—fifty dollars a week. That boosted my weekly pretax paycheck to $530, more than I'd ever earned in my life. But I still lived in New York, where a cheeseburger can cost five bucks and a parking ticket can cost fifty. Although I knew that George, the man I was replacing, had earned several thousand dollars a year more than I would be paid for the same work, quibbling over money seemed wrong. I was too grateful for my good fortune, and too worried about measuring up to expectations, to hardball it for a few extra bucks. Besides, I reasoned, I'll do such a good job they'll be throwing money at me.

Pinkerton introduced me to my new boss, Dick Rustin, about whom I knew little. George had described him as a tough but smart editor who had a knack for making him feel like a stooge. Rustin had just been promoted to supervising editor of the stock, bond, and commodities coverage after fifteen years as a *Journal* reporter covering the securities industry. He was the paper's reigning Wall Street expert.

Over lunch with him a week after I was hired, I learned that he grew up Jewish in New York City, was a student of the Civil War, and lived in New Jersey with his wife, kids, and mother. He still wore his black hair over his ears, and his complexion was ruddy.

His personality type was one I'd had little experience with. Rustin could be abrupt, although I didn't mind that in an editor as good as he. But I also found him intimidating and uninviting as a boss. He projected a leathery veneer, a drill sergeant's machismo, that was part company man and part Brooklyn wiseguy. He walked with his head forward like a bull ready to charge, and avoided eye contact, which I found especially unsettling. His voice talked to me but the eyes were looking at something just over my shoulder or on the wall. Sometimes I tried to loosen him up with a couple of jokes, but his laughter was too polite and not worth the effort.

"You've been getting good stories on the ticker," Rustin said over our first lunch. "But you'll find the column a different animal. It requires a more sophisticated approach than the quick and dirty kind of stuff you're used to doing. The column is longer, goes into greater depth, and takes a more analytical point of view."

He talked a lot about getting columns in before deadline and urged me to beef up my network of Wall Street sources. He really hammered at the deadline thing.

"You've got to concentrate on getting your stories in on time. You should have your first take [page] to me by between four o'clock and four-thirty at the latest. By five-thirty the whole column has to be in the works. But in the beginning I want you to try to get it in a little earlier. You're the new boy here and we may need extra time to edit your stuff until you get the swing of the thing."

On sources, he said: "Try to get away from the talking heads stuff—quoting a string of analysts who just want to get their names in the paper. Sometimes the best people are money managers and investors, people who own the stocks you're writing about and have put their money where their mouths are, so to speak. You have to work on your sources. Get out there and meet people. Take them to lunch or dinner.

"And be skeptical about what they're telling you. Everybody has an ax to grind."

Dick's deadline speech left me with my recurring nightmare: that one day at 5:30 my column wouldn't be done and there would be hell to pay. The column was a fixed size in the same spot in the paper every day. No exceptions and no excuses. The space couldn't be filled with black dots or a cartoon.

For the next couple of weeks, I tidied up my affairs at the ticker. The recession had steadily chipped away at stock prices. Earlier that summer I bet five dollars with another editor at the ticker that the Dow Jones Industrial Average would stay above 750 that year. On August 10 the Dow hit a 27-month low at 779.30. A small dealer in government securities went bust two days later, pushing prices lower still. The Dow fell to 776.92. But I was about to win my bet.

Six days later, about an hour or so after the market opened, Rustin was standing at my desk.

"The market's going crazy. Looks like we might have a record-
volume day. Check out what's happening and maybe we'll run a
story on the inside of the paper."

My first byline in the *Wall Street Journal* as a full-time reporter
appeared the next morning:

> *Volume Surges*
> *On Big Board*
> *To 1-Day Record*

What later proved to be the most powerful bull market of the
century had thundered out of the gate just a few days earlier. I had
stumbled onto the stock market column at *The Wall Street Journal* at
an historic moment.

I had picked up only scraps of the history of the "Heard"
column and the stock market during my days on the ticker. The
recurring market cycles and the rich heritages of Wall Street, the
paper, and the column were lost to me in the scramble to keep up
with my work. Had I taken the time, I would have learned that, in
one form or another, the "Heard" is as old as Dow Jones itself. The
first handwritten, hand-delivered newsletters in 1882 were full of
market gossip and rumor. The entire length of those early sheets
averaged eight hundred words, about the length of just one
"Heard" column in a two-section, 62-page newspaper one hundred
years later. The armies of analysts and professional money managers begging to get their names in print remained to be born.

I occasionally joked with friends and sources that the name of
the column ought to be "Heard on the Phone" and announced
myself to sources I knew as the "Nerd on the Phone." We spent
almost all of our reporting time dialing telephone numbers until we
found somebody to interview. Reporters for financial news organizations in the early days of Dow Jones used to hang out at the
Windsor Hotel in Manhattan, where deal makers and corporate
moguls met to concoct their stock market capers. Their descendants one hundred years later did their best work with Rolodexes,
push-button phones, and on-line data bases.

The mechanics of covering Wall Street changed over the years,
but not the veil of secrecy behind which market operators have
always preferred to work. Wall Street, after all, is about secrets—

especially trading secrets. Like a high-stakes game of poker, the good players feint and bluff and never show their cards, even when they lose. When money talks, Mark Twain wrote, the truth is silent. Knowledge can be converted on Wall Street into money. The value of knowledge is inversely diminished by the number of people who have access to it. In other words, the only reason to invest in the market is because you think you know something others don't. A successful investment profits when that same bulb lights up in the heads of other investors. They also think they know something that someone else hasn't yet divined and the party grows, with a line forming at the door and the cover charge rising. This is the central psychology of the market.

The ethics of journalism, like the laws governing the markets, were much looser in the early days of Dow Jones. Edward Jones, cofounder of the company, moved with a glitzy crowd. Jones had rich pals, like William Rockefeller of the Standard Oil Company family, and some of his cronies were among the most notorious stock riggers of their period. He even occupied a seat on the New York Stock Exchange for a time and is thought by some to have participated in the fabled Northern Pacific stock manipulation of 1901, which triggered a general panic in the market.

The "Heard" and its sister column, "Abreast of the Market," actually came into being in the "fat years" of the 1920s, just before the Crash of 1929. The first columnist was Oliver Gingold, cousin of the actress, Hermione. Gingold started with the paper as a copyboy at $4 a week in 1900. He wrote the columns at first and in later years edited them. He also parlayed a $2,500 loan into a fortune estimated at $3 million—in the stock market. It's said that Wall Street brokers used to seek him out for advice.

Out of the wreckage of the 1929 Crash and the Depression grew a public outcry that sought to pin blame for the nation's ills on the stock market and everyone associated with it. During that outcry, in 1932, Fiorello La Guardia, who would become New York's mayor, appeared as a surprise witness before a Senate committee and charged that some financial writers had been paid off to tout stocks. La Guardia produced three checks totaling $633.50 he claimed a Dow Jones reporter named Gomber received from a publicist whose clients included operators of large stock pools. The payments apparently were made when Gomber worked at his last job at another paper.

The *Journal* covered the story of allegations about its reporter on page eleven but let the matter die after the first installment. Gomber resigned the day La Guardia gave his testimony. La Guardia leveled a similar allegation, apparently without canceled checks, at another *Journal* reporter who wrote the "Abreast of the Market" column. He stayed on staff.

The only ethical instruction I received at the *Journal* came from Charles Elia, a "Heard" alumnus and my ticker guru, who once told me, "It's probably not a good idea to invest in stocks while you write the column. I never did."

The *Journal*'s main concern, I came to understand, was that its employees not bring the paper any public embarrassment, especially in political matters. I had been talking to editors and reporters at other newspapers about forming a group of gay journalists. I was invited to participate in or lend my name to public forums on gay issues because I worked for the *Journal*. I discussed going public with a senior editor in the New York bureau at the time. He was openly gay and had once tried to persuade the company to put in writing its verbal commitment against discrimination on the basis of sexual orientation. The company refused.

"I get invitations all the time to appear on television talk shows," he told me. "But I don't accept them. The paper doesn't allow any political activity under its flag. Strictly verboten."

For a couple of weeks after Pinkerton's welcome, my disappointment with the raise festered. I had to say something. One day I gathered my courage and poked my head into his office.

"Got a minute?"

"Just about," he said.

"It's about the raise. I probably should have said something when you told me what it was going to be." I explained that I had been doing freelance work to supplement my salary and with my new job I wanted to quit these assignments. But the raise didn't quite compensate for the income I'd be giving up.

"Is there some way we can work it out that my raise could be adjusted a bit?"

Pinkerton waved his hand and turned his head away, brushing the question aside like a gnat. "That's the raise O'Donnell approved and I can't go back to him about changing it now. Anyway, it's the standard raise for a promotion within the company."

He shuffled a few papers on his desk. Interview over. I wrote him a follow-up letter in which I said I would quit all my freelancing. I hoped this would provide fuel later to press for more money.

The *Journal*'s reputation for stinginess with salaries was legend. In 1922, a new managing editor wrote to his boss asking permission to give out raises. "That 'cheap talent' to which you refer got on *The Wall Street Journal* because it has been the policy of the paper to hire those who would work cheaply." Things didn't change much in the sixty years that followed.

Starting pay for a young reporter at *The New York Times* in 1982 was about $30,000 a year. The *Journal* paid the same young reporter about $20,000. The discrepancy was even more startling when circulations were compared. The *Times* sold about 800,000 papers a day versus the *Journal*'s two million. The *Journal* occasionally would dig a little deeper into its pockets to lure a whiz kid from another publication, to snare an expert or match a competing offer for a valuable writer or editor. But the paper never had trouble finding eager young men and women to work at those prices. It was a first-quality paper, the best in the country by most estimates.

Just about any association with the *Journal* had some value. A junior ticker editor who spent two weeks on a spot news assignment, his first and last stint at the *Journal*, was offered $1,000 to write a short proposal for a venture capitalist he happened to talk to on the phone. The financier had no way of knowing that this ticker editor didn't really work for the *Journal* and had no more expertise in venture capital than someone rewriting press releases from the Ladies' Auxiliary in West Plowshare. But he didn't seem to care either. The mystique associated with the *Journal* was enough to establish the editor's bona fides.

Lyndon Johnson called it "the rich man's paper." The *Journal*, however, is largely written by middle-class men and women, many of them young reporters struggling to meet their living expenses and pay off their college loans. Many were hired right out of college. They learned the business at the top, instant experts. The paper protected itself from youthful overenthusiasm and bad judgment with layers of experienced editors, like Georgette Jasen, who kept the recruits in line and out of trouble. It was a cheap, efficient way to run a sprawling news operation but it rankled the staff and became a growing source of irritation to me.

There were, however, distinct and compelling advantages to

writing the "Heard" at any price. The column I inherited had made stars out of some of the writers assigned to it. Two who preceded me in the decade before I came aboard were Elia, who had helped me when I wrote for the ticker, and Dan Dorfman, who went on to write a similar syndicated column for the *New York Daily News* and for Rupert Murdoch's *New York* magazine. Of the two, Dorfman was more colorful. He was a short, balding, nervous man who freely talked about his frustrating love life and how he was over-worked and unappreciated (his column appeared in more than 100 newspapers around the country and he claimed he earned close to $200,000 a year). I doubt that anyone will ever equal his network of sources. He was a fair writer and a fantastic reporter—he broke more big stock market stories than any other journalist. He was always ahead of the pack on some takeover, executive resignation, or scandal.

I spent my first month or so at the paper getting my bearings, working for a couple of weeks on the bond market column. I understood by now what made bond prices rise and fall (interest rates), but not much else. Mostly I collected numbers and statistics for the two reporters who regularly wrote the column. I also did another tour on spot news, under Georgette's eagle eye. *Journal* reporters hated the drudge work of spot news and tried to avoid it when possible. "Heard" writers ordinarily didn't pull spot news duty, but I was new and the editors wanted me to get some general experience on the paper before I went "live" on the column. This time on spot news proved particularly embarrassing—and just as I was trying my hardest to score points. Georgette gave me a press release one day from Newmont Mining, a big silver mining and processing company. The press release was about some new mine and the story, although slightly more complicated than average, seemed routine.

The next day a Newmont Mining executive called up, very politely, to point out an error in my story. It took me some thirty minutes on the phone with the guy before I thought I had the problem figured out. Instead of a correction, Georgette decided there was a bit of news yet to be reported, so I wrote another story for the next day's paper. I was saved from having an error on my record.

The following morning, I was horrified to hear again from the company that the second story contained a new error. Georgette, hand on her hip, let out a sad sigh when I told her. I was prepared to pack my bags and return to Trenton. But she didn't get hostile.

Elia and Dorfman each wrote the "Heard" column mostly solo. They had to come up with seventy-seven lines of typewritten material for every edition, five days a week. I don't know how they did it. The pressure was so intense some days that *Journal* employees would find Elia in the men's room trying to clear his senses by pouring water over his head.

By the time I arrived, the column was a joint effort. George Anders had shared the responsibility with Gary Putka, another young reporter who was recruited from *Business Week*. Both were good newsmen and had an eye for the unusual twist that makes a story interesting. But I liked Gary's writing better. He had a well-developed sense of humor and a flippancy that made his columns read well and hold my interest.

Gary's background was a little different from most *Journal* reporters'. He had worked for *High Times*, the magazine for the sophisticated dope smoker and drug user. He'd gone on to work for *Securities Week*, an industry newsletter, and later for *Business Week*. He was one of the stars the *Journal* had anted up to hire.

He was the more relaxed of the two "Heard" writers. Gary's laugh was explosive and hearty. He'd throw his head back and erupt in laughter several times when he was on the phone interviewing someone. With his long brown hair, wire-rimmed glasses, and the backpack he carried wherever he went, he looked more like a college student or a *High Times* editor than a stock market reporter. He wore skinny ties around the collars of all kinds of funky shirts. I can't ever remember him wearing a traditional dress shirt. His jackets and overcoat looked as though he'd found them in the bottom of a pile in the corner of a secondhand store. Gary didn't believe in underarm deodorants.

I admired Gary for his writing and his independence from the company mold. We shared a demented sense of humor and a healthy disregard for authority. Over the next eighteen months I would also grow to consider him a friend I could trust.

It was nearly the end of September by the time I actually started cowriting the column with Gary. Stock prices had continued to march higher from the bottom less than two months earlier. By the end of September the Dow hovered just below 900, but it had been as high as 934.79, 158 points or 20 percent higher than it was six weeks earlier. The move was gargantuan by any measure but especially because the economy was still weakening. Most of the statistics coming out of Washington showed persistent deterioration in employment and business activity.

But I paid little heed to the cosmic picture. My blood raced on rumors and gossip about individual stocks or industries. This was the way I had learned to cover the market at the ticker. I also was taking most of my cues from Gary, who helped me with sources and story ideas. We were both gunslingers. We preferred to jump on a sudden movement in a particular stock and ferret out the reasons. Or find a stock that appeared overpriced or undepriced. This way, we were telling readers something they didn't already know. The model to avoid was the "Market Place" column in *The New York Times*, which typically served up yesterday's warmed-over research.

"Market Place" was our most direct daily competition. I would have considered Dorfman the competition but his column then appeared in the *Daily News*, not a must-read on Wall Street which was Wall Street's loss. The *Times* column often provided us with the first laugh of the day. It was written alternately by Robert Metz and Vartanig G. Vartan, whom we nicknamed "Var-Var" or "Tan-Tan." Usually they covered stories that were old news to our sources, following up weeks later on major changes that, in the world of finance, qualified as ancient history. Their columns focused on a stock, or group of stocks, and listed the opinions of a string of analysts. The conclusion was usually something along the lines of: the stock might go up, unless it goes down, or stays the same. Their work lacked muscle and offered no real insights or logical thinking that readers could put to any valuable use. That was the problem with a lot of stock and stock market analysis. Investors want action and heavy breathing, not equivocation.

The "Heard" philosophy was to pick a corner and defend it. We never thought of ourselves as experts or geniuses on the market. We relied on the money managers, traders, and analysts we talked to on the Street for our leads. But we added a healthy dose of common sense and skepticism to the process. We actively sought sources who invested in the market, people with track records for being right more often than they were wrong.

The *Times* would report a rumor of a takeover of a troubled company by saying: "Some analysts think the company might be taken over. In the meantime, analysts think earnings next year will be dismal."

Gary's message would be: "Talk that the company might be acquired had investors wolfing down stock. They'd better be right because the company's business is in the trash."

"The 'Heard on the Street' column is like nothing else in the *Journal* in that it isn't necessary, or probably even desirable, that you should present all sides," Gary would say later. "But . . . it is incumbent upon [us], at least, to know all sides of the story, and choose what [we] think the market might be missing."

I bounced around the newsroom for the first month or so, using desks of people who were on vacation or out of the office that day. I had no ticker to keep track of the market, and no Quotron machine, a computer terminal that supplied stock prices and market data that helped me identify what was on the move. These essential resources were my window into the market. Without them I was driving on a dark road without headlights.

In the beginning of October, I finally moved to George's old desk, where I had my own ticker and Quotron machine. The desk was bolted to Gary's and we were separated only by a low divider, just high enough so we couldn't see each other without standing up. Unlike many reporters at the *Journal*, Gary and I lived in a world of our own. Our desks were off the tattered carpet paths that criss-crossed the rows of other desks in the newsroom.

We took turns writing the column but the arrangement was loose. If either of us had written the column several days in a row, the other guy would take over. Whose turn it was on any given day was dictated as much by doctor's appointments and by which of us dug up the most compelling idea for a column as by whose "turn" it was.

My calendar book grew crowded with breakfast appointments across the street at the Vista Hotel, at the Plaza Hotel—with its elegant European dining room—and at other hotel dining rooms that doubled as pit stops for the power-breakfast crowd. I was introduced to the $3.50 glass of orange juice and $5 croissant. The tab for breakfast for two ran as much as $25, which I guessed was what it cost to feed an Ethiopian village for a week. I rarely went out for lunch. There wasn't time to gather together all the information required to craft a column *and* spend two hours consuming and commuting to and from a fancy lunch. The folks we talked to were used to dining in the best restaurants. It was how they salved their bruised psyches when the market had punished them, and how they rewarded themselves when they were hot and making money. I found no added value to interviewing a news source over hotel silver and linen. But the *Journal's* offices were shabby. The blue carpeting was worn to its sisal backing in the aisles and someone had put down carpet tape to keep it from coming loose and tripping people. Only a handful of people—just the top news executives— had private offices. Everyone else worked in big open spaces at dirty-beige metal desks with Formica tops, some of which had privacy dividers clamped to them. The lighting was fluorescent and harsh, the air conditioning always broke down on the most humid days, the phone system was prehistoric and we were always missing important calls, and the cafeteria looked like it belonged on the Staten Island ferry. The paper had long ago outgrown its space, so there were few comfortable places to sit and chat over a cup of coffee. The executive offices two floors up, with cozy conference rooms and antique furniture, were off limits unless, of course, you needed a quiet spot to interview Henry Kissinger or Lee Iacocca.

My day typically started with an expensive breakfast in a hotel dining room with an investment manager from out of town. I grew to hate these breakfasts because they forced me out of bed an hour or so early. But once in a while I'd come away with a good idea for that day's column.

Occasionally I visited some of the big Wall Street securities firms to interview a partner or a research director. These were the heights of ambience and gastronomy. The partners' dining rooms at Salomon Brothers, the old-line German-Jewish firm that did a big bond-trading business, was a four-star operation. I had an appointment there one morning, on the 42nd floor of a financial-district skyscraper, to meet the research director. It was a bitter cold day.

The elevator door opened onto a sprawling lobby decorated like a living room in a mansion. Oriental carpets covered the floors. The walls were hung with original oil and acrylic paintings, a couple of which I recognized from posters I had seen. Wood trim and brass lighting sconces set off floral wallpaper in yellow and beige tones. Scattered around the lobby were about six living-room arrangements, each with three wing chairs, covered in light yellow or gold tapestry, clustered around a dark wood coffee table.

A tall man with snow-white hair and ruddy complexion, dressed in a doorman's uniform, sat behind a large handsome wood desk in the middle of the room, facing the elevators.

As I waited for my interview, I exchanged small talk with a public relations man for the firm and gaped out the window at the Hudson River forty stories below and at the haze-smudged New Jersey landscape in the distance.

The man I was supposed to meet finally arrived (his limousine got stuck in traffic). He wore a dark, sleek suit and smoked a cigarette through a holder. I followed him down the hall like a tourist in a castle, past more original art and a series of doorways that were open to reveal one small dining room after another. Sparkling chandeliers hung over the highly-waxed tables and the antique English sideboards.

Fussy English bone china in a dull reddish color with fluted coffee cups sat on a brillant white linen tablecloth. The silver reflected the warm light. Everything in the room glistened.

"What'll you have?" my host asked when we were seated. A waitress wearing a starched uniform poured water into crystal water glasses.

There was no menu. "Well, uh, do you have anything like eggs Benedict?" I asked. No big deal, I figured. Egg, hunk of ham, muffin, and some sauce. He looked at me funny. "Would you like some eggs?"

I got the message. "Sure. Over easy."

Such visits were rare and usually produced little in the way of juicy tidbits that might be expanded into a "Heard" column. The bigwigs at these firms rarely gossiped like the men and women who worked in the trenches on trading desks, juggling a dozen phone lines and three computer screens, and barking buy and sell orders all day long.

I tried to be in the office by ten o'clock, when the opening bell sounded on the exchanges and my Quotron machine's emerald screen would begin winking updated stock prices and trading volume.

The first thirty to sixty minutes of trading I continuously scanned the Quotron monitor on my desk as well as the ticker teleprinter on its tubular stand at my shoulder. The Quotron machine showed me price changes and volume on stocks I had heard stories about and thought I might write up in the future. It also gave me a list, updated every few minutes, of the stocks that had risen or fallen the most that day. The ticker gave me market data, especially sudden ups and downs in stocks and reports of big blocks of stocks that were changing hands. It also told me the stocks in which trading had been halted or delayed on the New York exchange because of a stampede of sellers or buyers. These trading gaps often were unleashed by investor reaction to an influential analyst having that morning issued a new forecast for the company's profits, its stock price, or its industry. Sometimes there was news or a fresh rumor that had broken overnight: a major new contract, the death of a key executive, or even a war. When England attacked the Falklands, the shares of companies in the business of making weapons rose sharply. A stock price might sink or soar after a company's executives met with a group of investors who, thinking they'd heard some good or bad news, rushed to the telephones to call their brokers.

In between monitoring the machines and sifting through piles of press releases and research reports sent to us by brokerage houses, I touched base with any of a handful of traders who were plugged into the electronic grapevine of Wall Street. These were guys who might work on the trading desk of a brokerage firm or for a money management company (Wall Street, even in the mid-1980s, is still a male-dominated industry). They were the stage-hands of Wall Street, pushing and pulling the switches and, in the process, picking up most of the backstage gossip. Their jobs were to make sure that a buy or sell decision upstairs was executed at the best possible price. They were bidders and sellers in a frenzied auction and their bonuses at the end of the year depended on their ability to shave costs on trades sometimes by as little as a sixteenth of a point, or six cents a share. Because they dealt in huge quantities, they could make or lose hundreds of thousands of dollars in a few minutes. They made it their business to know all the gossip that might be affecting the prices of stocks in which their firms had an interest.

They worked in a pressure cooker and usually let off steam by telling jokes, most of them too sick, offensive, or digusting to repeat. But that never stopped me.

My morning phone calls typically began, "Bill, it's Foster, 'Nerd on the Street.' How are ya?"

"Okay, buddy. Busy market." I could hear the sounds of

phones ringing and people shouting in the background. "Did ya hear that the Bank of Poland is going to start opening branches in this country?"

"No kiddin'?" I said.

"Yeah! For their first promotion they're gonna give away a thousand bucks to anybody who brings in a toaster."

I laughed. "Not bad. I like that one. So what's the poop this morning?"

"Ahhh, let me see. Seems Bache put the oil stocks on their buy list this morning and a bunch of the drillers and domestics are doing nicely. I heard a rumor that Maxwell at Lawrence did the same but I won't swear to it."

I scribbed on a piece of scrap paper as he rattled off a list of stocks that were up sharply in early trading. The next call went out to the analyst at Bache. Charles Maxwell at C. J. Lawrence was considered the most influential oil-stock analyst on Wall Street. His recommendations nearly always had an effect on stock prices but he rarely talked to the press and never returned my phone calls. In this case, it turned out that Maxwell had not issued a new report on the oil industry, but the stocks got a temporary boost from the rumor that he had.

Gary and I chatted over the divider whenever we weren't on the phone. Sometimes we heard the same gossip or noticed the same trends in the market that day. Other times we'd find ourselves chasing completely unrelated stories. We compared notes on what we'd come up with in the first hour and a half of trading. At about 11:30, we negotiated a consensus: who would do the column and what it would be about. There was a good-natured competition between us over who could come up with the freshest column idea each day. We never fought about it. Whoever was elected would tell Rustin if Rustin hadn't already made a pass by our desks to find out how we were coming along. I can't remember an instance when he vetoed our offering.

At noon, the *Journal's* top editors, just like in the "Lou Grant" show, met in a conference room down the hall. Rustin presented the subject of the "Heard" column and the group decided which stories were going into the paper the next day and where.

By noon or one o'clock I was at full tilt, dialing up a list of analysts who cover the oil industry and some money managers to pull together a kind of consensus on the oil stocks. For every source

I actually reached, I left messages for three or four others who were busy or out of town. I rarely took lunch out, grabbing a sandwich from the cafeteria and eating at my desk between phone calls instead. The pressure always was to have more information than I needed. Most important was to understand the subject well enough to be able to form some reasonable conclusions. In the space of a few hours, from about 11 o'clock to 3:30 or 4, when I started writing the column, I had to become a quasi-expert on the subject and make sense out of the statistical and analytical gibberish I had picked up.

The point of all this, as George Anders once said, was "to look forward instead of backward. By the time a stock gets to a fifty-two-week high or low, we want to give people an idea where the Street thinks it is headed next, rather than just explain a move that investors are already aware of."

A column, like the columns in the *Times*, that said, "Golly, this here stock's down 50 percent and here's why" wasn't news. A column that said, "This here stock's down 50 percent and here's a bunch of savvy investors and analysts who think it's just about to go back up again" said something new, something readers could use. Of course, we wanted our conclusions to be right.

The measure of our success was whether the stock price moved the way the column indicated it would, and whether, over the long haul, the people we talked to and quoted had made the right forecasts. Neither Gary nor I kept any statistics on whether we were right more often than not. Mostly we bragged to each other about our successes, and joked about our mistakes.

Dick Rustin's deadline admonitions gave me religion. I didn't wait until 4 o'clock to start writing. I launched into my columns by 3:30. Gary started slower. Sometimes he'd begin writing as late as 4:30. By the time I was ready to write, my desk was obliterated by drifts of white paper with my typewritten notes on them (I almost always typed my notes during my phone interviews, using an operator's headset to free my hands). In addition, the clutter consisted of research reports, photocopies of past articles from the *Journal*, an overflowing ashtray, a couple of old coffee cups and the paper plate from my lunch, a smudge of mayonnaise on it growing translucent. I handed the column in a page at a time to Rustin, who edited it, suggested changes, additions or omissions, corrected the typographical errors, and added the editing marks. He walked it over to the news desk where another editor combed through it line by line. Rustin seemed pleased that I was getting my stories in so early. Because I still was feeling my way along, he had time to edit them closely.

"You must be setting some kind of record around here," he said. He was used to the death-defying habits of Gary who played chicken with, but never lost, the deadline game.

The length of the column Monday through Thursday was seventy-seven typewritten lines—exactly. If it ran over (I never remember writing a column that was too short) the news desk would suggest sentences or paragraphs that could be cut. The last piece had to be out of my typewriter and on its way by 5:30. A news clerk in the New York office fed the four pages or so into a photofax machine. At the other end of a phone connection a similar device printed copies of the pages out in the main printing plant and composing room in Chicopee, Massachusetts. There it was re-edited, set into type, pasted into its berth on the page and the page transmitted by satellite to seventeen other printing plants around the country where the signal was translated into images suitable for making printing plates. The first copies of the first edition rolled off the presses at about 7 P.M. in some locations.

My first few months on the column I occasionally stumbled while trying to capture the rhythm of the thing. A few columns seemed naive or downright stupid. And I got a lesson on *Journal* telephone manners.

One early afternoon I was on the phone interviewing a source. Rustin had a habit, when I was on the phone and he needed an answer to a question or wanted to tell me something, of looming over me with one hand on his hip, the other resting on my file cabinet with a cigarette burning in it. He would stare at my desk, waiting for me to hang up, which usually intimidated me into doing just that.

This day I was on the phone saying something like, "Listen, I'm working on a column about the increase in sales among breadbox manufacturers. Seems a lot of people are excited. I know you cover the industry, what do you think the outlook is?"

When I hung up, Dick pointed at me with a finger on the hand with the cigarette in it. His eyes looked at my desk and he said, in an urgent, almost accusative low voice, "Who was that you were just talking to?"

My hackles perked up a bit. I thought, what business is it of yours who I was talking to? I stopped reporting my phone conversations when I moved away from home.

"Just an analyst who was giving some dope on the column," I said, a defensive tone rising in my voice.

"Well, Jesus Christ, Foster. Don't ever start your phone conversations off like that. What the hell are you doing, telling the guy what you're working on?"

"Well, I just wanted to give him an idea what the gist was so he could comment on it intelligently." A drop of sweat formed in my armpit and trickled down my side. "Why? What did I do wrong?"

"You don't *ever* tell people what you're doing. Be evasive, dissemble with your sources. Tell them, 'I want to know what you think about so-and-so.' Be discreet, for chrissakes. We don't want every bozo out there knowing what we're working on."

"Okay," I said. "I'm sorry. I'll try not to do it again." These habits were second nature. I didn't think it mattered a whole helluvalot whether I opened my telephone interviews one way of another. Some reporters, not I, would tell a source the opposite thrust of his story just to get a reaction. Like calling up a neighbor of a mass murderer and saying, "We're doing this nice tribute about your neighbor. What did you think of him?"

Besides, I thought, after spending a half hour on the phone talking to an analyst or money manager about a stock, my source knew I was working on a column anyway. He probably guessed from my questions whether it would be positive or negative. Hell, sometimes I had to call him back two or three times to check a quote or a fact.

I was starting to understand what George meant when he said Rustin made him feel like a stooge.

It took me a few months to break the habit, with Gary's help. He corrected me a couple of times also, but he did it with kindness. We could hear just about every word of each other's conversations. Gary was better than Rustin at giving advice. At least criticism was easier to take coming from him. A couple of times his head popped up above the divider and he ran a hand through his hair. With a chuckle forming in his throat and a half-smile on his face, he said, "Try not to be so open with sources. It's probably none of my business, but try some other approaches. Say: 'I'm watching the stock movement of thus-and-so,' or 'I'm doing some reporting on,' or 'I have been following thus-and-so.' Make it vague."

The part of the job we both seemed to hate the most was writing the "Abreast of the Market" column, a kind of play-by-play wrap-up of the action in the market each day. On Mondays, the "Abreast" was supposed to be a thumb sucker: the writer was obligated to step back and take a longer-range view of the big picture. Every other week Gary or I wrote this Monday version of the "Abreast," called the "Appraisal," and it was always a downer when I realized that it was my week to do it. We also filled in when the regular columnist was on vacation.

The "Abreast" ran directly above the "Heard" on the same page and was written by Vic Hillery, a tall, white-haired man who seemed uneasy with the youthful tenor of the newsroom crowd. But then I didn't know him well. Vic was a Dow Jones lifer nearing retirement. His ways were set in concrete. He practically owned the "Abreast," having written it for twenty years. He arrived and left at the same time every day. His routine never varied and his columns reflected it, many of them reading like scripts for a tennis game. But he had his fans, too. When an editor many years his junior handed down changes in deadlines or schedules, he complained bitterly, usually to me because my desk sat in front of his. The *Journal's* highly visible columns were closely followed by competing news organizations. Whenever any of us unearthed and quoted a smart new source, other print and television reporters glommed right on to him and soon his name was everywhere and his unique value as a source was diminished. This was a fact of our lives, as *Journal* columnists. But after all those years, it still drove Vic Hillery nuts.

"Look at this, just look at this," he said to me one day as he walked from behind his desk gingerly holding a piece of paper from the ticker as though it were soaked in toxic waste. His eyes were wide with horror and his voice had a hurt tone to it. "I quote one of *my* sources in the column and the next damned thing you know the ticker uses him. Honest to God. Can't these people find their *own* sources?"

Vic retired in 1984.

Gary and I were too engrossed in the gossip about individual stocks and industries to welcome the chance to fill in for Vic, especially when it entailed writing the Monday-morning "Appraisal." It meant taking a step backward to look at the market as a whole. A takeover rumor meant tracking down concrete facts. But the market sometimes seemed like a big mushy swamp, and writing the "Appraisal" column was like trying to sprint through quick-sand. Fortunately, no one remembered or seemed to care when we blew it. No readers ever called me a jerk because, six months later, one of my "Appraisal" columns turned out to be all wet about the stock market. In fact, all of Wall Street was mostly forgiving, or oblivious to, everyone's mistakes. I wondered if maybe people really did have a need to lose and a fear of winning.

David had been promoted by this time from his *Journal* news clerkship. In his new job he assisted the editors on the news desk, the funnel through which nearly all *Journal* stories flowed before they appeared in print. Our combined salaries covered our ex-penses, and we decided to take our first real vacation together in nine years the following spring, in 1983. We planned a trip to France. The dollar had been strong, especially against the franc, but our trip was about six months away and I worried that the dollar would weaken in the meantime and throw our budget out of kilter.

To lock in the cheap franc and to bet on the dollar weakening, I bought about $2,000 in franc-denominated American Express traveler's checks. The money came from a loan account attached to our checking account.

I poked my head over the divider and told Gary about it later.

"Well, Gary, I made my first real investment. I bought a bunch of French francs. You've been mouthing off for months now about the dollar declining. Now let's see some action."

My continuing interest in covering the market at the time was new issues. Gary got stuck on the dollar. He was convinced that the international value of the dollar was poised to fall any time, which would help a whole raft of U.S. companies whose overseas profits had been hurt by unfavorable exchange rates. (He wrote a couple of columns arguing the point and, of course, the dollar ignored him and went on to hit record highs against most curren-cies.)

Gary threw his head back and laughed. "So, taking a little fling on margin, huh, Foster? Well, we'll see. We'll see."

I paid fifteen cents a franc (the franc had traded before the dollar's surge at tewnty-five cents U.S.) and I hoped to get a big discount on our vacation. But within a few months the currency sank a couple of cents. I debated holding on or selling the traveler's checks when an even better investment opportunity sailed through my transom and landed on my cluttered desk.

We got many unsolicited phone calls as "Heard" writers from analysts and brokers peddling investment ideas for the column. In mid-December 1982, a fast-talking broker from Los Angeles named Jack Kennedy got me on the horn and started filling my ear with a tale about a tiny Arizona company that operated outpatient surgery centers. The company, American Surgery Centers, was hot, the broker assured me.

"Mr. Winans, I don't have to tell you about how the government and insurance companies are crawling up the asses of these hospitals looking for ways to cut health care costs." The guy sounded like he was in danger of wearing out his lips. I had to shout to get him to stop long enough so I could ask a question.

"Anyway," he plowed on, "the company's doing an equity financing and they're raising about ten or fifteen million bucks to start expanding and opening up these walk-in surgery centers all across the country. They'll have one hundred and seventy-five of these babies in operation by the end of 1984. They're the only ones doing it. All the insurance companies are pushing it and it's a potential four-billion-to-five-billion-dollar industry. And," he said, with a trace of reverence, "*Mormons* run it!"

Only a broker from the West Coast could get away with a line like that. I knew what he meant. The Mormons like to think of themselves as one of the lost tribes of Israel. They share another reputation with Jews. Mormons, I had learned in my travels in the Northwest were considered great businessmen with an uncanny knack for making money.

It took me a while to decelerate the mouth and get him off the phone.

"Send me some information" was the standard line and I gave it to him. It was a way to get the persistent ones off the phone. And I couldn't go any further until I had some documentation about the company.

A week or so later, just after Christmas, I got a letter in the mail from American Surgery with a package of information. The stock was trading at about $2.50 a share and started to percolate near the end of the year and into the first week of January. By January 7, the shares had jumped to more than $4 in heavy trading. As I poked around a potential story I became more and more interested. The wild man from Los Angeles called me a few times but gave me nothing new. I was intrigued, however, by the fact that a conservative management consulting firm had done extensive research on the company and its president, Lynn Singley. The firm not only gave American Surgery a clean bill of health, it was prepared to coordinate a financing and had found a number of insurance companies interested in the concept. The company had an air of authenticity about it. Singley, I learned, had a respectable track record as a consultant setting up surgery centers for doctors' groups. "Singley," said the management consultant, "is a winner." And brokers besides fast-talking Jack Kennedy were drooling over the stock. "It's a story," said one, "that leaves my clients panting."

Me too. I was convinced I'd found the stock of 1983, the one that in December would pop up at the top of the list of best-performing issues for the year. It would make a great column *and* a great investment. I hustled down to American Express and converted my French francs back into dollars. I wanted to own some of this hot stock.

The *Journal* editors, I knew, would choke if they learned I was investing in the market. If I opened a brokerage account in my own name, I was sure they would find out. Few brokers failed to read the "Heard" column each morning. It was must reading everywhere in the investment business and my name appeared at the top of every column I wrote. So I decided David should open an account in his name. But where? I knew nothing about brokerage accounts or buying and selling stock. Merrill Lynch's headquarters were across the street from the *Journal*, where both David and I worked.

David, in all our years together, had little interest in our financial affairs. He left to me all the major decisions. I filled out the forms and applications and earned the larger share of our combined income. So I carefully instructed David to get a new-account form from Merrill Lynch, take a check, and buy 100 shares of American Surgery. The next day I was seized with an attack of greed. Maybe we didn't buy enough! So I sent David back with a second check and instructions to buy another 300 shares. We were into the stock for $1,800, about $4.50 a share, all of it borrowed. I was excited and nervous. In just two weeks or so the price had soared more than 60 percent. Maybe we were too late. Maybe the big move was over and we'd get stuck!

Somehow I managed to isolate my plunge in the market as just another example of an investment idea I might have passed on to someone else, like the guy who made $6,000 on G. D. Searle options when I gave him a tip while I was at the ticker. But this time I was going to make the profit, not somebody else. I knew what I was doing was technically unethical for a journalist. But since I knew that I wasn't letting my investment alter my judgment at work in any way, the ethical question was purely one of appearances. There was nothing intrinsically or factually corrupt about what I was doing. If no one ever found out, no one would perceive a potential conflict and, therefore, I would not have done anything unethical. It was slightly circular reasoning but it got me past the big hurdle.

I also wanted to make more money. And owning stock got me a little closer to the heat of the battle I covered every day.

I knocked out a draft of the American Surgery column. Usually I got my ideas and wrote them up the same day. This one had taken some time to develop because no analysts covered the company, which hadn't yet earned a nickel and was a fly speck compared with most of the companies we covered. The first draft began, "American Surgery Centers limped onto the health-care scene just over two years ago . . . and has been bleeding red ink ever since." Parts of the column were flawed, a little too enthusiastic. Rustin quibbled over some of the language and he worried that the *Journal* would be giving too much positive publicity to a small, unknown company.

He liked nothing better, however, than to run a column blasting a little company whose stock price had soared. It seemed to me inconsistent and biased to argue against one while embracing the other. But his editing comments were good and helped strengthen the piece.

"Let's take out some of this gushy stuff and let the people know that the president may be its single biggest asset," he told me after he'd read the draft. One of my most important sources had requested anonymity but Rustin wanted a name attached to the comments. I called the guy back and talked him into letting me use his name.

"This column still makes me nervous," Rustin said. "I want you to tone it down. Some people are likely to run out and buy the stock when the story appears and I want to make sure we aren't overstating the case. A 'Heard' on a outfit like this is like shooting a mosquito with a howitzer."

I was a little miffed. For one thing, these little company stocks were zooming in the market surge, attracting widespread investor interest. We wrote a lot about corporate Goliaths that were well covered and well known. Getting the goods on this tiny company no one had heard of was real detective work and I had enjoyed it. I also was catching the fever of greed: the market's big bull surge and the panting over American Surgery.

I polished the column as Rustin suggested, and it ran a day later. The stock rose 94 cents a share to $5 the day the column appeared. The market, it seemed, agreed with the thesis of the column. But during the next three days it settled back to just about where it had been. I debated about buying more but decided to wait and see how things developed.

At the same time, a money manager talked me into meeting with him about another small company. This time, however, the thrust was bearish. The money manager was a small-time operator from New Jersey, another motor mouth, who claimed the stock, Radiation Technology, was grossly overpriced. Another detective story and I dove right in.

Radiation Technology, I learned, was in the business of zapping food products with gamma rays. This killed off all the bacteria that caused spoilage without leaving any radiation residue. The raw concept actually was more exciting than American Surgery's. Irradiated food had been sent into space with the astronauts and the process had attracted international interest, especially for storing and shipping foods for starving third-world countries. Irradiated fish, I was told, would keep for weeks. Some foods remained stable for months after treatment.

But the company was run by a fanatic named Martin Welt who had been living and breathing the religion of irradiated foods for twenty years in the face of stubborn resistance. People weren't quite ready to marry the bomb to their diets. The company did a little business sterilizing medical products with gamma rays. But, Welt was telling anyone who would listen, the FDA was just about to approve widespread use of the process and the Pentagon was just about to give *his* company a contract to nuke *millions* of meals for its troops.

Welt was a table-thumping evangelist. I listened with growing skepticism to his tirades on the phone against the FDA for its delays in approving the process and against his detractors in general. I never met the man but he reminded me of the scene in the film *Frankenstein* when the crazed doctor realizes his monster lives and shouts, "It's alive! It's alive!"

Welt's claims about huge Army contracts and imminent government approval turned out to be so much fluff. The Army denied ever suggesting that anyone would receive such a contract and the FDA's projected approval was a year or so away. Rustin loved the column ("One of your best") and clapped his hands with delight when the stock, which closed at about $28 a share the night before publication, burned and crashed the next morning. It opened at $14. Investors who hadn't read the "Heard" thought the company had declared a two-for-one stock split.

It is accepted wisdom in the market that people only complain when they lose money. I got a couple of angry calls after the Radiation Technology column, including one from a spluttering Dr. Frankenstein. And a fellow from New Jersey reached me on the phone and told me a tale of woe.

"Mr. Winans, I just want you to know that I mortgaged my house and put my life savings in this stock, $100,000, two days ago at $32 a share. Your column just wiped me out."

The guy was really shaken, and it was obvious to me that some slick broker had talked this pigeon into plunging all he had into Radiation shares "before the stock gets away from you."

I tried to calm him down. "Sir, I'm sorry you feel hurt but a question immediately pops into my mind. What in the world were you doing risking your nest egg and your home on a speculative stock like this?"

He rambled about how the broker had assured him it was a solid investment and how could I have done this to him.

"First of all," I said, "I didn't do anything to you. The company obviously was overconfident in its comments to shareholders and the investment community. You had an obligation to check it out before you bought it. Secondly, you don't lose money until you sell. The *value* of your investment has fallen but, over the long haul, you may end up to the good. You don't lose until you sell."

"I sold this morning," he said, dejectedly. I was dumbfounded. The guy was beyond hope, a classroom example of market psychology. Blind greed had him drooling over an unsubstantiated story. The moment there was bad news, he jumped ship. In fact, if he had stayed with the stock for another year while it recovered to its high he would have saved himself a $50,000 loss.

Through the early months of 1983 I began to meet a whole cast of Wall Street characters, including Eddie the Weasel (a fictitious name for a real person). Eddie was a stump of a man who seemed to have no history and inhabited the dark and dank recesses of the investment community. He scurried from shadow to shadow scavenging for scraps that the rest of the world had discarded or rejected.

Eddie was short, very round, and his graying hair was piled up on top of his head in a pompadour. His face was round as well, with full lips, a beak of a nose, and wire-rimmed glasses. He spoke Brooklynese in a wheezy, nasal tone and claimed he had good connections overseas, "very good Swiss banking sources." He made me swear I'd never quote him or use his name, a request I found easy to grant. "I have a lot of tax problems," he explained. Eddie never said anything quotable, and the cats and dogs he put me in touch with barely were worth my time and not at all worth writing about. Every couple of weeks I got a truncated phone call from him almost as though he were reporting a crime but unwilling to provide details.

"Foster? It's Eddie. Have you had a chance to check out Rubber Nipple Industries? It's acting very well, the volume is higher, and there has to be something going on there. I can't tell you what it is. Gotta run. Bye." Click.

Other times he would beg me to meet with one of his funny little companies. I usually did, on the same theory I'd meet with anyone else: occasionally I'd get a story idea and even if not, it was part of my education. Eddie was the only source who gave me a peek into the dirty creases of Wall Street. His strangeness was amusing, comic relief in the pressure cooker. I would learn a year or more later that he was a convicted felon whose scam had been to short a stock and then tell the Securities and Exchange Commission what a bad company it was. Then he spread the word in the market that the SEC was investigating, the stock would tumble on this rumor, and Eddie would take his profit. It was brilliantly simple, kind of like letting the system work for you.

Those were wild days on Wall Street. The market continued its northbound march into new, uncharted territory. It seemed that any dry cleaner with a corner location could go public and raise a few million in the stock market. American Surgery was chugging

right along with the rest of them. Kidder, Peabody and Shearson/
American Express (now Shearson Lehman Brothers, Inc.) were
buying the hell out of it. In March, when the price had gotten up to
more than $8 a share, American Surgery announced termination of
a financing agreement which would have accelerated its expansion
plans. The price skidded to about $6 a share.

Remembering Rustin's worries about my column on the company, I pointed out the stock action and asked him if he wanted me
to do a short follow-up item that would appear at the tail end of the
"Heard." I called the company, and the comments of the chairman—that $25 million in financing was expected over the coming
months—appeared in the "Heard" the next day along with a
description of the violent plunge in the stock price.

The stock eventually resumed its advance. David and I decided the vacation to France was a little rich for our budget,
especially now that we had money tied up in the market. We spent
a rainy, snowy week in April, instead, driving to Montreal and
down through New England to Martha's Vineyard. We had by
then invested some money in a few other stocks as well, junky
companies in weird businesses whose shares sold cheap and had
been touted by some source. Most of them weren't worth writing
about but in the euphoric atmosphere that gripped the market
anything was possible.

By May, American Surgery's climb steepened. My brother,
Chris, an editor at a newspaper in suburban Philadelphia, wanted
to take a plunge in the market after hearing of the success of my
American Surgery investment. He borrowed $5,000 from his bank
and bought 150 shares at $12. A few days later I decided David and
I had too much money, a total of about $4,000, tied up in the
market. American Surgery was the only one showing a profit.
After calling my brother to let him know that we were selling but
that I thought he should hold on, we cashed in at $12 for a total
profit of just over $3,000. At the end of May the shares reached $15
and I convinced Chris to sell his shares, too. The spirit of the
market had infected just about everyone. If I had had a sense of
history, I might have recognized that this spirit invades the market
just before a big downdraft. I would have known that something
was askew when I got a phone call at work from a friend, his voice
full of pride, bragging about his first independent investment
decision.

"I just bought Telcom International," he shouted into the phone.

"What in the world is that?" I asked. "Where did you hear about it? What do they do, telephones or something?"

He paused and his voice suddenly was soft and vulnerable. "I don't know. I'm not sure. I saw it in the paper. It was going up and it was cheap."

"Let me see what I can dig up and I'll call you back." I looked the company up in my stock guide. Trucking and transportation, not telephones. Then I got a dope sheet on it from the Standard & Poor's stock books the *Journal* kept in the office. The company was in bankruptcy. Oh brother, I thought. Doesn't look good. I called him back.

"Get rid of it," I said. "The company's bankrupt and I have no idea why the stock was up. I think you ought to sell it in case it's just about to roll over and die." He did and the stock subsequently sank.

The publicity and huge price advance in American Surgery were starting to attract sharks who smelled an easy meal. The price was way higher than anybody, including me, thought possible. The company still hadn't earned any money, and to wiser investors than I it looked top-heavy and ready to crash. They call such stocks screaming shorts: so top-heavy that you'd have to be a screaming idiot not to see that the price is headed for a tumble. In other words, American Surgery was screaming to be sold short.

The folks at American Surgery called me from time to time to exchange expressions of disbelief over what was happening to the stock. One of them called me one day late in May.

"Well," I said, "How's it feel to be a paper millionaire?" The company's employees had gotten cheap stock in lieu of full salaries. The shares were restricted: they couldn't be sold in the market for two years or more. But on paper they felt like lottery winners.

"It's wild," he said. "But the stock is beginning to look like a short. I wish I could sell. I'd retire and live in the mountains somewhere. Listen, are you interested in a lead for a story?"

"Sure," I said. "I'm always looking for good ideas. You think you've got a good one?"

"I don't know. There's this guy, a stockbroker, who is supposed to be the top broker on Wall Street. I thought maybe he'd be an interesting person to talk to or maybe worth a story."

I rarely talked to brokers, especially retail brokers as opposed to the salesmen who handle large bank and pension fund accounts. Retail brokers spend most of their time cheering on their clients when prices are rising and trying to placate them when they fall. They don't do their own research and typically handle small trades that have no detectable effect on stock prices or corporate developments. When I wrote the rare story about the activity of individual investors in the market, I had to scrounge for brokers to interview.

But a top retail broker might be somebody worth knowing and maybe a good subject for a profile.

"Well, why don't you give me his name and number. Maybe I'll give him a call," I said.

"His name is Peter Brant, B-R-A-N-T, and he's at Kidder, Peabody." I jotted the name and number down on a scrap of paper and threw it on a pile of similar scraps in the corner of my desk.

5

Superbroker

The pressure to outperform your neighbor be-
comes intense in a greedy, upward market. In
many ways it is a time of unhappiness, producing
the kind of mental exhaustion that tells you that,
sooner or later, you are doomed to fail.

—John D. Spooner, *Sex and Money*

A hot-dog vendor working the corner of Broad and Wall Streets in
July 1982 was an expert on the stock market compared to Ken
Felis. He'd spent his working years after Babson College bent over
printing presses, wiping his hands on his ink-stained jeans. He
wore a sports jacket to see customers but he didn't own a suit. The
day he reported to work at Peter Brant's Park Avenue office he
rushed in to Brooks Brothers and paid an extra $50 to have a suit
fitted and altered while he waited. A week after he was on board,
Peter walked into Ken's office and said:

"Well, pal, guess what. I just ordered eight new suits for you
at Brooks."

Peter set Ken up with an Oldsmobile 98 and a driver to ferry
him back and forth from his home in Connecticut. Ken had an
office and a secretary next to Peter's at Kidder, Peabody's Park
Avenue office. It was in a suite that was designed and furnished for
Peter, by now the firm's undisputed top-grossing retail salesman.

It was almost as though they were back in college again, with
Peter providing the props for the millionaire dress-up game. But
instead of horses, they were betting on stocks.

Ken went through a Cinderella-like transformation. He entered the brokerage business at the top of the heap in a well-known firm, with a posh office, chauffeur, secretary, and a guaranteed 10 percent of the take of one of Wall Street's top salesmen—all of this, and he didn't have his broker's license yet.

Peter needed Ken because he was the only person in the world he felt he could trust to work with him as his brokerage business grew. He didn't trust the other people at Kidder, Peabody. He seduced Ken away from the label business with talk that the market was like a loaded gun just waiting for someone to pull the trigger. He'd said, "We'll make millions overnight." But it wasn't the money that changed Ken's mind. He missed the camaraderie he and Peter shared in college—the capers, the millionaire goofs, and especially Peter's sense of humor. He had no pressing desire to make millions and no burning interest in the brokerage business. In fact, he harbored middle-class suspicions about and antagonism toward the phoniness he associated with the power elite of the New York business world. Peter hung out with a Waspy crowd of wealthy jet-setters Ken couldn't understand or stomach. Once he and Peter were having drinks in the Racquet Club with one of Peter's wealthy clients who Ken thought was trying too hard to be witty and intellectual. It sounded like a load of crap and a funny thought popped into his head:

"Boy," he told himself, "one shot in the mouth and this guy would run away crying. Look at this wimp. He doesn't even know what life and work is about with his screwed-up sense of values. Just a spoiled, self-indulgent baby."

Peter was the only person in the world Ken would have joined in such a partnership. Peter was his best friend and soulmate, like a brother. If nothing else, they would share some good laughs.

Within four weeks of Ken's arrival, the stock market took off like a cannon shot, just as Peter predicted. But Ken still had four months to go before he would have his broker's license. He had to sit and watch Peter work. He was mesmerized.

Peter invested every spare dollar of clients' funds and his own in stocks as the market lurched into high gear. Then he proceeded to margin every account to the eyeballs (a method of buying stock on credit).

Digital Switch, Peter's pet stock and the one he'd loaded up his accounts with, had been rising all year. With the onset of the bull market, the curve of its trajectory steepened. Peter bought still more shares on credit that was tied to his paper profits. The pattern repeated itself again and again. The process is called leveraging up and essentially gave him and his clients a free ride beyond their initial cash purchase. An investment of $100 which rose to a value of $150 allowed the investor to make additional purchases equal to half of his paper profit—or $25—without putting up a nickel. Peter, however, was dealing in millions.

His success with Digital Switch and the feeding frenzy that had seized the market unleashed a flood of new business and fresh cash. Both the stock and the market had become cocktail party conversation. Digital Switch (brokers and traders referred to it by its stock symbol—DIGI) was *the* hot stock in a historic bull market.

Investors bragged over drinks, "We're making so much money in the market," which brought to their feet anyone still sitting on the sidelines, breathlessly asking, "Oh yeah? Who's your broker?"

Referrals started to pour in to Peter's office. Clients who already had accounts sent him more money to invest. Those who were out of the market begged to be let in. He had accumulated such a huge chunk of Digital Switch, perhaps the largest single piece, that anyone who wanted to know about the stock eventually was referred to him. Even Kidder, Peabody's own traders begged for tidbits of gossip that helped them buy and sell the stock more profitably.

The traders at the firm worried about Peter's huge position in DIGI. The firm was a market-maker: it maintained an inventory of stocks like DIGI.* The traders' year-end bonuses depended on the profit their operations showed. Peter's buying had helped drive the stock up. In fact, his continous purchasing of the stock may have been responsible for a good portion of its huge rise to a high of $147 from about $20. The traders lived in terror that their inventory of DIGI shares, acquired at steadily higher prices, might be vulnerable to a sudden huge downdraft and a devastating loss if Peter started dumping the stock.

---

*Smaller brokerage firms which aren't market makers execute buy and sell orders for clients by going out and purchasing from other firms or selling to them. Large brokerage houses tend to maintain their own in-house inventory of securities. Some smaller firms make a market in small quantities of smaller stocks or penny stocks.

Ken was like a youngster on his first visit to Disneyland. He couldn't wait to see how much they were going to make each day. It seemed he and Peter were running into each other's offices exchanging expletives of disbelief and joy every twenty minutes. This daily upswing continued for eight months, with few days when a profit somehow eluded them. Ken thought that was the way it was going to be forever and that Peter was a genius. Their roles had been reversed from the days at Babson when Peter looked to Ken for advice on major decisions. Now, Peter knew it all and Ken followed him around like a loyal puppy.

Peter sat at his mahogany desk, eyes fixed on his Quotron machine. He'd watch the trading volume and each movement, each tiny wobble or jiggle, in prices. A stock would rise an eighth of a point—12.5 cents a share—for just a few moments and Peter was able to read some profitable meaning into it. He'd turn to Ken and say, "They're about to run this stock price up." Peter bought and, like magic, the stock started to rise. He was a day-trader, buying in the morning and selling in the afternoon, clipping a fraction of a point or more on trades of a few thousand shares.

One day Ken noticed an account statement lying on the desk of one of the secretaries. It was for a huge account with a name he didn't recognize: David Clark. Ken put two and two together, and Peter confirmed that this was the "lawyer friend" he'd met at a Connecticut polo club and who he had talked about as being a partner—the same one in whose account Peter shared trading profits. Ken realized this was the same guy Peter talked to four or five times every day. Clark was a heavy hitter and Peter's mentor. He introduced Peter to his clients, like Roger Wilson, the aspiring actor, and opened other doors so Peter could land prime new accounts such as Richard Leakey, son of the famed archaeologist.

At the end of a day of this Wall Street madness, Ken wanted only to get home to his wife and children. He relaxed by throwing off his suit, pulling on a pair of sweats, and shooting a few baskets or playing paddle tennis with his friends in Connecticut. Peter spent increasing time in the city at a co-op apartment on the Upper East Side, going home less and less to Locust Valley on weeknights. Lynn confided to a friend that she suspected Peter was being unfaithful to her some of his nights in the city. But she insisted that she loved him anyway. At least life was easier for her now that her second husband was making a fortune. She may have even welcomed his nights away as respites from Peter's high-velocity personality, supervising the redecorating of the house and watching over her two children. Peter was home on weekends and some weeknights.

Peter and David Clark spent some evenings in the city to-gether, at social functions and places like the Racquet Club, the "21" club, and an exclusive supper club called Doubles in the basement of the Sherry-Netherland Hotel. Peter rubbed shoulders with celebrities like Frank Sinatra, whose music he had favored in college—especially the song "My Way."

Clark took Peter on a bird shoot to England and showed him how to travel in style, helping him set up an account at Coutts & Co., an exclusive London bank, and Claridge's, a first-class hotel. One of Peter's big coups was talking Lloyd's of London, the huge insurance syndicate, into opening a stock account with him. He also signed up two Greek brothers who were moguls in the shipping business.

The senior partners at Kidder, Peabody were delighted with Peter's performance, and he learned early how to turn their pleasure to his advantage. He convinced the firm to put his driver, Ricardo, on the payroll at $30,000 a year, to which Peter added a year-end bonus of $5,000. He learned how to keep the bosses in line. They wanted the juicy business he generated, and Peter always held over the firm, without saying it, the horrible possibil-ity that he might defect. Especially during a big bull market, Wall Street firms routinely paid fat bonuses up to hundreds of thousands to lure a major leaguer like Peter from his roost.

His immediate "boss" was Evan Collins, manager of the Park Avenue office. Collins was, at best, a junior partner. But the size of his bonus at the end of the year depended on how well his brokers did, especially Peter, whose gross was a big chunk of the branch's business. Collins's earnings were calculated as a percentage of the total business flowing through the office. In fact, Collins worked for Peter and Peter never let him forget it.

One day Ken walked into Peter's office in the middle of a shouting match between the superbroker and the office manager. They were arguing over the monthly fees Kidder paid to have the plants watered. Peter did most of the shouting:

"Of all the *stupid* fucking things," Peter roared, the look of mock disgust forming on his face. "You pay somebody $25 a month to come in here and water these fucking plants which cost $40 apiece and they're dead in two months anyway. Why don't you just quit watering them and let the fucking plants die? It'd be cheaper."

The subject was not exactly crucial to the future of Kidder, Peabody but he relished any chance to humiliate Collins. Peter wasn't happy until Collins was out the door of his office and crawling down the hall. After Collins slinked away, Ken and Peter looked at each other and burst out laughing. But Ken disapproved of Peter's browbeating. Collins needed his job and he couldn't talk back to his number one boy.

"Why are you always giving the poor guy such a hard time over bullshit?" Ken asked.

"You've got to understand," Peter said with a straight face. "It's like having a dog. You've got to whip him every once in a while to make sure he knows he belongs to you."

He treated Ricardo, his driver, the same way. Ricardo would be negotiating the black Cadillac through midtown New York traffic and suddenly Peter would erupt in a stream of obscenities from the back seat.

"Why the fuck did you do that? Why didn't you just go through the goddamned light! Of all the *stupid* fucking things. How could you be so fucking *stupid*?" Peter badgered Ricardo about the way he changed lanes, the way he stopped at a light, the way he'd pull out of an intersection. Peter treated the whole Kidder organization like his personal kennel. He got along with just one or two other brokers at the firm and never attended the mandatory morning pep rallies. Ken wanted to attend these sessions when he came on board. Peter told him not to bother but Ken went once or twice anyway.

He realized Peter was right. These were mass meetings in the "boiler room" where all the other brokers in the office sat at desks lined up like a steno pool. Ken came to Kidder with an image: that he would learn to be one of the financial professionals—the words had a solid ring to them—looking out for their clients' best interests. But these sales meetings were a joke. They were talking about IRAs, tax shelters, and stuff like that but they presented them like supermarket products. "Today we're selling apple pies and we'll give you two points for every apple pie you sell."

The next day it might as well have been Bibles. There was nothing about being money managers or financial professionals or doing what was right for the client. After Kidder, Peabody, Ken decided, he would be qualified to be a Fuller Brush salesman.

Peter wrung all kinds of concessions out of Kidder—from the car and driver to his office, which was a throne room in a royal suite compared to the "boiler room" where everyone else worked. His fiefdom was on the quiet, more private side of the elevator banks on the same floor. Peter's private office was laid out like a truncated triangle with windows on three sides giving it a kind of bay window feel and placing it among the most luxurious offices in all of New York City. And it was high—on the 42nd floor. But Peter kept the curtains drawn on the downtown view because it fronted on another office and on the uptown view because it was visible from the Kidder cafeteria, disturbing his privacy. He left open the view across the East River toward Queens and Long Island. Ken's office was next door, and both offices opened into an outer area where two young secretaries, Casey and Diane, worked at desks sorting trade confirmations, checking account statements, and keeping track of portfolios.

Diane was twenty-six, married, and had been Peter's sales assistant for a year. She had a broker's license, but mainly so that she could take care of business and sign papers for Peter when he was out of the office. Casey was twenty-four, attractive and single. She had been with Kidder for two years and Peter was her third or fourth boss. She handled his personal finances, checking accounts, and the like as well as general office duties. Both women were originally from Brooklyn and both of them liked working for Peter, in spite of his hair-trigger temper, foul language, and shouting attacks. Casey was devoted to him.

A half-wall separated Peter's fiefdom from three other offices that had been set aside for other big-grossing brokers (another concession Peter talked Kidder into making) but which remained empty most of the time. In effect, Peter controlled half the floor from the best office in the joint. Collins's private office was on the other side of the floor and opened directly into the boiler room.

Kidder furnished Peter's office with topnotch details: mahogany desk, brown leather club chairs, a down-filled sofa and an antique dining table with four chairs. The walls were papered with designer grasscloth, tinted blue. Peter kept a soiled baseball, signed by a bunch of players from some team somewhere, on his desk next to a toy truck given him by Toys 'R' Us (a retail toy chain whose stock he owned) and a picture of himself on a horse playing polo. Kidder paid an estimated $50,000 to furnish and decorate the room. Here Peter watched the screen of his Quotron machine, entertained clients, and talked on the phone several times a day with David Clark.

"Mr. DIGI," or "Mr. Digital Switch," as Peter came to be known at Kidder, found his second big stock early in 1983. About three weeks after my "Heard" column on American Surgery appeared, Peter started buying the stock for his clients at prices just above $5 a share. Ken bought some, and Peter began loading his clients up with it in much the same way that he had enriched them with Digital Switch, which by this time had reached $108 a share and kept going. But his success with DIGI had its down side—he had attracted too much attention. One day Peter sent orders to buy American Surgery down to the Kidder trading desk. A few minutes later the trader called back.

"Sorry," he said, "but I can't fill your ticket on Surgery at the price you want."

"Why not?" Peter demanded. He expected the best service in the place.

"There's somebody else bidding against you," the trader explained.

Peter was fuming but not half as angry as he became when he discovered that he was bidding for the stock against members of his own firm! He learned that Collins, the office manager, had seen Peter's success with Digital Switch. Collins routinely got copies of all Peter's trade confirmations and he had figured out that by sifting through them he could pick up a few ideas for himself. When he saw a flurry of buy orders flowing out of Peter's office for American Surgery, he dove right in. A group of Kidder employees were tailing Peter the way a flock of starlings scratch for worms in the furrows behind a plow. It drove him crazy. By trading in David Clark's account, in which he shared the profits, he thought he would attract less attention. But it didn't work like that. His groupies were too smart.

By March Peter was snapping up Surgery shares like a true believer. That month alone he bought nearly 200,000 shares just for one of David Clark's accounts. The stock, naturally, reacted to this pressure by rising, trading as high as $8 and finishing the month at more than $7 a share, up from $4, where it traded when my column appeared. Word spread that Mr. DIGI had found another hot stock. The tailgating by Kidder employees spread outside the firm and the stock was getting away from him. He searched for a better way. In early spring he called American Surgery at its headquarters in Phoenix.

"I've seen the publicity about your company and watched your stock go up," he told Surgery's executives. "Now, I'm a big broker here in New York with a respected investment firm and I have a lot of clients who would be interested in putting up a sizable amount of money for some stock."

If he could put together a package deal for private stock at a fixed price, he wouldn't have to chase the thing in the market. Private stock, or restricted stock, usually is sold at below-market prices because its sale is restricted for two years after it's acquired. But by all appearances, the bull market was going to thunder ahead forever. Besides, American Surgery was involved in a hot area in a business, health care, which flourished during good times and bad. Two years? Hell, in early 1983 two years seemed just around the corner. What could go wrong in two years?

Peter met several times with American Surgery officials hammering out an agreement. He and his clients would buy 750,000 shares at $4, raising a much-needed $3 million to help finance the company's ambitious expansion plans—to become the McDonald's of the walk-in surgery racket. When Peter inked this deal and then sat down to figure out how much of the stock to feed each account, some of his clients almost took his hand off trying to get the biggest bite. Small wonder. The deal stock was to be sold for $4 a share and Surgery was trading in the open market at more than twice the price.

Peter made some of his clients feel as though he was handing out free winning lottery tickets. He told more than one that American Surgery was a stock that "will change your lifestyle," the same thing he'd told them about Digital Switch. None of his clients got as much of this "deal" stock as they wanted but few of them complained as loudly as David Clark and another client, Nancy Huang. She appeared in the office one day after receiving her confirmation of the restricted stock in the mail. She was fuming that she'd gotten just half the shares she expected. Peter was away so she shouted at Ken, who, in Peter's absence, spent most of his time making sure his chair didn't roll away. He didn't trade or make any decisions when his buddy was out of town. Ken had never learned how to fill out an order ticket.

By June, American Surgery had escaped earth's gravity, trading as high as $20 a share. This flyspeck of a company—with its big ideas, annual revenue of $1.3 million, and hemorrhaging red ink at the rate of $4 million a year—was worth in the stock market nearly a quarter of a *billion* dollars! Ken's little label business in Connecticut—which was racking up more sales, employed ten times as many people, earned a profit, and paid him a six-figure salary in absentia besides—was several times bigger than American Surgery.

Peter, meanwhile, was spending his profits, in the form of loans against the paper profits in his stocks, like a drunken sailor on liberty. With David Clark, he bought a 52-foot yacht for about $200,000 and arranged for a complete overhaul that would cost about $200,000. Together they also bought the apartment for $1.8 million on the Upper East Side of Manhattan. He purchased several eighteenth-century oil paintings including "Lioness and Lion in a Cave" by George Stubbs, a well-known English artist. The Stubbs cost Peter more than a half million dollars. He spent close to another half million sprucing up the house in Locust Valley, including more than $100,000 just reslating the roof. He built the enormous garage abutting the driveway that was designed to look like a carriage house he'd seen on a neighboring estate. A large television screen was installed so that it descended from a slot in the ceiling of the living room. He had a closet full of audiovisual equipment. Peter had the installers design uniform Plexiglas face plates for the receivers, amplifiers, and players so that, stacked together, the boxes looked like a control board in a recording studio. He bought horses and paid to have them stabled. He owned the Cadillac that Kidder paid Ricardo $30,000 to drive, an Aston-Martin, a BMW, and a full-sized station wagon. He commuted to work in a helicopter which picked him up in the morning in a field on a neighboring estate and dropped him at a heliport on the East River in Manhattan.

Of course, he had it to spend. Who wouldn't reward himself richly after running his assets from a few hundred thou up to $20 million or so? But his worth existed mainly on paper. He didn't sell stock and buy with cash. He borrowed against his net worth. Debt gave him drive. Cash burned a hole in his pocket; he spent it wisely, on things of value that could be resold, but he couldn't have money in the bank.

Peter's prediction that they would make millions overnight had come true. Ken, who started out the preceding July with a grubstake of $28,000, owned about $1 million of Digital Switch by March and twice that much by June when the stock approached its peak price of about $150 a share. He also jumped on the American Surgery bandwagon and by May or so that stock was worth an additional $1 million.

He still had his label business, which was worth about $1.5 million. So, in the space of about ten months, his net worth had jumped to between $4 million and $5 million. He built a house for about $500,000 and paid to have it decorated, all for cash.

Peter hadn't been in touch with his father for nearly eight years, rarely spoke to his brother, Chuckie, and saw his mother infrequently. Every once in a while he and Ken would share a chuckle about his background. A client would be in the office cracking antisemitic jokes and they would look at each other and burst into uncontrolled laughter. The client would never know that they were laughing harder at Peter's secret than at a joke.

But there were moments when his heritage threatened to surface at an inopportune time.

He had been blackballed once when he tried to join the Piping Rock Club, a super-exclusive country club in Locust Valley, by a Kidder employee who didn't like him. Now he tried again. One day in the office, another Kidder broker stopped Ken in the hall.

"There's talk that Peter is trying to get into Piping Rock," he said.

"Yeah," Ken said, "I guess so."

"Well, I heard a rumor that Peter changed his name. Do you know?"

Ken thought fast. While he never cared much to play Peter's games, he was loyal and would never do anything to hurt him.

"No, no," he said. "You must have him mixed up with the other Peter Brant"—a wealthy investor and avid polo player from Connecticut who was fairly visible in the jet set and had the same name. People were always confusing Peter Brant of Kidder with Peter Brant of Connecticut and Palm Beach. Peter said it never did him any good, though. He never did get into Piping Rock.

Once again Ken had covered for Peter and Peter was grateful.

He generally avoided contact with the group from Babson. They knew his background and represented a threat to his successful efforts to pass undetected as a gentile. He poked fun at Ken's clients, some of whom were Babson graduates or people down on their luck whom Ken wanted to help with the soaring stocks.

"Jesus Christ," Peter would say. "You take in every stray dog you run into." He didn't like having some of these clients in his office and from time to time tried to talk Ken into dumping them.

One of the Babson group with whom Ken had kept in touch stopped by the office one day to say hello. He was one of the college men who had razzed Peter unmercifully with nicknames like BornJew. After chatting a few minutes with Ken, he poked his head into Peter's private office to say hello. Peter, whom he hadn't seen in three years, was on the phone. Peter looked up, saw who it was, put his hand over the receiver, and shouted, "Get the fuck out of my office!"

Peter kept Ken separate from his social and business life. Ken wasn't interested anyway, but with his jet black hair, brown eyes, olive complexion, and ethnic name, he figured he didn't fit in with Peter's crowd. He didn't ask why but Peter never offered, for instance, to sponsor Ken at the Racquet Club or any of the other clubs or groups to which he belonged.

Ken accepted this dichotomy. He understood Peter's act from the beginning and assumed that in order to infiltrate high society Peter had made all the right moves. He believed that Peter never would have been able to land a job at Kidder in the first place with the name Bornstein and never would have captured the premier clients. Always at the root of their frendship, Peter was the overdressed kid with the irreverent sense of humor he'd met in a college dorm years earlier over a quarter-stakes game of poker. Ken wasn't interested in Peter's other world.

No one could question Peter's investment prowess. He had guessed correctly that a bull market was coming and jumped in with both feet at the beginning. He picked two of the best-performing stocks of the bull market and rode them like bucking broncos to dizzying heights. Kidder, Peabody executives openly discussed him as a star and the great white hope of the company. Peter convinced the research department at Kidder to put Digital Switch on its recommended list, a move he knew would give the stock an extra shove higher. He convinced the firm's corporate finance department to work on a major underwriting for American Surgery, a possibility he knew would give Surgery credibility and access to other financing. He began agitating for a seat on Surgery's board. He was riding the crest of a wave, a golden boy on his surfboard under a crystal-blue summer sky.

Peter had good reason to feel self-assured and maybe even a little giddy. But he also grew full of himself, like a peacock emboldened by the grand spread of its iridescent tail. He started to believe in his abilities, and he increasingly demanded unquestioned fealty from his accounts. He told clients like Robert Turner, his former Locust Valley landlord, that he had to do things Peter's way or not at all. Turner saw respectable profits in his portfolio, grew nervous about giving those profits back and wanted to sell, a reasonable investment decision. Turner said Peter either refused or ignored his pleas.

"You can't sell," Peter said. "First of all, these stocks are going much, much higher. Digital Switch is a two-hundred-dollar stock and Surgery is a one-hundred-dollar stock. I'm very close to these companies. I know better than you or anyone what's going on.

"Secondly," he said, the tenor of his voice rising with evangelical fervor, "how do you think it would look if sell orders started coming out of my office for these stocks? People would look at that and say, 'Holy shit! Peter Brant is selling, we better get out.' That would just kill the stock, all these people dumping because they think I've turned negative. It would just kill the price and we'd all lose money." He had a knack for making clients feel guilty for even suggesting such heresy.

His logic had merit, though. The flock continued to follow Peter around, watching his every move. The perception that Mr. DIGI, who had also become Mr. Surgery, was a seller instead of a buyer could only be interpreted as an ominous signal for the stock price. The nervous traders at Kidder, Peabody would wonder whether Peter was about to sneak up on them and dump tons of stock in their laps, sending the price off a cliff and devaluing their inventory. But they wouldn't wait for a definitive answer. They would start selling ahead of him. Peter couldn't trust his own traders not to screw him.

But there was another, far more pressing reason why Peter couldn't allow clients to start selling. He and David Clark had bought millions of dollars worth of Digital Switch on margin, the credit they enjoyed from the increased value of their original cash purchases. He had operated the same way in many of his clients' accounts. Peter also had drawn out substantial loans against his profits in DIGI to fund his lifestyle. If the stock were to fall, he and Clark, whose fortunes also were tied up in DIGI, might get margin calls: demands to put up additional cash to cover the reduced value of the shares. Leveraging up, or buying on credit as the stock rises, was a free ride. The return trip could be costly because Peter had used up all the credit tied to his paper profits. This meant that he kept his stock account in as much hock as the law allowed. So did Clark. If a panic hit the stock, both might find themselves facing serious cash squeezes.

If they didn't have cash lying around to bolster the value of the accounts back up to the legal requirement, the only alternative was to sell stock. That decision might not be theirs. If they didn't have the cash to cover a margin call, Kidder traders automatically sold stock to raise it. Such forced selling could beat the stock price still lower, which, in turn, could generate new margin calls, etc., etc. This was exactly how the Crash of 1929 began.

But by June 1983 the Dow Jones Industrial Average had soared nearly 60 percent, and investors everywhere were making great leaps of faith. Few were the voices of doom and many were the believers, like Peter, that the world had entered a golden age of prosperity that would allow the bull market to charge ahead forever.

6
Full Boil

"I learned a lesson years ago," Herbert says to me, "and it's become Herbert's market rule number one. When anyone calls and tells me a six-dollar stock is going to a hundred, I immediately become a seller."

—John D. Spooner, *Sex and Money*

In the same fashion that Peter mesmerized Ken with his "genius," the stock market in early 1983 became my fixation. I got hooked on my job. The pressure to churn out timely and well-written columns left me weak at the end of the day, good mainly for watching dopey shows on television. I was greedy to do more than my share of the work. I hated days, like weekends for instance, when there were no stock prices to watch. I was a card-carrying member of the Thank-God-It's-Monday Club. Returning to the column after the occasional day off left me rusty and sluggish, in need of a fix. I'd pump Gary for details of the previous day's session, but his replay was never the same as the real thing. I started going to the office on Sundays, telling myself that it was the only way I'd ever be able to keep up with the weekly stacks of mail and the torrent of column ideas. To uncover the best investment ideas before the rest of the world, I had to be there all the time. That was how good money managers operated: rarely more than fifty yards from a telephone so they always could call their offices and check prices. I was having so much fun I privately worried that someday there might not be a stock market anymore.

I took Dick Rustin's sermon on deadlines to heart and made it a compulsive game to see by how many minutes I could beat deadline. The last page of my column often was out of the typewriter and on his desk a half-hour before deadline. I was running full tilt and then some. Besides having fun, I thought my diligence would count toward the raise I thought I'd have coming after my first six months or so on the job. Rustin complimented me once or twice on a good column, but generally he kept silent about the overall quality of my work. Part of the *Journal*'s corporate machismo, it was once explained to me, is that you can assume you're doing a good job if nobody tells you otherwise.

And then I stumbled.

My column in January on Radiation Technology, after which the stock sank like a stone tied to a cannonball, contained a minor error. A word, "operating," was omitted in reporting the company's losses for the preceding year. It was a stupid mistake that didn't change the thrust of the column and was insignificant by any measure, equivalent to a typographical error. I was embarrassed and Dick was irritated.

He rolled his eyes, grimaced, and shook his head like I'd borrowed his car and dented the fender. "You've gotta watch these things. That was a strong column that knocked the hell out of the stock. These columns have got to be error-free, bulletproof."

He was right but I didn't give it much thought. I figured it was a fluke. Besides, it was nothing compared with a whopper of a screwup, the kind that cause nightmares, that Gary faced a month earlier. He'd written a glowing piece about Worldwide Energy, an oil company. Analysts liked the stock and thought it was worth closer to $17 a share than the $6 price it fetched in the market. The day the column appeared, Worldwide shares jumped more than $2, or about 30 percent. Gary was gratified. We assumed our columns were on target when the stock prices moved in sympathy. When they stayed flat, or ran in the opposite direction, we assumed we had missed the real story.

"Well, I guess I caught that one just about right," he joked when he saw the big surge in Worldwide. But his good humor soon turned to misery. A phone caller told him that he had overlooked a few facts about the company. Such as an expected massive write-off for unsuccessful drilling, "exhausted" lines of credit, and plans by a major investor to dump 200,000 Worldwide shares on the market.

The worst part of it was that all this negative information was available in a public document the company had filed weeks earlier with the Securities and Exchange Commission. Gary could have obtained it before writing his column. His sources, if they knew about it, should have mentioned it to him. Had he known all this other stuff, Gary probably would have tossed the whole thing in the trash or written a negative column. At the very least, the negatives ought to have been included. His face was taut and his shoulders drooped as he rose from his desk to give Rustin the bad news.

The next day Gary wrote a tail-end item for the "Heard" that effectively canceled out the good news he had reported twenty-four hours earlier. Worldwide sank back to near where it had traded before he discovered it. I felt terrible for him. It could have happened to me. In the rush to turn out a timely, interesting column, we didn't always have spare minutes to assemble every shred of evidence necessary to confirm what our sources were telling us. In this case, the analysts and money managers Gary talked to must have been too busy calculating their expected stock market profits to notice the negatives.

About two months later, in March 1983, I stumbled again. Another stupid mistake. I reported a company had a $5.1 million loss in its last year instead of $2.1 million, the correct number. The two had become a five. Again, the column's thrust was unaffected and few people even noticed the error. Besides, the company's previous loss was old news. But it was another mark against me and I felt bad about it. I wanted every column to be bulletproof.

Meanwhile, Gary and I unwittingly scratched a few egos in the company in the process of writing our columns. The *Journal* news empire sometimes resembled a network of tiny fiefdoms run by feudal lords who, to varying degrees, resented the power flowing from the paper's "capital" in New York. Some of these bureau chiefs welcomed Gary and me when we picked up a good column about a company in their area. The local *Journal* reporters often were overworked, and they barely understood the stock market anyway. In fact, most *Journal* reporters professed little or no understanding of the market and how it functioned. They were glad to learn that we were on the scene, shortstopping the ground balls with the bad hops.

Just a handful of bureau chiefs wore their high self-regard on their sleeves. Anyone who passed across their estates had to pay fealty—or else. Barnie Calame, the Los Angeles bureau chief, was possibly the worst. He had a low regard for anything New York did and was the first to react when he thought protocol had been violated. He had no detectable sense of humor.

Several times we forgot to call Barnie before writing columns about his companies and each time he complained to Rustin. I did it twice. I apologized to Rustin and Calame. Rustin made little of these instances. He understood better than anyone that in the heat of battle we sometimes forgot to brush our teeth.

A week or so after the second error (when $2.1 came out $5.1), I wrote a column in which I misidentified the firm with which an analyst was affiliated. Stupid mistake number three. I realized the error first thing in the morning and called the analyst to apologize. He laughed and said everyone in his office had laughed about it, too.

"Now that we've all had a good laugh over this," I said, "I think we should run a correction in the paper."

"Nah," the analyst said. "It's not important. Everybody knows where I really work."

"Well, I think I'll do it anyway just to set the record straight." Stupid mistake number four.

"This is no good," Rustin told me. "These are inexcusable kinds of errors and, frankly, I'm really beginning to worry. I'm doing the best I can to protect you. But I'd hate to have to recommend to Pinkerton that we yank you off the column." The words reverberated in my head. *Yank me off the column?* I made some stupid mistakes, one of which I didn't even have to report! I felt lousy about it and it was clear that I had sacrificed accuracy for speed. But "yank me off the column" seemed a little like, well, shooting a mosquito with a howitzer. I knew Rustin hadn't threatened Gary like that. But then, Gary was an established star who'd been writing the column before Rustin took it over. Rustin was less likely to try to bully him.

Rustin clearly mistrusted me and now the feeling was mutual.

A week later I did it again. In a "Heard" column listing a group of stocks that looked risky to some analysts, I wrote the wrong name for one of the companies—I wrote Four Phase Systems, which had long ago been acquired and didn't even trade anymore, instead of Floating Point Systems, the company I meant to mention. Same initials, wrong company.

I learned of my error from Rustin. He had a look of disgust on his face and my heart sank. My career was going down the drain because of my dopey mistakes and he wasn't making it any easier.

"The goddamned company doesn't even trade on the exchange anymore, Foster. How the hell could you have made a mistake like that?"

The next day I was at my desk working when Rustin wheeled around the corner of my file cabinet like a squad car arriving at a crime scene.

"C'mon," he said impatiently, waving his hand. "Let's go talk to Stew [Pinkerton]."

My heart pounded into high gear. Now what? I followed him down the aisle into Pinkerton's office like an errant schoolboy being towed by the ear to the principal's office. I sat down in front of Pinkerton's desk and Rustin sat next to it so that they were on one side and I was on the other. It was a trap.

"Dick tells me you've had a string of unfortunate errors in the column so far this year, more than any other reporter on the paper," Pinkerton began.

Sure, I thought to myself. And I probably wrote five times as many stories as any other reporter on this newspaper.

"You know how important and sensitive the integrity of the column is," Pinkerton continued. "It's one of the best-read features in the *Journal* and we can't afford to have the readers questioning our accuracy. Without that we have nothing."

I started to explain that the errors Rustin was so exercised about were minor but Pinkerton raised his hand, palm out like a traffic cop, and cut me off. "I don't want to hear any explanations," he said. "Now, I'm going to write a letter for your file outlining the discussion. I want to make it clear to you that this is serious."

The audience was over.

"I'm doing the best I can to save your job," Rustin said later. "But you've got to work on this problem. Take extra time after you've written the column to doublecheck all your facts. The columns are in early anyway. There's no excuse for not taking the time."

He was right. I hadn't taken this whole issue seriously enough. I deserved a trip to the woodshed.

A week later a news clerk dropped on my desk a bright yellow envelope with the words HAND CARRY printed in red and my name handwritten across the front. It was the letter to my file and it read like a bill of indictment, listing all my mistakes plus the additional sin of having failed to call the Los Angeles bureau twice. It was embarrassing to see all this in black and white and, I thought, kind of unnecessary. Then I got to the last paragraph and I almost choked on my coffee.

". . . Should these problems recur, we will have no choice but to take additional steps that could jeopardize your continued employment here."

"Oh, my God!" I said under my breath. The adrenaline started to pump into my veins. I was frightened and angry. I had been working harder than I had ever worked in my life, writing more than my share of columns. I had been getting them in early, before deadline. My story ideas were good and getting better. I had even managed to squeeze time to report and write a front-page feature. I accepted my verbal thrashing. Stupid mistakes shouldn't be ignored. A letter threatening my job, however, was too much. I felt like I'd been set up for a mugging.

I showed the letter to Gary and he agreed. We brainstormed to try to divine why Rustin was in such a hurry to kick my brains in.

"Do you think it has anything to do with being gay?"

"I don't think so," I said. "Do you?"

"Well, one of the other reporters was telling me that he was making some particularly vicious faggot jokes and I wondered if maybe he just couldn't handle the subject."

Gary and I had drawn close over the months working together. I shared with him the ebb and flow of my personal life and vice versa.

"This is chickenshit, Gary, and you know it. I don't know what to do about it but I've got to do something."

I showed the letter to Groseclose, my former boss on the ticker, and he agreed with my assessment. The letter was too harsh. I also showed it to my father confessor at the *Journal*, Bernie Wysocki, a quiet-spoken, gentle editor whom I respected and who was supportive of my efforts to win a berth on the "Heard." He also agreed and offered to try to run interference with higher-ups.

In the meantime, I lived in daily terror. Every fact in every column became a landmine waiting for me to step on it and blow myself right out of the newsroom. I was distracted, intimidated by the work I enjoyed so much. I started excising facts I wasn't absolutely sure of. My concentration faltered. A week after I got the letter, and none too soon for my deteriorating state of mind, David and I left for vacation in Montreal.

A week after we returned, a *Journal* friend took me aside. "You didn't hear this from anyone let alone me," he said. "Stew Pinkerton and Rustin are going to invite you to lunch to apologize for the harsh treatment. It's Larry O'Donnell's [the managing editor's] idea. Act surprised."

A day or so later, Rustin appeared at my desk. He was grinning and acting very friendly.

"Uh, Stew and I would like to take you to lunch on Friday. Are you free?"

"Sure, what time?"

"Let's say around twelve-thirty or so. We just want to let you know your life isn't in jeopardy here," he said, wheeling and disappearing around my file cabinet before I could react.

Lunch was at the Union League Club, a private men's dining club on Park Avenue that looked frayed at the edges and well past its prime. All the waiters were black and wore white jackets. All the guests were white and wore dark suits. I thought of *Gone with the Wind*.

We small-talked our way through drinks, appetizer, entree, and coffee without a single mention of problems or apologies. I was beginning to worry that it would all be over and I would be cheated out of my reparations.

"Um, about the accuracy thing," I said, lighting a cigarette as the waiter poured more coffee. "I'm really trying harder and I get copies now of the edited version of the story so I can recheck the facts before I go home at night."

"That's good," Pinkerton said. "Whatever it takes not to have a problem is all we care about."

By the time I got back to the office—after a long, painful ride through stop-and-go traffic seated hip-to-hip with these two in a battered cab—I was as bewildered as ever. Of all the great people who worked at the *Journal*, people I liked personally as well as professionally, how had I managed to wind up with these guys? I wondered how Gary was able to shrug off and trivialize these corporate types. He didn't take them nearly as seriously as I, who practically shuddered every time I had to walk past Rustin's desk to the water fountain.

A week later, I introduced myself to a graceful and handsome young stockbroker I was thinking might make an interesting profile.

"Mr. Brant, my name is Foster Winans. I'm a stock market writer at *The Wall Street Journal*," I said when I called to arrange the interview. "I've been thinking, what with the fantastic rise in the market, of writing a feature story about some top stockbrokers and someone gave me your name."

"I've seen your name in the paper," he said. "What kind of story did you have in mind?"

"Kind of a profile describing how they work, how they get their clients, that sort of thing. Someone gave me your name and suggested you might be a good subject. Whattaya think?"

"It's an interesting idea," he said, "but I'm not sure I want to be profiled. Seems to me the people I see profiled, like in *People* magazine, end up looking like jerks."

He was right, of course, but I offered to meet with him on an off-the-record basis and he accepted.

Peter's office was in a new glass tower on Park Avenue a few blocks south of Grand Central Station. The day of my first visit was springlike—warm, gentle breezes and small puffy clouds in a bright sky. A secretary ushered me in to his office. The first thing I usually noticed about these high-floor perches was the view. This one was okay, with its view of the East River and the ship traffic moving upstream and down. But it didn't compare with the vistas that spread out before the high floors of the financial district.

He sat at his desk, a massive dark-wood thing with columns on the front, as I outlined my story idea. We both chose our words with care, kind of circling each other and sizing up the situation. I wanted to ease any jitters he had about me while learning if he really was all that interesting.

"I had an idea to do a 'hanging around' piece," I explained. "That's when a reporter spends a lot of time just following the subject around, getting to know his routine, his habits, his associations. It makes for an interesting portrait, sort of like a camera following you around." I hoped for an inside look at the high-stakes world of a big-time broker.

Peter repeated his fears, but as the preliminaries deepened my questions became more specific and an interview took place.

He told me he managed about $70 million in assets, a huge sum for a retail broker, even if most of it was in bonds that just sat there collecting dust and interest. He had gotten his start at Kidder selling bonds to country doctors at a beginning annual salary of $11,000. Seven years later, he was at the top of his profession and personally worth more than $20 million. Peter was thirty years old. He was born on Christmas Day, so his parents gave him the middle name Noel, which Peter pronounced "knoll." The numbers were staggering. I knew a small money manager in New Jersey who danced a jig when all the money he managed finally rose above the $15 million mark.

The interview lasted less than an hour. I left with an agreement to meet again. We had established enough of a rapport that I thought there was a good chance the story might pan out.

"Sounds good," Rustin said when I got back to the office. "Try to focus on how the guy gets his business, what his social contacts are, where he hangs out, how he sucks up to people to get his business."

I drafted a one-page outline of the story, Rustin suggested some changes, and he started the process of trying to find it a home. Each department of the paper—page one, second front page, statistics, editorial, etc.—had its own chief. Rustin thought maybe he could get the front page to run the story. The only other place to try to sell a feature like that was second front page, which we called just "second front."

The weather was cloudy June 1 and the streets still damp from a late-afternoon drizzle when I arrived at the Racquet Club, where Peter and I had agreed to meet. I didn't see him in the lobby so I signed myself into the guestbook. An attendant tried to track him down upstairs by telephone.

"He's in the gymnasium," he said when he got off the phone. "He should be down in a few minutes. Unless you want to go find him."

I climbed a grand staircase to the second floor where I found a large open dining room and bar. The bartender, dressed in a white jacket, made a few more phone calls.

"I'm not sure where he is," he said. "I know he's here. I saw him. You can wait for him here, if you want."

I went back downstairs. Finally, Peter showed up.

"I looked all over for you," I said. "This place is a rabbit warren."

"Have you ever been here?" he asked.

"Never. It's quite a joint, though."

"Let me give you a tour. It's really very interesting."

We climbed two flights of stairs to the third floor where he led me into a huge concrete chamber that looked like a tennis court but not like any tennis court I had ever seen. A net was strung across the room, but it drooped in the middle as though overstretched and in need of repair. That was the way it was supposed to hang during play. The walls, with small windows on the side that were covered with netting, met the foul lines and, after rising eight or ten feet, sloped outward and then up again toward a huge vaulted ceiling with a skylight.

It took me a while to get Peter to explain the thing in plain language. This, I learned, was one of the few places left in the world where court tennis, as opposed to the popular lawn tennis, was still played. Instead of just pounding the ball back and forth, you somehow scored points by bouncing it off the sloped walls. The way he explained it, the game sounded like a cross between squash, tennis, handball, paddle tennis, and a few other games I'd never played. Scoring practically required a calculator. Court tennis had been a favorite of English royalty years ago and was the ancestor of lawn tennis.

We toured a polo practice room. At one end was a high wooden saw horse with a saddle seat. Polo mallets rested against the wall. At the other end of the room was a net.

"This is where you can practice your polo shots," he explained. "It's my favorite game. I found this practice horse in an auction somewhere and donated it to the club."

As we walked by one of the many alcoves lined with bookshelves, he touched a few covers, selected a volume on horses and removed it from the stack. "I donated some books to the club on horses and polo."

The club had its own tobacco humidor, an oversized closet the size of a small retail store with drawers full of expensive cigars and tobacco. The rich dank smell of cured leaf, which I recognized from my days in the family business, filled my nostrils. An attendant brought Peter a box of his cigars. He chose two and we went into the lounge/dining room where I snacked on cheese and canapés over a Campari and soda. Peter drank his usual, a light beer.

We talked about the market, which had continued its initial surge upward and now was more than 400 points, or about 35 percent, above its low back in August when I first transferred to the *Journal*. Peter said his favorite stocks were Digital Switch, American Surgery, and something called Ferrofluidics, which supplied manufacturing equipment to the semiconductor industry.

"It's a great stock," he said. "It's going to go to one hundred dollars a share." So was American Surgery. Ferrofluidics was trading at about ten dollars a share and Surgery was up around fifteen dollars. Digital Switch I'd never heard of. It was trading at more than one hundred dollars a share. Digital Switch, he assured me, was headed for two hundred dollars.

My column that morning in the *Journal* was about Institutional Investors Trust, a real estate trust company whose shares I asked David to buy in his Merrill Lynch account. We bought the stock six weeks earlier after a stockbroker from the Midwest called me breathing heavy about how cheap it was. The shares traded at less than $1, my kind of stock because with our limited funds, we could buy tons of it—1,000 shares. Just as the broker predicted, the price rose to nearly $2 a share. But there wasn't much to write about the company until just a few days before Peter and I met at the Racquet Club. Another company had agreed to buy a big chunk of Institutional Investors. I updated my research and wrote the column.

We had a respectable profit on the stock and I thought maybe we should sell and roll the money into Ferrofluidics, Peter's $100 stock. He'd hit big winners in Digital Switch, whatever that was, and American Surgery. How wrong could he be on Ferrofluidics?

Peter proposed dinner at "21," the tony uptown place I'd read about in the gossip columns. It was the reputed hangout of lots of New York celebs and it was supposed to be unbelievably expensive. I was ambivalent. This, after all, was just another source meeting. I preferred to be home relaxing off duty. I debated for a moment and decided, what the hell.

"Sure," I said. "Why not? It's a first for me."

When we got to the sidewalk, a slender young man in a dark

suit jumped out of a black Cadillac parked at the curb. Eyes fixed on Peter like a devoted pet, he sprinted to the passenger door and opened it. Peter led the way.

I was pretty impressed. It was a simple limousine, no bar or television. But the back seat had lots of room to stretch out as the chauffeur, whom Peter introduced to me as Ricardo, pulled out into traffic for the short trip to "21."

"This is part of what making and having money means to me," Peter said. "I hate traveling in public transportation. I'm tall and in this thing I can stretch out and take it easy. Being rich means I don't have to ride in cars with other people or in crowded elevators." Peter was posturing, but against the scenery of his wealth his statements gained weight. And he was entertaining to be around—the tones of his husky voice, his vitality, and his physical energy and grace.

The maître d' recognized Peter when we arrived at "21." Peter stopped to say hello to someone at another table on our way to our seats. Throughout dinner we talked about the market and I kept stealing glances at other tables to see if I could spot any famous faces. They were there, I was sure, but I didn't recognize any of them. Celebrity watching was not my forte. I once spent an entire restaurant meal furtively watching Peter Boyle, the actor, eat sweet-and-sour pork at the next table. It wasn't until he and his weird-looking dinner pals left the restaurant that I learned he was dining with Mick Jagger, John Lennon, and Yoko Ono.

The conversation during dinner, which cost Peter $140 (gasp!), rambled aimlessly over the state of the market and Peter's business. The thread of his personal philosophy, he made clear, was money. And money meant to him privilege, privacy, and security from an ugly, dirty, hostile world. Peter's basic rap was that everyone ought to be rich. It was the most outrageous thing I had ever heard uttered with a straight face by a man in a suit. But I was intrigued by Peter. He was a character unlike any I'd ever stumbled across, and I was a journalist with a strong natural curiosity.

We walked out of the restaurant into the warm night air. Peter gestured toward the car and offered to give me a ride home.

"I'm staying in town tonight anyway," he said. "It's no bother. Hop in."

I had never ridden in a limousine before that night and felt out of place during the trip to 14th Street. This was not where I belonged, and I felt too guilty about enjoying it to enjoy it. I wondered what Peter's reaction would be when he saw the deteriorated buildings, the porno theater, and the young dope dealers who hung out on the streets twenty-four hours a day. What would the neighbors think if they saw me getting out of this big shiny black car in front of the door? Peter was silent about the neighborhood as I got out. The car pulled away and I glanced at the license plate to see if it bore the telltale numbers of a leased limo. But it read, simply, "PNB."

David was home when I walked in the door.

"Wow," I said. "I just got a ride home in a limousine. What a trip! It sure beats the miserable subways. Let's buy a limousine!"

"Sure," he said. "First thing in the morning."

David had just quit his job at the *Journal* to devote himself full time to a small business he was developing, selling advertising on tourist maps of New York. I wasn't thrilled with his decision. We had been holding our own between our two regular weekly paychecks. Now we would be vulnerable to the ups and downs of a young business. We had to count on living on my paycheck until the business started to generate income.

The next day Peter called me at work.

"Listen, I was thinking. You know I try to help people out when I can. Like Ricardo's mother. I made her $50,000 in the stock market. I don't usually take small accounts like that but if you could come up with $5,000, I'd like to open an account for you."

I told no one about David's stock account, which was where all the money we could borrow was tied up. But I hardly knew Peter well enough, nor was I inclined, to share this fact with him.

"It's a generous offer, Peter, but I don't think so. Thanks anyway."

"Look, it's no problem. We can open it up today and I can start making money for you."

"I'll give it some thought," I said.

We sold the Institutional Investors a few days after the Racquet Club meeting and bought 100 shares of Peter's $100 stock, Ferrofluidics, which then traded at $10.38 a share. At $100 a share it would be worth $10,000. I could hardly wait!

Two weeks later Peter and I met again, this time in his office. We hadn't really talked about the story per se, but he told me on the phone, "A guy is coming in about becoming a client. I'll let you sit in so long as it's off the record. That way you can get a feel for how I work."

The view out his office window this time was murky. The city was in the grip of an early heat wave, with humid smog bathing the Queens suburbs in a grimy-looking haze.

Peter had grown more relaxed in my presence and resumed working a trade he'd been involved in when I arrived. I pulled out my notebook and settled into a chair in front of his desk as he stared at the screen of his Quotron machine, his chin in his hand.

"I shorted Texas Instruments this morning," he explained. Shareholders had given the stock a violent thrashing the day before, chopping roughly a third off its value in twenty-four hours. The violence began when the company announced plans to bail out of its troubled videogame business and take a $100 million loss. Peter had bet the stock would fall again the second day after the bad news.

"These big institutions don't react the first day," he said, outlining his theory. "The banks, insurance companies—they have to have a meeting of their investment policy people before they do anything and that takes a day or so. Then, finally, they figure out that they don't want to own the stock anymore. So they sell the day after the first big plunge and the stock takes a second hit, which I caught by going short at the opening."

He got on the phone to his trading desk. "Joel, it's Peter. How are we doing on that TI short? . . . Good. Well, let's get it off. . . . You got it? . . . Okay, buddy." He turned to me and flashed a broad self-confident smile, "Well, I just made $20,000 on that one. Not bad for a day's work."

I had witnessed such transactions before, yielding even larger profits. I also knew that sums just as large were often lost. But I never got bored watching. All my working years I slaved long hours for pennies a word. People like Peter shuffled in a day as much capital as the average American family might expect to earn in a generation.

"You've obviously done well for yourself," I said, looking around the office with its antiques, down-filled sofa and silver water pitcher. "You've made yourself millions. But what's it all for? Why knock yourself out? What's the motivation?"

"I want to make enough money so I can afford to donate large sums to charitable foundations or maybe even start my own foundation. I have an interest in wildlife. I could do some good with all the money I've made. I'd like to be the kind of man that someone—I think it was Jefferson—said he wanted to be. Accomplished at many things. Able to perform surgery and fly a hot-air balloon."

This fluff sounded a little disingenuous, but Peter, for all I knew him and his industry at the time, could just as well have been the next John D. Rockefeller under construction. He projected sincerity, he had the trappings his business required, and his life suggested a man who had already accomplished some amazing feats. He was just thirty and had earned from scratch a fortune that defied my imagination. I saw no reason to disbelieve his abilities. His physical presence only added to the image. He was handsome and poised. I was particularly struck by the seductive quality of his voice and speech pattern—it was pleasant to my ears.

The prospective client finally called to cancel.

"You know, I have a yacht I keep up here in the summer. Sometimes on Friday nights I sail it home with some other folks from Wall Street," Peter said. "Why don't you join us sometime?"

"You're kidding," I said. "You *sail* home from Manhattan to Long Island?"

"Sure, if the weather's good. And then sometimes we sail it in on Monday morning. It's tied up at a dock on the East River."

"Well, I'll think about it. Sounds like fun."

"And I'm having a party on the boat the Fourth of July. That might be a good chance for you to see where I live and meet some of the people I do business with. Why don't you come out?"

"Let me see what's doing and I'll get back to you."

"Um, did you have a chance to think about opening an account? We can do it right now, if you have a check with you."

"Look," I said. "The truth is I don't have any extra cash."

"It's okay," he said. "I'll open the account for you and we can worry about that later."

"I appreciate the offer but no thanks," I said.

I took no offense at his effort to link us together. Sources often dropped such anvil hints: "Here's a great stock. You ought to buy some in your mother's account." Peter was just more direct about it. I had learned that on Wall Street people were always scratching backs. Sometimes this presented a problem for reporters. For instance, we were supposed to pay for meals with sources. But many of my sources, high-powered investment types who viewed expense account largesse as a common courtesy, wouldn't take no for an answer. I asked Rustin what to do after nearly getting into an argument over a breakfast bill early in my days on the column.

"Well, if you can pay for it gracefully do it. But don't fight with them if they insist. A meal isn't going to make the difference," he had said.

As I rose to leave, Peter picked up a small cloth-bound book from the credenza behind his desk.

"Here, this is a rare copy of a book I want you to have. It's about a famous stock market trader. I think you'll enjoy reading it."

He pulled a fountain pen from his pocket, opened it, and made an entry on the flyleaf as I stood waiting to leave. It seemed to take him forever, and I was a touch uneasy about this unexpected intimacy. Finally he finished and handed me the book. I stuck it in my briefcase without looking, we shook hands, and I left.

In the subway on the way back to the office, I pulled out the book. It was a hardback with a deep orange cover which had on it a drawing of a bear wearing a three-piece suit and a top hat and smoking a cigar. It was titled *Reminiscences of a Stock Operator*. Peter had written on a slant inside with a fountain pen:

> To Foster W—
>
> This most entertaining book has tremendous virtue. Quality, timing, common sense all important here & great influence on me & my success in my business & trading. Hope you enjoy it as much as I did,
>
> Regards,   Peter Brant

The book was written by Edwin Lefevre and dedicated to Jesse Laurston Livermore. But history records it as Livermore's thinly-disguised authorized biography at the age of forty in 1923. It was a fascinating read. Livermore was one of the most famous stock manipulators of Wall Street. His heyday was before the Crash and the advent of the SEC. Livermore was a fiercely private man who got his start at fourteen years of age trading stocks in crooked bucket shops (the owners often threw buy or sell orders into the trash—a bucket—instead of executing them for clients because prices were rigged so that the little guy usually lost). Livermore figured out how to beat these shops at their own game. With his blond hair and smooth skin, he gained the lifelong nickname of "The Boy Plunger." He became a legend in his own time, kind of an anti-hero like the corporate raiders of today, a lovable rascal to the business press. He also made, and lost, several multimillion-dollar fortunes during his lifetime.

One November afternoon in 1940, Livermore downed two drinks in the bar at the Sherry-Netherland Hotel in New York, walked downstairs to a bathroom in the basement and blew his brains out. He died nearly penniless. Forty-three years later, a boy plunger of another era named Peter Brant would rub shoulders with the likes of Frank Sinatra in an exclusive supper club called Doubles on the same spot.

7

The Balloon Bursts

That the hotshots will resurface is not doubted by any old-timer—nowadays this means anyone who managed to survive the 1960s intact. If the pattern of the past is repeated in the present, they will shine brightest just before the market collapses.

—Robert Sobel, *Inside Wall Street*

The superbroker story was aborted. The *Journal*'s front-page editor rejected it and Rustin submitted it to the editor of the front page of the second section and we got the same reaction: Who cares about a broker and his clients getting rich in a bull market? Everybody was getting rich. My concept of the story differed from Rustin's. I wanted to do my "hanging around" piece. He wanted to make the guy look like a playboy dilettante who sucked up to the rich. That may have been Peter, but Rustin was prejudiced from the start. It was a theme in *Journal* feature stories. We were encouraged to expose subjects to ridicule.

George Anders, the former "Heard" columnist who had transferred to the London bureau, lamented this practice in a letter to me. George was working on a story for the European edition about London's most expensive dry cleaner. The proprietor was a bold self-promoter who drove a Porsche badly, claimed to do Margaret

Thatcher's undies, and had changed his name so it would be more European sounding.

"It would be easy to write a bitingly funny story about this guy, but it would be tinged with a bit of meanness," George wrote me. "I've been encouraged [by *Journal* editors] to write those kinds of stories. But I think they give journalism a bad name, and I think it is a much greater art to write a critical story that doesn't make the subject embarrassed to go home to his family."

I actually was relieved when our efforts to "shop" the story around to different sections of the paper proved fruitless. I didn't like the feeling that I was boxed in to a story that reflected Rustin's prejudice.

Peter and I kept in touch by telephone during the summer. We talked every couple of weeks, mostly market gossip in general and Digital Switch in particular since it was Peter's favorite. The company had declared a three-for-one-stock split in May. Shareholders got in the mail two extra certificates for each one they owned and the price of the stock was divided by three to compensate. Stock splits usually are considered bullish because the lower price, in theory, makes the stock attractive and accessible to a broader audience. Individual investors are more likely to buy lower-priced stocks—like me, who could only buy a few shares of a $50 stock but could afford a thousand shares of a $1 stock. These investors mistakenly call such low-priced issues "cheap stocks," as though they had been discounted to make room for the new models. In fact, they can be more overpriced than a $100 stock.

But in the case of Digital Switch, the stock split boomeranged. The shares had soared in about a year from $14 to $147. People knew they had made money in the stock but the reality of it hit home when, in the mailbox, they found extra stock certificates. Peter complained that DIGI had waited too long to declare a split.

"They should have done it when it got above $50," he said in one of our phone talks. "Now these little investors got more stock certificates and they treat it like it's a gift or something. Fred and Edna get this 'free' stock and they think, 'Hey, let's buy that new car.' So they start selling."

DIGI started to sag as the summer wore on. American Surgery did too, retracing some of its huge gain but holding above $10 a share.

The stock market itself began to level off. The bull looked a little tired, and market experts began saying the second half of the year would bring only modest additional gains. Peter convinced himself that the plateau was just a resting period after which the market, and his stocks, would resume their rise.

But something was going wrong, slowly and imperceptibly at first but definitely wrong. Perhaps the first signs of rot in the market's foundation showed up as early as May. Certainly the crash of Texas Instruments in June should have been a sign. The big money had been made in technology and health-care stocks. Anything exotic—companies with names that ended in "xonics," for instance—had made people rich. The American Surgeries and the Digital Switches had been the best action in the best stock market in generations. These same stocks started to wobble as summer broke. The wobble grew more pronounced as the summer wore on and the stocks began to crack and disintegrate.

The other sign of trouble was in the new-issues market. Peter had been an active player of these stocks. As Kidder's top broker, he had dibs on shares of companies that were going public for the first time. While the market was hot, everyone wanted a piece of the action. Investment firms would put together an offering of stock to the public to raise fresh capital for some young, unproven company. The firms set a fixed price and would sell the shares to willing buyers before the stock actually traded in the market. On Day One of public trading, the shares often would jump a few points and those lucky enough to have gotten stock on the offering would sell and pocket an instant profit. Investment firms used these new issues to curry favor with, or as gifts to, productive employees or big customers. The profit was practically guaranteed.

As the bull slowed down to rest, these profits, or "premiums" as they were called, evaporated and new-issue stocks started to fall in the open market instead of rising. I wrote a column in which I quoted Peter, by name, saying, "I haven't touched one in the past six or eight weeks, after months of taking everything I could get my hands on. The bubble has burst for now. The easy money's been made."

Peter had the rap but he wasn't listening to his own words. I was too involved in the daily routine to catch the significance of what was happening until August. And I had no sense of Wall Street's history. Neither did most of the people who were managing money. Except for some old-timers left over from the go-go years of the sixties and the bloodbath that followed it, most of us covering the market and many of those managing the money were children of the 1970s who had never lived through a major bull market.

Peter's comments about new issues fit perfectly into my column, but I suspected he would probably pay for his honesty. I made sure he understood I intended to quote him and use his name. I guessed right. Kidder, Peabody's executives gagged on their fresh-squeezed orange juice the next morning when they read my column and saw their top salesman thumbing his nose at an important source of the firm's revenue and profit.

"Boy, that quote sure made some people pissed off around here," he said the next day.

"I sort of wondered whether you might get some flak. That's why I made sure it was okay to quote you."

"Yeah," he laughed. "The bosses wanted to know how I could be so fucking stupid."

Peter's ties to American Surgery continued to strengthen. Kidder executives were a little miffed when they learned of Peter's arrangement to sell 750,000 shares of restricted stock (stock that couldn't be sold in the market for two years or more) to his clients without Kidder's approval. He had acted as an investment banker under Kidder's umbrella, but the firm got cheated out of its customary fee for arranging such deals. Peter, meanwhile, was complaining about American Surgery. He said that he'd been promised 40,000 free shares for having arranged the deal, but American Surgery seemed to be dragging its feet on delivery. In the meantime, he convinced the investment banking department at Kidder to consider doing a major underwriting for the company. The investment banking folks met with Surgery officials and the negotiations were going smoothly until, in August, the stock was broadsided by a fiercely bearish syndicated column written by Dan Dorfman, the former "Heard" writer.

American Surgery had announced on the ticker that it was a potential bidder in a possible deal to build and operate hospitals in the Middle East. The company said it hoped to participate in bidding for a multimillion-dollar contract with Bechtel Group, one of the largest and most prestigious construction and engineering firms in the world. The announcement sent the stock soaring some 30 percent to more than $13 a share. The excitement attracted the attention of a group of short-sellers who recognized that the stock had gotten way ahead of itself and was due for a big tumble. The company was still losing money on an annual sales rate of just more than $2 million. Yet the total value of the company, based on its stock price, was $156 million.

Dorfman accused the company of hyping the stock and quoted Bechtel officials as saying the possibility of the contracts was unclear, that they were still in the planning stage. The stock plunged the day Dorfman's column appeared in the *Daily News* in New York. The Kidder investment bankers, who were close to completing a major financing for the company, suddenly were tied up in meetings and couldn't be disturbed. Big respectable securities firms hate controversy, and Peter received a few phone calls that morning that fueled his fury.

"Those *stupid* fucking assholes!!" he screamed. He phoned Lynn Singley, American Surgery's president, a tubby middle-aged man with a balding pate whom Peter nicknamed Jabba the Hut. Singley liked to portray himself as an aw-shucks kind of Midwesterner, precisely the kind of person Peter would ridicule behind his back. But Dorfman's column, and the stock drop, squelched Peter's sense of humor that morning.

"You *stupid* fucking assholes!!" he screamed at Singley. "What the *hell* were you doing making that goddamned Bechtel announcement? You don't even have a fucking contract. Now you got everyone riled up and made an ass of yourself with the press. I had this goddamned financing all set up here at Kidder and now the fucking thing is down the drain! How could *anybody* be so fucking *stupid?*"

I saw Dorfman's column that morning and wired a copy of it to the *Journal's* Los Angeles bureau so they could follow it up. Somehow I convinced myself that the company still had its act together, even if they had screwed up their public relations. Dorfman was playing handmaiden to the short-sellers, something he did regularly. That was part of the game of covering the stock market. Like Gary and me, Dorfman's approach was to pick a corner and defend it. In this case he was shooting fish in a barrel. The company's market valuation was way out of whack with its true value, and the big Middle East hospital contract was just pie in the sky until a deal was inked. Besides, the hospital was going to be in Lebanon, where armed factions had been busy reducing the capital, Beirut, to mounds of shattered concrete and dust. The talk among the short-sellers, who had the scent of blood in their nostrils, was, "Yeah, they're going to build hospitals in Lebanon, all right. If there is a Lebanon."

The Los Angeles bureau bounced the follow-up back to me, and I wrote a short item that ran at the end of the lead "Heard" item the day after Dorfman's column appeared. I thought it only fair to mention that the stock sank after Dan's column. I put Dan's name in the story and submitted it to Pinkerton, who was filling in for Rustin.

Pinkerton read the story and smiled when he got to Dorfman's name. He knew Dan from his days at the *Journal*.

"Oh no. Oh, no," he said, shaking his head and grinning slightly. "I'm not putting Dan's name in *this* newspaper." I thought it was unfair to leave Dan out. After all, the stock crashed after his column appeared. But I assumed Pinkerton wanted to nettle Dan a little. Dan would read the "Heard" and *he* would notice that his name was missing.

Sure enough, like clockwork, I answered the phone the next morning and it was Dan Dorfman. I'd never spoken to him before.

"Foster, this is Dan Dorfman." he said in a high-pitched squeaky voice that had become familiar to viewers of the Cable News Network. He did a market commentary every night on "Money Line."

"Is this *the* Dan Dorfman, of stage, screen, and supermarket openings?"

He laughed. "Listen, I don't know whose idea it was but I just want you to know that I think it was lousy of you guys not to put my name in your story this morning."

"Yeah, Dan. I have to agree. It was in there the way I wrote it but the editors took it out. Maybe they wanted to see if you'd call and complain."

We chatted about American Surgery. He clearly was a bear on the stock and I clung stubbornly to my bullish view. I wanted to meet this legendary columnist, one of my predecessors, and we agreed to have dinner a few days later at an Italian restaurant near the financial district. Over dinner we discussed the market, market coverage, and, inevitably, American Surgery.

"I think you're all wet on Surgery," I told him. "Sure, the

stock got ahead of itself but my sources on the Middle East thing told me a different story than what you wrote in your column."

"The company's no good and the stock is no good," he persisted. "And it's going to go a lot lower."

I couldn't ignore the challenge. "I say the stock will be ten dollars a share or more by the end of the year. What do you say?"

"How much are you willing to bet?"

I thought a second. "Okay, if I'm right, you buy a dinner. If I'm wrong, I owe you a dinner."

"It's a deal," he said.

What had happened to American Surgery was symptomatic of the steady deterioration taking place that summer in the entire market. A few months earlier, the slightest breeze of good news sent stocks like Surgery soaring. Now, the psychology had reversed. You could knock most of these stocks over with a feather. The top-tier stocks, such as IBM and the other huge corporations whose shares made up the Dow Average, had ceased rising and flattened out. But underneath this placid surface, hundreds of overblown little technology and health-care stocks were burning out of control. For the first part of the summer, Peter wasn't too concerned. He and his clients still had good profits in Surgery and DIGI. But as the carnage widened and accelerated, he started to sweat.

The market was already wobbly late in August when news from Washington produced a sudden, spasmodic decline in DIGI. The Federal Communications Commission announced its decision regarding the cost to long-distance telephone companies such as MCI for plugging into the AT&T network. The cost structure the FCC adopted was much higher than anyone was expecting. If costs were to spiral up for companies like MCI, they wouldn't have as much money left to expand and buy the fancy telephone switching equipment that DIGI made. The bulk of DIGI's business was with these long-distance competitors to AT&T. MCI was its biggest customer, accounting for about 25 percent of DIGI's revenue.

The FCC decision sent MCI off a cliff, clipping 20 percent off its share price in a matter of hours. Digital Switch lost more than 10 percent, trading for the first time in months at just under $100 a share, or $33 adjusted for the three-for-one stock split.

The stocks continued to crash as the effect of the FCC

decision, helped along by the market's flaccid tone, began to ripple through the investment world. By the beginning of September, Digital Switch had fallen to half its June high—$75 a share, or $25 adjusted for the split. The breakup of AT&T was the biggest business-news story of the year, and we covered it closely. The time was ripe for a column examining the issues and the outlook. I remembered that Peter had said he owned a bunch of DIGI, so I called his office to find out what he knew and whether he might be selling. I had heard there were margin calls and forced selling in the stock.

Peter's secretary said he was out of town, in England, but he returned my call later in the afternoon. He gave me the bullish liturgy. "People don't think this FCC decision will stand and DIGI's customers will need to buy its switches just as much as before." He gave me the names of a few sources to call for additional gossip.

"So what are you doing with the stock?" I asked.

"It's murder," he said. "There are margin calls all over the place. People are getting sold out. If this keeps up, I'm going to be wiped out."

I didn't believe for a second that Peter Brant, who sailed a yacht home on Fridays, commuted in a helicopter, and built a fortune from scratch, was anywhere within $10 or $15 million of being wiped out. I had no independent knowledge of his finances or the details of his business but it was a colorful quote, appropriate to the cataclysmic nature of the action in the stocks. I used the statement in the column anonymously, describing Peter as "one broker and money manager who, on behalf of his clients, holds a large position in Digital."

We talked again early in September—about Apple Computer. The stock skidded sharply the day we spoke and I was preparing to write a column examining the drop and the reasons behind it.

"What do you hear about Apple?" I asked. "The stock's getting hammered. There's talk IBM is giving Apple a tough time."

Peter rattled off something I considered uninformed. But he thought he had learned something from the conversation. After he hung up he dashed into Ken's office all excited and talking as fast as his lips would let him.

"I just talked to Foster. I'm pretty sure he's doing a negative story about Apple." Peter called the Kidder trading desk and put in an order to short Apple.

We talked again the next day. "Boy," Peter said, "that was really amazing. We talked yesterday and I was short Apple and you ended up doing a negative column on the stock. I couldn't believe it when I saw the paper this morning. What a coincidence."

As far as I knew, that's all it was—a freak coincidence.

Peter never let on that anything was really amiss in his life. But as September grew older, his spirits declined. The battering of Digital Switch was beginning to take its toll. He and David Clark had been hit with heavy forced margin selling. He wasn't exactly facing disaster but his two favorite stocks, DIGI and Surgery, both had changed direction with ferocity. His net worth fell from millions and millions to just millions. His lifestyle didn't change, but Peter suffered emotionally when his net worth dropped a few million. It was the same as it would be for an office clerk whose landlord raises the rent by $25 a month. Peter's numbers were bigger, but the psychological effect was no less pronounced. Fear of poverty stalks even the best neighborhoods. When he had made $10,000, he once told me, he needed $100,000. When he'd made $100,000 he needed a million. When I met Peter, he was up to tens of millions and aiming for his first $100 million.

A month after the Apple Computer column, a woman with whom Ken Felis had trained for his broker's license called him up with a stock tip. People were always calling Peter's office with stock tips. He had a reputation as a heavy hitter. If he could be romanced into liking a stock, he was in a position to pour millions into it and give it visibility and buoyancy.

Ken looked at the literature she sent him on Widergren Communications. He thought it looked interesting so he took it in to Peter.

"What is this mongrel?" Peter said as he flipped impatiently through the pages. He always disparaged Ken's investment ideas. After all, they'd made so much money on Peter's ideas, why screw it up? "Look at this stock. It's overinflated. We shouldn't be buying it, we should be selling it short!"

He picked up the phone and dialed my number.

"How you doing?" I asked.

"Great," he said. "Listen, if you're looking for an idea here's one you might find interesting. I'm short the stock. It's Widergren Communications and its a real piece of shit. The stock is way up and they don't even have any business yet."

"Sounds interesting," I said. "Who did the underwriting? Where can I get more information?"

He turned to Ken as he hung up, a smile lighting up his face. "I think he's going to do it," he said.

In fact, he hadn't shorted the stock yet. But he sure did then.

I got copies of the company's prospectus rushed to me by courier that day and wrote a small item at the end of the column describing how the stock had soared 450 percent in the preceding two months. Widergren's sales were meager, about $500,000, and it hadn't even begun manufacturing the computer device on which it had staked its future. The shares fell the day the column appeard.

"Thanks a lot, pal," he said, laughing, when he called the next morning. "That was a great piece you wrote and I ended up covering my short at a profit."

"Don't thank me," I said. "It was a good tip and an interesting item. If it hadn't been interesting, the stock wouldn't have fallen. You did the favor, not me."

Sources would do that from time to time—call up and say thanks. But I didn't care where my ideas came from or whether people had positions in the stocks they touted as raging buys or screaming shorts. I assumed that they gave me these ideas *because* they had an interest in the stocks. What other motivation could anyone possibly have for giving a stock market columnist an idea? If they made money, so what? We didn't print puff pieces and we never accepted one person's word as gospel. If our reporting undermined the original thesis, either there was no column or we took the opposite tack. Even if we came to the same conclusions as our sources, the stock market didn't necessarily obey the "Heard." Sometimes we were just plain wrong.

Peter made money on Apple and Widergren, but everywhere else his empire was beginning to crumble at an alarming rate. Ken, who had stuck by Peter, made tons of money, and endured the pretension of Wall Street and Peter's jet-set clients, by now was bored and itched to get back to his label business in Connecticut. He never intended to make a career of Kidder, Peabody, and now that the market was no fun anymore, he wanted out. Peter fought him every time he wanted to sell stock and Peter had been wrong. The stocks continued to slide. Ken finally got himself and his clients out of American Surgery, at least those shares that weren't part of the private placement and restricted from sale. Digital Switch was another story.

Ken made plans with his business partner to return to Connecticut around the first of the year, 1984. But before he had a chance to discuss it with Peter, the worst disaster yet struck Digital Switch. The stock, which had managed to struggle back to about $33 a split share, suddenly turned and went into a free-fall. The price sank more than 30 percent, or $12 a share, in the space of a week or so, triggering massive forced margin sales in Peter's account and in the accounts of clients such as David Clark. Selling begot selling, just as it had in 1929. In the space of a few days, the value of the 320,000 Digital Switch shares remaining in Peter's and Clark's accounts had dropped almost $4 million. And that didn't include shares buried in other accounts.

Peter panicked. He still was well fixed by any standard, worth a few million or so. But he suddenly saw himself in a precarious situation. Maybe he was wondering how he would explain the $2.3 million that had been transferred out of the Roger Wilson account. Or his obligation to fix up the yacht for $200,000. Yet, inexplicably, he couldn't bring himself to sell Digital Switch voluntarily. He had made the same dumb mistake that the most unsophisticated investor makes. The stock had been good to him and he fell in love with it. As bad as Digital Switch had been to him since it peaked in June, Peter couldn't bring himself to make the decision to get out. It was still a $200 stock. Peter no longer owned DIGI. It owned him.

Ken was more pragmatic. He sold the remaining shares of DIGI and washed his hands of it. He pleaded with Peter to do the same.

Peter continued to try to impose his loyalty to the stock on his clients, either talking them out of selling or ignoring their requests to do so. Robert Turner, his former landlord, managed to sneak through a sell order when Peter was out of the office. When Peter returned and saw the trade, he flew into a rage.

"He had already started to get hyper and nervous before the big plunge," Turner said. "We were friendly but his mood worsened and this began to strain the friendship. Then when my sell order went through against his wishes, he exploded, yelling and screaming at me on the phone about 'How could I do this to him?' and 'Didn't I realize how much damage this could do to his reputation?' I had had it with the roller-coaster ride on Digital Switch. Selling the stock was the happiest day of my life."

Clients who had bought the restricted shares of American Surgery started putting pressure on Peter. As part of the stock deal, Peter told some clients they'd be able to sell some of their restricted shares early when there was another stock offering, presumably the one Kidder had been working on before the Dorfman column killed it. But this promise could no longer be fulfilled. Surgery was sinking, there would be no financing, and Peter's clients were getting fidgety. The stock market wasn't booming anymore and they wanted out.

"Don't worry," he told Turner. "These stocks have just hit air pockets and they'll be coming back. Besides, next year we'll find another Surgery or Digital Switch."

Meanwhile, Kidder, Peabody arranged to run full-page ads for Peter in *Avenue* magazine, a glossy publication aimed at wealthy New Yorkers. The ad showed Peter sitting on the edge of his desk in his office and flashing his half-smile. "Thinking of investing in stocks and bonds?" the headline read. "Kidder, Peabody has someone you should talk to!"

The copy read:

> Now that your investments require more thought, you need a stockbroker who is an accomplished professional. A broker who knows the American markets and how to assist upper-income individuals make the most of their money. A broker who, moreover, understands the subtleties involved in international transactions. And the importance discretion plays in any business relationship.
>
> Peter Brant is such a broker. Experienced. Straight talking. He spends an enormous amount of time and energy going after the unusual situation with potential for massive gains. And believes in maximizing return by taking a large position in a small number of securities and staying with them as they develop fully.

What's more, Peter Brant's considerable skills
are backed by Kidder Peabody's vast resources. . . .
That's important because it allows Peter Brant . . .
to hear of promising situations before the herd.

On October 6, six days before I sat with Peter in the Racquet
and Tennis Club and he suggested I tell him what was going to be
in the "Heard" column, he submitted a financial statement to
Morgan Guaranty Trust to support a loan to purchase a painting.
He listed $16.5 million in assets and a net worth of $11 million, up
from $1.4 million a year earlier. His biggest assets, unsalable shares
of Kidder, Peabody and American Surgery plus tons of Digital
Switch, he valued at a total of $12 million. But the restricted
Surgery and Kidder stock couldn't be converted into cash. The
Digital shares he listed at $10.3 million, but he owed nearly $5
million of margin debt. Within six days of the date on the financial
statement, his Digital stock lost a third of its value. The rest of his
assets were tied up in art, real estate, horses, and personal belong-
ings.

By the time of our meeting at the Racquet Club on October
12, Peter's liquid assets weren't anywhere near the $12 million
he listed on his financial statement, but closer to $2 million.
His commission income had soared, of course. The year-to-date
$875,000 income he showed on a September 1982 financial state-
ment grew to $1.8 million for the same period a year later. But the
bulk of his fortune had evaporated like a morning mist, as though it
never existed. And there was still the matter of the depleted Wilson
account. The walls were beginning to close in on him.

Similar pressures, on a much smaller scale, were beginning to
dog me. David's small publishing business had yet to earn a profit.
We might have lived on my salary alone, but the extra cash we had
to pump into the business to keep it going proved too great a
burden. We had made a total of about $4,000 in American Surgery
and Institutional Investor, but subsequent investments managed to
cancel out a chunk of our gains. My bank statement for the
beginning of October showed a balance of zero—we were overdrawn.

The tension of working for Rustin, the many breakfasts and
dinners that extended an already lengthy day, and my continuing

dissatisfaction with my salary had me musing about a job change. A couple of mornings I had appointments scheduled for eight o'clock at the Plaza Hotel in midtown but was so exhausted I went to the Vista by mistake. These were days when I couldn't remember the name of the person I was supposed to meet and had to elicit it in a roundabout fashion.

I was to have breakfast one morning with a money manager whom I'd only known by his voice over the phone. I arrived on time and spotted a white-haired guy in a conservative suit. He spotted me and we sat down, ordered breakfast, and chatted about the market. It wasn't until our plates arrived and we had starting eating that we realized each of us had arrangements to meet someone different.

I thought I might be able to edit analysts' reports for a brokerage firm and maybe learn to become an analyst. I had learned a lot about the stock market in a year, and more about reporting and writing than I had learned in all my previous jobs.

A friend who was a producer at CBS urged to me to consider television news.

"Look at the crap they call business news on TV today," he said one night as we dined in Soho. "It's lousy, uninspired and uninformed. You've got the contacts to do a great job of it, and business news is where it's at right now."

In September the *Journal* sent me to San Francisco to attend an annual investment conference sponsored by Montgomery Securities, one of the larger brokerage firms on the coast. At a cocktail party after a day of non-stop dog and pony shows by participating companies, a senior partner in the firm took me aside.

"So, what are your future plans?"

"That's a good question," I said. "I'm enjoying what I do but I doubt I'll want to do it forever. I figure I could use another six months or a year writing the column. What do *you* think my future is after the *Journal*?"

"I was thinking that we could use a good writer to help sharpen up our research reports and maybe run interference for the analysts to make sure they aren't missing something in the market. To sort of keep them in touch with the rest of the world. These guys get so wrapped up in their areas they lose touch with what's going on elsewhere."

It sounded like a good idea. Most of the research reports

coming out of Wall Street were badly written. Analysts don't make great writers, yet writing is their most important form of communication.

"When you're ready to make a move, give me a call."

The *Journal*, meanwhile, was in a state of upheaval. Norm Pearlstine, the *Journal*'s golden boy who successfully launched the paper's European edition, returned triumphant to New York to take over as managing editor of the *Journal* itself. The mood in the newsroom was expectant and a little nervous. It was akin to the second coming. Pearlstine promised to bring with him a completely different, more open style of management. But his arrival also carried with it an implied threat: that some people might find their careers suddenly stalled or deflected.

The reorganization that followed his return resembled a chess game filmed at high speed. Almost as soon as Pearlstine's jet hit the tarmac, people were being promoted and reassigned. He hired dozens of new reporters and editors. The editing system was completely reshuffled. The paper began to assume the structure of an Italian postal bureaucracy. Every day a new stack of interoffice memos from Pearlstine appeared on the bulletin boards. They all began, "We are pleased to announce . . ." and listed the latest moves in the companywide chess game. There was only one I really cared about. Dick Rustin was transferred to the foreign desk. It was the second happiest day of my tenure at the *Journal*, after the day I was hired.

"Gary," I said that morning, "I feel like Martin Luther King. Free at last. Thank God almighty, I am free at last."

8

No One Gets Hurt

Wall Street professionals know that acting on "inside tips" will break a man more quickly than famine, pestilence, crop failure, political readjustments or what may be called normal accidents.
—Edwin Lefevre, *Reminiscences of a Stock Operator*

The Peter Brant I met at the Racquet Club on October 12, 1983, appeared serene and self-confident. The $12 a share crash of Digital Switch never came up in the conversation and neither did the extensive damage he and his clients had sustained in the previous two weeks.

Peter invited me out to his house in Locust Valley that weekend to discuss his proposal about trading on the "Heard" stocks. I was sure I would go but less sure about his proposal. He would be more specific during the weekend, I thought, so I delayed a decision until then.

Peter dropped me off in front of my apartment house and I got upstairs without having to explain to any of my neighbors—all of whom I knew from my work on the tenants' committee—why I had just stepped out of a limousine. The only limos we saw in our neighborhood, none of them bearing my neighbors, stopped further up the street so the dope dealers could negotiate through a slightly opened window the price of a small plastic bag of grass.

Our building was going co-op, equivalent in New York City to winning the lottery. To accelerate sales, building owners typically offered their tenants a discount on their apartments of forty to sixty percent off the "retail" price to outsiders. It usually was a hell of a deal. Some New Yorkers built small fortunes by renting and subletting dozens of apartments. Eventually a few of them would turn co-op and these entrepreneurs would sell at retail, pocketing between $50,000 and $150,000 a pop.

My neighbors consisted of a ragtag collection of college students, aspiring actors and actresses, travel agents, and senior citizens. All of us were big-city poor. Our rents were cheap, $400 to $600, compared with the $800 to $2,000 rents many people in New York labored to pay. But none of us earned big incomes. David and I were better off than most. My salary, about $30,000 a year, paid the rent and left us some money to invest in David's business. But everyone in the building was frightened. Some feared they'd lose their homes. Some of them worried that if they bought their apartments, they wouldn't be able to pay the mortgage and the maintenance. I lay awake at nights worrying that we wouldn't have the down payment for a mortgage. We needed about $6,000. Housing in New York was such a nightmare that I intended to buy and stay. For a change, we wouldn't have to scrounge around for an apartment ever again. We'd be our own landlords. I had worked hard to find our apartment, getting up at 4:30 in the morning every Wednesday and running down to the newsstand to catch the early delivery of the *Village Voice*. At one apartment I saw advertised, thirty people showed up for the viewing. Competition for affordable space was frenzied.

I had an unreasonable compulsion and anxiety about the apartment. David and I argued over our budget. There just wasn't anything left over at the end of the week to sock away toward a down payment. I made lists of people I thought might help us. I dropped hints to my family. Our plunges in the market, in addition to satisfying my curiosity and gambling instincts, aimed to raise enough cash to make the down payment. It was an obsession that Peter unknowingly fed with his proposal to trade on advance knowledge of my columns. The checking account was overdrawn, and although we'd made a little money in the stock market the prospect of raising the entire $6,000 by the time we'd need it seemed bleak.

David was home when I got inside. We rarely discussed my work. Sometimes I'd bring home office gossip about people he knew from his time as a news clerk at the paper. But David was quickly bored by the details of what I did, even when he worked at the paper. If he had any feelings about my work, they tended toward resentment of the time I spent rushing off to breakfasts, and staying late for dinners, with sources.

"I'm going out this weekend to visit a broker source of mine on Long Island," I told him, once I'd gotten settled in for the evening. "He's a rich stockbroker who wants to do some trading with me. He wants me to give him stock ideas and share the profit—if there is any."

A look of suspicion crossed David's face. He objected to my long hours during the week. Now I was going to be away a whole weekend. He had heard me talk often enough about possible career moves that hadn't come to pass. This was just another possibility.

"We don't have money for that kind of thing," he said, lighting a cigarette.

"We don't have to put up any money. It's supposed to be my ideas and his money."

Peter's idea intrigued the hell out of me. Gary and I sometimes made a game of guessing whether stocks would rise or fall, and by how much, the day our columns appeared. Like the Radiation Technology column, after which the stock price collapsed by half. Gary had said, "Well, Foster, this ought to knock the stuffing out of the stock." Neither of us expected the drubbing it actually took. Then there were the columns that completely missed the mark. I once wrote a bearish piece about Digital Equipment, but the stock rose a point or so the day the column appeared and soared $10 a share the day after.

As I pondered Peter's proposal, I gave the ethical questions short shrift. My one concern was getting fired from the *Journal*. But that was a possibility I had learned to live with. Dick Rustin fixed that. Every day I arrived at work could have been my last. In spite of the praise I'd received from other editors and from Gary about the work I was doing, I still considered Rustin a threat, and then after he moved to the foreign desk, Pinkerton remained the troll under the bridge.

The constant state of insecurity, coupled with frustration about my salary, helped make me a bad employee. I compared my work poorly to Gary's and never felt I quite measured up to the high quality of the columns he wrote or the work that most other reporters on the paper turned out. I valued Gary's judgment above my own and must have asked him two dozen times, "How am I doing?" Each time he responded, "Great!" But as much as I needed this reinforcement, and as hard as Gary tried to give it, I never could bring myself to believe it. I hated reading my columns in the paper, seeing in them all the flaws I had missed while I was writing them. Maybe six of them I was truly proud of. The rest seemed like so much unsophisticated blather. In a weird way, I may have been trying to get myself fired. A parasite of self-doubt and self-destruction gnawed at my psyche.

And then there was the atmosphere of Wall Street. I had learned from my sources and from covering the markets that just about anything goes when it comes to trading and making money. One source seemed to know ahead of time about a whole host of takeovers. He hit some six or seven deals in a row. Yet there was never any talk of his trading on inside information. He was just doing business the way everyone did business. On one of his hits, he claimed he got the tip from a lawyer for an investment banking firm that represented one side of the deal. If it was true, he'd committed a crime. But he sure didn't behave or talk like a criminal, and acted as though this was the way every hot shot did business.

There were lots of other examples as well. Gary or I had learned on occasion of influential analysts who, the afternoon before they told all of their firm's customers of a major recommendation change, tipped off their best and biggest institutional clients. This allowed a few clients to make their trades before everyone else.

Then there were the hordes of aggressive bears, short-sellers, who cultivated the press to their advantage. Gary knew more of these people than I did. They were great sources for leads on grossly overpriced stocks and knew better than anyone that negative press could pound these stocks down and give them a chance to cover their short sales at a profit. The same thing worked in reverse, of course. Positive coverage could boost a stock price. But newspaper reporters are more interested in exposing puffery and fraud than they are in praising great little companies with bright futures. Scandal always sells more papers than good news.

These short-sellers worked in packs, like wolves, spreading the bad news among themselves, to the investment community and, finally and most importantly for them, to the press. In one sense, they performed a public service in much the same way that wolves only kill the weakest and sickest game. A stock is overpriced whether or not anyone says so. Ultimately it will crash, just as American Surgery and Digital Switch crashed. The pack of short-sellers were highly organized and just accelerated the process. And, of course, they got to feed on the carcass. As stock market writers, we knew we were being used all the time. A good, solid story exposing puffery and even fraud was our payback. The pack of hungry short-sellers ran down the overpriced stocks with fact sheets and rumors of cash flow problems, canceled contracts, and corporate misdeeds. Once cornered, it was left to the press to put these stocks out of their misery and, as a by-product, enrich the short-sellers.

Sometimes, when stock prices tumbled after a negative column or soared after a positive mention in the "Heard," Gary and I would joke, "Hey, maybe we're in the wrong end of this business!" It was an easy trap to fall into—believing in our ability to identify successful investments. Our sources—investors and short-sellers—had already done their homework and handed us some of these stories ready to heat and serve. We worked hard to verify information and dig up facts, whether they proved or demolished a point of view. But we weren't analysts or brilliant money managers. It was easy to imagine, when a stock jumped or sank after a column, that we were the geniuses. In a few instances, we might have been. But most of the time, we were only as smart as the people feeding us our tips and ideas. Our real talent, if we had one, lay in the ability to tune in only the most promising and logical investment ideas from the constant static that bombarded us.

All of these facts of life on the Street were known to me and part of my consciousness when Peter made his proposal. I was anxious about my job, worried about money, and disbelieving in myself. And by now my sense of morality had been altered by my experiences. I had come a long way from my days on local newspapers as a young reporter chasing stories about the little guy getting screwed. I had served on the board of a local chapter of the

Foster Winans's picture as it appeared in
the 1966 high school yearbook for
Germantown Academy, near Philadelphia.

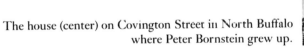

Peter Bornstein's picture as it appeared in the
1970 yearbook for Bennett High School in Buffalo.

The house (center) on Covington Street in North Buffalo
where Peter Bornstein grew up.

The Bombay Club, the informal social group to which Peter Bornstein and Ken Felis belonged. Peter is in back, fourth from the right. Ken is in front holding a drink, second from the right.

The social group Peter Bornstein adopted at Babson College formalized itself with blazer patches, bordered in gold, that featured as a logo a pair of crossed polo mallets and a martini with an olive. The Bombay Club had no official standing on campus and its function, other than as a vehicle for college pranks, was limited.

Peter, in his early 20's, with Lynn, whom he would later marry, at a formal dance near Boston during his college days in the mid-1970's.

The Racquet & Tennis Club on Park Avenue in New York, an exclusive private men's club to which Peter Brant belonged. It was here that Peter first proposed to Foster Winans that they trade on advance knowledge of articles scheduled to appear in *The Wall Street Journal*.

Peter in a photo taken in his Kidder, Peabody office on Park Avenue for an advertisement which appeared in *Avenue* magazine in 1984, just as his stock-trading arrangement with Foster Winans was first surfacing in the press.

R. Foster Winans

The view from the links of the clubhouse at the Meadowbrook Club. It was here that Peter Brant and Foster Winans sealed their arrangement.

David Carpenter, dressed up to attend the Dow Jones 100th anniversary party in 1982 at the Metropolitan Museum of Art in New York.

Left: Ken Felis at his home in Connecticut.

Above: David W. C. Clark as he appeared in April 1984 in Manhattan being chased by an NBC film crew. *(NBC News)*

The apartment building on East 14th Street in Manhattan where Foster Winans and David Carpenter lived in the early 1980's. The one-bedroom apartment was on the fifth floor, far right.

The *Finesse*, a 52-foot sail and motor vessel designed by Sparkman & Stevens and built in 1958, which Peter Brant kept on the north shore of Long Island in the summer and near Palm Beach in the winter. When he owned it, the hull was navy blue and the decking and upper works were all dark wood.

The section of the condominium development at the Palm Beach Polo and Country Club where Peter and Lynn owned a one-bedroom apartment. It was here, in 1984, that Ken and Peter had their last face-to-face meeting and it was here that Peter and Lynn moved with their infant daughter after selling the house on Long Island. *(David Murry)*

American Civil Liberties Union, worried and written about discrimination against blacks, marched against the war in Vietnam,
and walked the straight and narrow on even the most minor issues.
I couldn't sleep one night when I worked at the *Trentonian* because I
had accepted a five-dollar bowl of spaghetti from a city councilman
at a city-funded dinner. The next morning I presented myself to
the city clerk's office at opening time and reimbursed Trenton for
one bowl of pasta. Now, four years later, I contemplated participating with Peter Brant in a scheme that could jeopardize the best
job I'd ever had. Something in me had warped.

If any troublesome caution flags popped into my mind during
the two days between the Racquet Club meeting and my planned
trip to Peter's house, I managed to rationalize them out of existence. Peter never gave me a reason to think that he was a desperate
man playing his last cards. And I never asked myself why a
millionaire stockbroker needed to indulge in such a caper. Instead,
I sat down with all of our bills and totaled up what we owed. It
came to about $18,000, including a $6,000 loan on a car. Before I
left that Saturday, I decided I would ask Peter for an advance
against the profits he expected if we made a deal. At least maybe
David and I would get out of hock. That was all I wanted. To get
out of the financial hole we'd dug.

Peter's house was tucked away in the trees on a small country
lane in a heavily-wooded section of the North Shore of Long
Island. Some of my ancestors had built ships in this part of the
country, but I had never explored the island—and especially not
this area, which was populated by very wealthy people who lived
in enormous houses on huge tracts of land. Peter's house was large,
but seemed modest compared to some of the leviathan estates I
passed on the way—built of stone at the end of long asphalt
driveways and surrounded by manicured lawns and gardens. Many
of these palaces were out of view, safely hidden in the woods. The
neighborhood was so exclusive that most houses didn't have mail-
boxes, just small tasteful black signs stuck in the ground with the
owner's last name in gold letters.

Peter's house was hidden from the road by stands of rhododen-
dron and tall trees with dense foliage. It had a short driveway,
covered with chipped stone, leading to two parking areas—one at
the front door and another at a large garage that looked like a horse
stable or a carriage house. The two were connected by a circle. The
house itself was painted white. It was modestly adorned, bland and

uninviting—an overgrown suburban tract house with several Greek-style pillars at the entrance.

Peter answered the door, and I stepped into a large and cheerless marble-floored foyer that echoed. He introduced me to his wife, Lynn, who was very poised but passive, almost deferential, as though she didn't want to infringe on Peter's role as master of the house. Peter accepted that role, paying her scant attention. She was stunning to look at, with her long wavy hair, which was reddish brown, and smooth rosy complexion. She was well into a pregnancy.

The house looked much bigger inside than it did from the outside. The ceilings on the first floor were very tall and the rooms large. We spent most of our time in the den, which was really a large informal living room with huge French doors that looked out on the lawn and swimming pool at the back of the house. The space was dominated by club chairs, a large coffee table that housed the TV projection equipment, and an overstuffed sofa piled with throw cushions. At the flick of a switch, a screen would descend from a slot in the ceiling. The walls had been painted a streaky blue, an attempt to give the room an antique feel. But it just looked like streaky blue paint to me and seemed to cheapen the grandeur of the space and the big French doors with brass handles. This was the warmest room in the house and even it had a chill.

We spent the afternoon and evening in small talk. Peter gave me a tour of the house and grounds. A long hall connected the living room with the kitchen, which had recently been redecorated with gray Formica and tile floors. Off the hallway were a sparsely decorated formal dining room and a formal parlor. The furniture looked expensive—antiques with brass handles, and stiff-looking sofas and straight-backed chairs. Both rooms looked like they belonged in museums, and I half expected to see felt ropes across the doorways and red ribbon tied across the arms of the chairs. No one, it seemed, ever used these rooms.

Peter showed me several eighteenth-century paintings in fussy gold frames and explained the history of one of them, which showed an eighteenth-century squire on his horse under a tree, with an estate in the background.

But his most prized possession was the carriage house. It was a large wooden structure with a ventilating cupola on top and heavy beams supporting a high roof.

"I had this thing almost completed, and I'd spent $40,000, when I realized it wasn't right," he told me. "So I had it torn down and we started again."

I couldn't figure out the purpose of the building. The house already had a garage, stuffed with expensive cars like an Auston-Martin and a BMW. And I was sure he didn't intend to keep horses in that neighborhood. But it was his pride and joy, as was the driveway which was undergoing some final touches. The chipped stone had recently been laid and was being bordered with marble curbstones. A mop of a dog, a West Highland Scottish terrier, followed us everywhere. The dog's name was Westy and he was Peter's pal. He had owned another dog, a white terrier, that was run over and killed by a car when I was first getting to know Peter. The dog's death threw him off for several days, and he still talked about how much he loved the mutt and how he wept when it was killed.

Peter mostly talked about the house and I mostly listened. When Lynn was around, we talked about the impending birth. She was worried about the risk of having a child at her age, forty or forty-one. But mostly she hung out in the kitchen or elsewhere in the house. Later her daughter, Stephanie, a teen knockout with long blonde hair and draped in high-fashion clothes like a model, showed up from the boarding school she attended in upstate New York. Peter started kidding her about the social station of her boyfriend, the son of a local garage mechanic, and about her expensive clothes.

"You like having a daddy who's a millionaire, don't you?" he teased at dinner. She smiled sheepishly but she didn't answer, so he said it again. I was embarrassed for both of them. It was a tasteless thing to say, especially in front of company. I wondered whether he said it for my benefit or just to razz the poor kid.

The cold house and all its trappings of new wealth made me wish I was back home in my cozy apartment in New York. Peter and I were connected by the market, and we seemed to enjoy each other's company most when we talked about stocks. The evening had been all small talk, family stuff about my background and work. I felt a little out of place. After dinner, I took him aside.

"When had you planned on having our talk?" I asked. I thought perhaps we could get this over with and I could go home that night.

"Tomorrow," he said. "We'll go out to my golf course."

The next morning we had breakfast and headed out to the Meadowbrook Club. Peter drove his BMW fast and with abandon. I was learning that this was a hallmark of his personality. He was usually in a big hurry, driven by some unseen and reckless force.

He signed us in, and we picked up an electric cart and started toward the first hole. The day ranked as one of the year's best, just on the cool side but with a clear, bright fall sun punctuating a perfect deep-blue sky. The leaves were just reaching their height of color. The land on which the course was built stretched away from the clubhouse in sweeping strokes of brilliant green bordered by flaming trees. The day was filled with promise.

"So did you think about what we talked about?" he asked.

"Yeah," I said. "But I want to hear more. I don't understand how such a thing could work." I don't play golf, so I watched and walked as Peter smashed the ball around the course. He couldn't seem to get it anywhere near where he wanted, but it didn't seem to matter. It was a great day for a walk and we both enjoyed it.

He explained to me that I would tell him the day before what was going to be in the "Heard." He would buy stock or call options on positive stories, and sell short or buy put options on negative stories.* The day the column appeared, he would close out the transaction and, presumably, there would be a profit.

"So, what do you think?"

"A couple of thoughts come to mind," I said. "First is that I'm no genius about the stock market. I mean, we've been wrong on our stories and we've been right. Maybe you won't make a profit like you think you will."

"That's the risk I take," he said. "But if we're right, we make a lot of money."

---

*Options on stocks work sort of like options on real estate. The option purchaser pays a premium just for the right to participate in a transaction some time in the future at a specific date. Options to buy a stock are referred to as "call" options, giving the holder the right to "call" the stock to him in the future at a set price. There is also an option, called a put, that gives the holder the right to sell or "put" to someone else a quantity of stock at a specific price by a specific date. Options trade on exchanges just like stocks. Most options are bought and sold many times over before expiring. The price to play options is much lower, as little as twenty-five cents a share, but the investor risks, and often loses, his entire investment. Occasionally investors make fortunes in options overnight, giving them a speculative or gambling appeal.

"The second thing is that under no circumstances would I ever screw up a column because of such a deal. I would want to feel I was sort of working in a vacuum, that I would continue to do the best job I can without regard for any deal we have." I respected the *Journal* and my profession, if not myself, and would not have agreed to any arrangement that required me to misinform in any way the editors or the readers of my columns.

"Oh, yeah!" he said enthusiastically. "That's right. You just keep doing what you're doing. The only difference is you tell me what the column's about. I won't bother you about your business and you won't bother me about mine."

"Another thing is I probably would be better off not knowing how much money you're making," I said. "I know that sounds funny, but in a way I think it might make my job harder if I knew we'd made a ton of money. If I need dough, I'll let you know. Otherwise, I'd rather you just kept it aside without saying anything.

"You know, this is the best job I've ever had," I continued. "If the *Journal* were ever to find out, I'd be fired on the spot."

"No, no, no!" he said. "No one will ever know. It's just between us. You write the columns and I'll make the trades. No one gets hurt, no one knows. Then, when we've got a few million bucks stashed away, I'll start my own firm and you'll come to work for me. Deal?"

"Yeah," I said, extending my hand to shake his. "Deal."

Peter's little black terrier sat in my lap as he negotiated the cart between the greens. I had total confidence in him, although I recognized that the part about making millions was hyperbolic. If we did make millions, I knew what I was going to do with it. I had my lottery fantasy all planned out a long time before I met Peter: first thing was to get my father a new car, pay off the mortgage on my mother's house, and pay all my brother's bills.

What really excited me, though, was the prospect of being linked to Peter in such an intimate way. He was still a pretty mysterious guy and I hungered to know more about him. He was my Jay Gatsby, and I was progressively more interested in what this elegant young roughneck really was about.

We continued walking as Peter hacked the ball around the course. You'd think he'd never played golf before the way he was knocking it into the woods and sand traps.

"How would you let me know what's in the column?"

"I guess I'll call you. How else?"

"Maybe you shouldn't call from your desk. Are there any pay phones nearby that you can use?"

"Um, I don't know." I thought for a minute. "There is a bank of pay phones across the street in the lobby of the AT&T building. I could call from there."

"Yeah, that sounds good," he said. "I guess that means that if I call you at the office you might not be able to talk."

"Depends. Our desks are back-to-back and it's pretty easy to overhear each other. Sometimes Gary's away from his desk or out of the office. But I'll let you know if it's a problem."

"There are a couple of things left on the agenda," I went on. "First is, I know I told you I'm not married. But I do live with someone, a guy, whom I share my life with. I just wanted you to know that in case you have any problems with it. You've brought me into your family and I want you to know my family as well."

"Sure," he said. "No problem. What's his name?"

"David Carpenter."

"How long have you known him?"

"Oh, I guess it's been close to ten years," I said, calculating the time. "Yeah. Ten years this January."

We rode a little further.

"The other thing is more embarrassing. David hasn't worked for a while. He's trying to start his own business but it doesn't look like it's going to go anywhere soon. Plus, he's had huge dental expenses. Anyway, we're in tough shape financially and I wondered whether you'd be in a position to advance us a little money against the profits, assuming there are any."

"Absolutely." He jumped in without any hesitation. "How much do you need—$15,000? $20,000?"

"Nah. That's high. I think $10,000 would probably keep us going for a while."

"Fine," he said. "But are you sure? You sure you don't need $20,000? It's no problem."

I thought about it for a minute. We had $18,000 in bills, including the car. But I didn't need to pay off the car. That would leave $12,000 or $13,000 in bills.

"Okay," I said. "Make it $15,000. I really appreciate it. You have no idea how much that helps us out."

"No problem," he said. "We're partners. We'll just take it out of whatever ends up being your share of the profits, after deducting

50 percent for taxes. I'll write you a check tomorrow. Except one problem. I can't make the check out to you. Do you trust David?"

"Absolutely," I said. "We're very close. I trust him completely."

"Well, that's great. I'll make it out to him, okay?"

"Sure, sounds fine."

When we weren't talking about the stock market, or family affairs, or our arrangement, Peter launched into an occasional sermon on the benefits of being rich. It was the central theme in his life. He told me that when he was a young trainee at Kidder, Peabody his wife developed an ear infection. He said he couldn't afford a specialist to treat her, and after a period of excruciating pain, she lost most of her hearing in the ear.

He shook his head and said with reverential conviction, "I'm never ever going to let something like that happen again."

By the time we were done, we must have gone around that golf course three times and lost six balls in the woods. It had all gone so easily. It all seemed to make so much sense. There weren't any victims. This was just a formalized version of the kind of guessing my sources did every day. And it was a gamble in which he was willing to take all the financial risk. I trusted him that no one would ever find out, so I didn't even conjure up the ultimate disaster scenario—being fired. As I contemplated my future on this glorious fall day, I thought how lucky I was.

When we got back to the house, I collected my things and drove back to the city, into a spectacular judgment-day sunset.

"Well," I told David, "it's all set. And the really good news is Peter is going to advance us fifteen thousand dollars. Now, maybe, we can finally get out of this hole and get some money set aside for the co-op. Also, I told him about you and he wants to make the check out to you."

I had always been the primary wage earner in our household and David frequently complained that if I died or if we split up, he'd have nothing to show for his years with me. The checking accounts, the loan accounts, the car, the apartment—all were in my name. I had only recently added his name to the checking account, and he still didn't have access to the loan account. I knew he'd be pleased that I considered him part of my business dealings with Peter, even if in name only. If something should happen to me, I thought, maybe Peter would be able to take care of David.

"Getting involved with a source of mine like this very easily could get me fired," I told David. "One whiff of this and the *Journal* would have me out the door so fast my head would spin. This is our business, nobody else's. So we keep it between us, right?"

"Okay," David said, lighting a cigarette. "But you're the blabbermouth around here."

Less than two hours after I left Peter's that Sunday night, he changed the rules without telling me. He spent more than an hour on the phone with Ken Felis describing the arrangement. But Peter's version of how it came to pass was quite different. He told Ken that I had lured *him* into the deal, instead of the reverse—that I already was doing the same kind of trading but was undercapitalized and sought Peter out as a partner. To Ken it made sense, the way Peter presented it. They had read stock market columns in the *Journal* and elsewhere and said to each other, "Boy, I wonder how many shares this guy owns."

"What about Clark? Are you going to include him?" Ken asked Peter that night on the phone. Peter and David Clark talked on the phone four or five times a day. They were partners. It seemed a natural progression that Peter would include him.

"Clark's a pig," Peter said. "He's a lunatic. I don't want anything to do with him."

The next day was Monday. I called Peter from the AT&T lobby and announced myself to his secretary as Foster Winans.

"Hi, it's me," I said, when he got on the line.

"Hi. What's the good word, buddy?"

"I'm working on a column that's been lying around on my desk for a while but I think it's timely now. Some analysts I've been talking to think the oil service stocks look cheap. You know, the drillers, the oil rig people. Anyway, some of them are recommending the stocks because the rig count looks like it's bottoming out and they're talking about a rebound."

"Which stocks?"

"Oh, let's see. Halliburton, Tidewater, Sedco, Western Companies, Schlumberger. A whole bunch of them."

"I can't go out and buy all those stocks," he said. "Which are the ones they like the best?"

"I can only tell you that the two biggest ones, the two most visible, probably are Halliburton and Schlumberger."

"Okay, pal. We're in business."

"Uh, did you have time to write that check?"

"Yeah," he said. "Spell the name for me again."

"Carpenter, like the guy with a hammer and saw."

"What's his first name?"

"David."

"Okay, how do you want me to get this to you? You want me to send it down by messenger?"

"Yeah. Actually, let me send a messenger from down here. Maybe you should put it in an envelope with something else just in case somebody accidentally opens it before it gets to me."

"Okay," he said. "All set."

"Listen," he continued, "I've got a partner I want you to meet. He's an old college friend whom I brought into my business and gave ten percent. He's a partner in everything I do."

Cripes, I thought. One day, and already there's someone else involved whom I don't know. I was angry but I hid my feelings.

"What's his name?"

"Ken Felis. He's a good friend. I trust him. We've known each other a long time. You'll like him. We'll get together later this week and you'll meet him." I deferred to Peter anyway, and he presented it in a way that didn't invite any objections on my part.

"So, it's this oil service thing for tomorrow, right?"

"Yeah," I said. "Talk to you later."

That same morning I had an interview in the office with a money manager from upstate New York. I had been putting the guy off for months about a possible column on his investment methods. They were unusual. The only stocks he bought for clients were the thirty stocks that make up the Dow Jones Industrial Average. After the interview he told me he was also being interviewed by another publication later that day. I was worried that I'd get beaten on my own story so I switched gears. The oil service column I'd told Peter about would have to wait for Wednesday and this money manager column would have to go the next day.

When I got a chance, I called him.

"Change of plans. The oil service column will run Wednesday. I've got something else that absolutely has to run tomorrow."

"Okay," he said. "Maybe we'll get lucky with the market tomorrow. I already did the trades. I bought Schlumberger. Let me know if there are any other changes."

The check arrived that afternoon in an envelope containing a

Kidder, Peabody research report. The check was drawn on an account at Morgan Guaranty Trust, a bank I knew catered to the very wealthy. Peter's name was printed at the top. As soon as I got home that night I sat down with our bills and made out a list of checks I wanted to write. God, it felt good to be able to pay the bills. We would finally be able to pay back about $5,000 we had borrowed from friends and another $4,000 owed to a loan account. Most of the rest would go to a host of smaller bills. I showed the check to David and he endorsed it.

"We've got to make this last," I said. "I don't know whether Peter is going to make any money or not. If he doesn't, we may have to pay this back. In any event, don't count on any more."

The next morning I deposited Peter's check in our joint account through an automatic teller machine. I got a little tingle when the machine, after swallowing the envelope, showed on its screen the balance in our account—$15,072.88. The same day the market flew into an air pocket. The averages sank sharply, taking most stocks with them, including Schlumberger.

Peter was about to leave his office that afternoon for a squash game when David Clark telephoned, according to Peter's testimony later, touching on other of the day's events; about which I knew nothing.

"You got anything to do?"

"Yeah," Peter said.

"Come over to my office." Clark sounded depressed.

"I'm just about to head out to a squash game. Can't we talk tomorrow?" Peter said.

"I've got to see you now." Clark was insistent and Peter gave in. Clark, after all, was his biggest customer, generating several hundred thousand dollars a year in commissions. They shared the profits in Clark's trading account, and Peter had received some of the money that used to be in Roger Wilson's account. Peter thought Clark was a pig, but he couldn't ignore the fact that he had put plenty of bacon on Peter's table.

He found Clark, at his law office on Madison Avenue, in a severe state of depression, talking suicide. He told Peter he had been diagnosed as an alcoholic and couldn't live with himself. Peter felt sorry for the guy and tried without success to console him. Then he had a brainstorm.

"Remember, I told you about that *Wall Street Journal* reporter who was coming over to my house last weekend?" Peter said. "Well, he did come out and we have a deal where he's going to tell me what's going in the paper the next day so I can trade on it. I'll share the profits with him."

Clark's spirits began to recover. "You know how I feel about that," he said. "It's the cheapest money you can pay." But he was skeptical. Peter told him that an article would be in the paper the next morning about oil service stocks.

"If the article is there, we know the plan is working," he said.

Very early the next morning the phone rang at Peter's house. He was barely awake. It was Clark, who lived in a house nearby in Locust Valley.

"Have you seen *The Wall Street Journal* this morning?"

"No," Peter said. "I just got up."

"Well, I haven't been standing out in the rain at 5:30 in the morning waiting for the first edition for nothing, kid."

"Is the article in there?"

"Looks like we got ourselves a deal."

When Peter got to the office he told Ken about the conversation with Clark.

"I saw Clark last night and the guy was really depressed about his drinking problem. So, to cheer him up, I let him in on the deal with Foster."

Ken said nothing but he thought, Isn't this the same guy who Peter two days ago called a pig? This small gesture of generosity on Peter's part—a gesture he neglected to mention to me then or later—proved to be an act of self-destruction. We were lost even as we were beginning.

Later, under oath at the Securities and Exchange Commission, Clark denied discussing our trading agreement in its early stages with Peter. Clark claimed he at first inferred that Peter had a source at the *Journal* after Peter began suggesting and making trades in Clark's accounts that bracketed the "Heard" column. Clark claimed he didn't know I was Peter's source, until two months after we began our trading scheme, when Peter told him.

Wednesday morning my column on the oil service stocks appeared. Schlumberger had fallen $1.50 a share the day before, along with the rest of the market. Peter had bought 100 call options on the stock, a riskier and more volatile investment, as well as 15,000 shares of stock. The day the column appeared, Schlumberger didn't do much, finishing the session at $54.13, up only 38 cents. Peter sold his options at a loss of nearly $50,000.00. I was working on my next column so I called him again from a phone booth in the AT&T building.

"Those industry group stories are no good for us. We lost a lot of money," he said when we talked that day. "You don't get as much of a pop when it's spread out among a whole bunch of companies. It just doesn't work. Plus we got stuck because of the market risk. That extra day, when the market fell, really killed us. We've got to avoid that market risk."

But he remained enthusiastic. This was just fine-tuning the system. I had warned him that sometimes stocks didn't perform the way we thought they might and that I wouldn't alter my schedules or change them to suit his needs. This was glaring evidence that the "Heard" wasn't a sure thing.

After he finished analyzing the Schlumberger trades, I told him about the next day's column.

"This is a good one," I said. "TIE/Communications. They make telephone sets, the ones with more than one line on them. Well, today AT&T announced it's going to write down the value of its installed phones. The betting is that the company will sell all this old equipment to customers at fire-sale prices. That could hurt sales for companies like TIE and force it to cut prices as well, killing their profit margins. Besides, the analysts I've been talking to think the stock is overpriced in any event."

"Sounds good. You're writing this for tomorrow?"

"So far." We made plans to meet the following night with his partner at the Racquet Club.

These trips to the phone booths were a bother but I couldn't speak freely from the phone at my desk. We had agreed that Peter wouldn't call me at work unless he really needed to. I always called Peter when I had done enough research that I was sure I had the gist of the story down. But that meant leaving my desk at a point when I still had calls to return and additional research to do. I wasn't used to leaving my desk anytime during the day, except maybe to get a sandwich from the cafeteria one floor up or to look something up in the *Journal*'s library.

Peter was anxious to reverse the loss on Schlumberger, and the TIE thesis sounded strong. He muscled his way into TIE like a refugee trying to catch the last helicopter out of Saigon. He traded in Ken's account, instead of his own, because—he said—Kidder employees wouldn't be as quick to jump on the bandwagon if the trades were in someone else's account. He bought 454 put options on TIE in Ken's account and, secretly, bought another 400 puts in David Clark's account. Plus he sold 22,500 TIE shares short in Clark's account. All of the trading added up to the equivalent of a 108,000-share, $3 million bet that TIE's price would fall. That was close to the total trading volume for TIE for a whole day by everybody in the world.

TIE stock and options were traded on the American Stock Exchange. Unknown to any of us but not surprising in light of Peter's lead foot, a computer in the surveillance department of the American Stock Exchange noticed unusually heavy activity in TIE and sounded a bell. The activity also drew notice in TIE's offices in Shelton, Connecticut, where the company's executives got phone calls from their sources on the Street. TIE had sunk 20 percent the week before and analysts were warning the company that a negative story seemed to be in the works for the "Heard" and that there appeared to a flurry of selling just before.

Meanwhile, Peter ran into some flak from the Pacific Exchange, where traders were having trouble coming up with the number of puts he was ordering through Kidder's New York office. He complained later that the Pacific Exchange traders were "just a bunch of stupid crybabies."

Fewer people would have noticed what Peter was doing if he'd hired a skywriter. He had managed to crunch the toes of just about anyone who had anything to do with TIE/Communications. None of us knew that these red flags had been raised. Peter only told me that some options traders were unhappy. He said it as though this was the kind of everyday aggravation that he had to contend with.

The next day TIE sank more than $2 a share. Because options are more volatile, they rose in value by a much greater percentage than the stock. When Peter finished closing out the transactions, Ken's account showed a profit of $51,000 and Clark had a profit of $55,400. Not bad for a day's work.

Peter and Ken were all smiles and giddy with the day's good fortune when I met them that night at the Racquet Club. I immediately liked Ken. He had Peter's good sense of humor but he was more relaxed than his college buddy, who took Valium to calm his jangled nerves. Peter gushed about how well they'd done in TIE and chattered away about the market. I tried to engage Ken in some of this market chatter but I soon learned that he always deferred to Peter, as though he was just along for the ride. He seemed unfamiliar with market talk and let Peter carry the ball. We had a few drinks and Ricardo drove us to Elaine's, another celebrity restaurant I'd heard of but never visited, on the Upper East Side. The place was packed, so we got back in the car and ended up at another place called Nicola's. The tables were full and we waited over drinks at the bar. Peter excitedly jabbered about potential profits and somehow got to talking about my split. There were three of us now where there had been two.

"We'll just have to wait and see how it goes," Peter said.

"Maybe we should just pay you twenty-five thousand dollars a story," Ken offered. I didn't take him seriously but the comment revealed an unsophisticated view of the market and journalism. Peter shot him a dark look and I, just as quickly, protested.

"That's ridiculous," I said. "If you make money, I participate. If you don't, fine." Paying per story I knew to be the same thing as a bribe. Our arrangement was profit-sharing. I didn't take bribes.

Just as he had at the Racquet Club that first night, Peter talked boldy about our arrangement, as though it was all good clean fun, just a college caper. I repeatedly had to ask him to lower his booming voice. Some great newspaper stories have started with overheard conversations. One "Heard" column, written by a reporter in the Atlanta bureau, began with a conversation overheard on an airplane by an analyst. He happened to sit behind some bank executives who were buzzing over their plans to take over another bank. Loose lips sink ships, especially on Wall Street where information is king.

Peter performed an encore of his TIE trades on Key Pharmaceuticals, a company about which I wrote a column a few days later. He was only slightly less aggressive.

During the afternoon, as I wrote my column, I noticed a report on the ticker of a block of 10,000 shares of Key Pharmaceuticals out of Kidder, Peabody. I called Peter.

"Ticker says your guys did a big block of Key. I guess that was you, huh?"

"No," he lied. Ken was standing next to him. "That must be somebody else in the place." Peter was secretive and he didn't want me bothering him about his business.

Another bell sounded at the American Stock Exchange, where Key was traded. Two exchange employees were assigned to check clearing sheets to determine which brokerage firms had been active in TIE and Key on days before "Heard" columns. The reports showed unusual and unexplained volume on behalf of a Kidder, Peabody client—an investor by the name of David W. C. Clark.

The weekend in between the TIE and Key columns, David and I visited Peter at home. Lynn and Stephanie were there along with Lynn's son, Todd, who was a year or two younger than Stephanie. The routine was basically the same. Peter gave David the tour. David had been in the upholstery and decorating business, and had sold drapes for a living. He and Peter chatted like a couple of suburban housewives. Peter was upset because the people who were laying the marble curbstones on the driveway had built a curve into it that he thought looked lousy. In fact, he seemed unhappy with the way the whole place was coming together.

"This is a customer I wouldn't want to work for," David told me later. "He probably drives everybody who works for him crazy."

Peter supported Lynn's kids, and claimed to love them as if they were his own. But he had a funny way of showing it. Peter teased them both unmercifully but saved his harshest treatment for Todd, a skinny kid about fourteen years old with brown hair and a quiet demeanor. We were outside looking at the driveway when Peter noticed Todd's moped parked on the gravel, dripping oil on the chipped stone. A stain about three inches in diameter had formed under the bike. Peter strode into the house, shouting at Lynn, "Where's Todd? The little bastard parked his goddamned bike on the driveway and now it's stained."

I would have burst out laughing if Peter hadn't looked so fierce. What the hell did it matter? He fumed about the oil stain all afternoon until Todd finally came home and he could chew him out.

"I told you not to park the damned bike out there in the driveway. Put it in the garage!"

Todd went and moved the bike without comment. He seemed accustomed to Peter's shouting attacks and didn't take them too seriously.

Stephanie had a date that Saturday night with her boyfriend, the mechanic's son. When the kid arrived to pick her up, Peter put on the stereo a Billy Joel album and played Joel's song "Uptown Girl."

He sat back down on the sofa with a mischievous look on his face.

"Listen to this! Listen to this!," he whispered to us. David and I exchanged blank stares. What was the joke?

"It's 'Uptown Girl.' I just love to drive the kid crazy," he said, a big grin on his face as the words filled the room and echoed through the house: "Uptown girl, she's been living in her white-bread world . . . She's looking for a downtown man. That's what I am." It was kind of amusing but only because the kid seemed oblivious to Peter's joke. If he'd figured it out, it would have been cruel. Stephanie understood and did her best to ignore Peter. I had never seen this side of him: a bully picking on those he thought couldn't or wouldn't fight back. Ken had seen it all before—taunting a college friend about his Polish background, goofing on the Boston yuppies, arguing with the Kidder office manager about plant-watering fees and swearing at Ricardo's driving. Peter couldn't sit still. He always had to have something going to keep himself amused.

David and I stayed overnight. The next morning we all went to the golf club again on another perfect fall day. We had lunch in the clubhouse, an old mansion, and just Peter, David, and I set out on the course. David whacked a few but mostly Peter hit the ball around. The dog ran alongside the cart as we drove. Peter was in a benevolent mood. It was another one of those days full of promise.

He offered to fix up a ramshackle guesthouse behind his place for us to live in. We talked about David going into the lawn-furniture business in Locust Valley with Peter's wife.

"Once she has the baby, I think she'd like to get into some line of work," he said. "I could put up the money for a retail store and with David's experience with furniture and decorating it should do well out here. People are always buying that stuff and it's mainly a summer business."

We talked about David getting a part-time job with Peter as a clerk. After we played golf, Peter drove us around to show us some of the huge estates in the neighborhood and the field where the helicopter picked him up each morning to go to work. He was selling us on the benefits of living out there.

Above and beyond my business deal with him, I thought Peter seemed to need our friendship. David wondered why Peter even had us out to the house. We were from a very different social and economic group, young city dwellers who never went to midtown, preferring to shop in the small second-hand stores, Ukrainian food shops, and bakeries that dotted our neighborhood. I enjoyed the racial and ethnic mix. Locust Valley, by comparison, was bland and lifeless. Nobody walking on the streets to look at, and everyone in their cars and in stores looking all the same. Peter traveled with a diamond stickpin crowd that we never sought out nor wanted to join. We both had the impression that Peter had few friends and was reaching out, trying in a clumsy but generous way to link us to him.

But David and I had our own social life in the city. Locust Valley held no allure for us.

Peter traded regularly on the column for the next three weeks, roughly every other day. I started telling him about other stories I knew would be in the paper, stories based on market rumors I'd heard in my telephone travels around the street.

In the first month of our arrangement, he traded on eleven *Journal* stories. The net profit in Ken's account, including a few losses, reached $250,000. I never asked for an accounting, but Peter told me the profits were up around $225,000. Clark did somewhat better. His account showed profits of $414,000. All told, between the accounts, Peter had generated profits of nearly $670,000. The only fly in the ointment I knew about was one comment Peter said his secretary made: that a broker from another firm asked her, "Who is this Brant guy at Kidder who keeps hitting all the home runs?"

"We gotta be careful we don't attract too much attention," Peter had said. "Everybody wants to know what I'm doing and if they figure this out, they'll be all over us like a cheap suit."

It was a little late for words of caution.

9

Rumblings

Stockbrokers are supposed to report all mention of
inside information to their firm and/or the authorities. However . . . we all struggle from our first
breath to be as unequal as we possibly can. I have
never heard of anyone reporting inside-informa-
tion leaks to the authorities unless he had a personal ax to grind.

—John D. Spooner, *Sex and Money*

About the only good that came to Peter from the crash of Digital
Switch was the commission revenue it spun off. He was going
down in flames, but from the executive suite it looked like he'd
launched himself into orbit. By the fall of 1983, he was more than
just a superbroker and number one hotshot at Kidder. He had
become a one-man profit center. The next broker down on the list
produced at most a quarter of the commissions Peter harvested
from his accounts.

For the ten months of the year through October, his trading
activity put $3.5 million of commission bacon in Kidder's larder.
Peter's cut was $1.8 million—about half. His clients owed loans
against stocks of $40 million to $50 million, debit balances on
which clients paid interest of between $300,000 to $400,000. The
forced margin selling in stocks like Digital Switch and American
Surgery should have yielded Kidder's trading desk another profit
estimated at $500,000 or more. All told, Peter's "shop" added to
Kidder, Peabody's annual revenue about $3 million—roughly the

same as Ken Felis's label business, which supported ten times as many families.

This was the dilemma Kidder executives faced near the end of October when they received word from underlings that a half-dozen trades in one of David Clark's accounts, and in Ken Felis's account, bracketed articles in *The Wall Street Journal*. The firm's senior partners worried that Clark or Ken were getting their tips from someone at the *Journal* or someone who knew someone at the paper. If true, Kidder might find itself entangled in a horrendous scandal. And worse: at odds with the most powerful and respected voice in the world of finance. It might bring down on the firm an investigation by the Securities and Exchange Commission. Those beautiful seven-digit numbers rolling out of Peter's office might dry up. So much was at stake. Nobody wanted to pull the plug on Clark, whose accounts were by far the biggest chunk of Peter's business.

Peter held the high cards. Other brokerage firms would have paid him plenty to defect—$500,000 and maybe more in cold hard cash plus luxury benefits. The Kidder partners knew of Peter's volatile temper—it was legendary. Pushed too hard on this *Journal*-story business with Clark, Peter might get offended and bolt. Nobody wanted to be responsible for igniting a conflagration over a mere coincidence. Maybe—it was a long shot—the correlation really was just a fluke.

Everyone involved was walking on glass and wondering who was going to be the first to get cut.

Bill Kennedy, manager of Kidder's Fifth Avenue branch and head sales manager of the New York region, received a packet of "Heard" articles along with Ken's trading records. Kennedy over-saw the firm's New York employees, and it was his unhappy job to quiz Peter and Ken about the bracketing trades. He paid Peter's office a visit one day in early November, after Peter had traded on nearly a dozen "Heard" columns. Kennedy pointed out some of the correlations and asked both brokers why they made the trades. Ken told Kennedy he was copying the trades in David Clark's account.

"Where do you think Clark is getting his information?" Kennedy asked.

"I don't know," Peter said. "The trades were totally unsolicited. I guess he's getting his information from friends on Wall Street."

"Do you know anybody on *The Wall Street Journal*?"

"No," Peter said. It was a dumb fib because he'd been repri-
manded not two months before for allowing me to quote him in my
new-issue column.

"Does Clark know anybody at the *Journal*?"

"No," Peter said.

"Have you done any of these trades in your own account?"

"No."

Kennedy decided the trades looked bad for the firm and at
least Kidder employees shouldn't be involved. Maybe Clark had an
unholy source but for now, at least, Kidder could be insulated. He
turned to Ken: "The trading in your account has to stop immediately." Then, to Peter, "As far as the unsolicited trades in the Clark
account, I'm not sure what the firm's position will be. But I'm
going to refer it to the legal department in the morning and they'll
be in touch with you."

Peter was worried, and he hit Kennedy with the obvious: "You
know, Clark is a very important client of mine. If he can't do his
trading here he's probably going to take his business elsewhere."
Peter was making good money from our deal but he also liked the
idea that it made him look good upstairs. In the space of three or
four weeks, he had traded about $1 million eleven times, generating
commissions on nearly $12 million of trades. Peter had visions of
moving up the ladder, maybe someday becoming the firm's president. Brokerage is a sales-driven business and his success depended
on maintaining his solid lead as top retail broker.

Kennedy had more bad news. Nancy Huang, the client who
stormed Peter's office in the spring complaining that she didn't get
her fair share of restricted Surgery stock, had filed a written
complaint. Now that the stock had tumbled, she was threatening to
sue Peter charging he'd misled her about the time she'd have to wait
before she could sell her restricted shares. Kennedy showed Peter
her letter and told him to produce all the documents pertaining to
the account as well as a signed statement from him answering her
allegations.

Peter was furious. Huang had just spoiled his perfect record—
no one had ever filed a complaint against him. And she was the
same person who in the spring griped because she didn't get
enough of the stock.

"The nerve of some people!" Peter raged.

The next day Kennedy turned over his file to Kidder's legal department and briefly met with Ken and Evan Collins, Peter's whipping dog and manager of the Park Avenue office, to reiterate the ban on Ken's trading around *Journal* articles.

"We've got to cool it," Peter told me the next time I talked to him.

"What's the problem?"

"Ah, those crybaby traders are complaining and some brokers at other firms are asking questions about all the home runs I've been hitting. We're attracting too much attention. We've got to cool it for a while, figure out something else."

The trading in Ken's acount around *Journal* stories stopped.

One day about a month after our arrangement began Peter told me, "By the way, your name now is Howard Cohen when you call." I had asked him before if he minded his secretaries' announcing my name out loud when I phoned. I understood he now wanted me to identify myself by the new name.

"Who's Howard Cohen," I asked.

"Just a client who used to call here a lot and doesn't anymore," he said.

But neither of Peter's secretaries doubted for a second that it still was Foster Winans on the wire. I made it easy for them. One time I called and said, "This is Peter Brant. Oh God. I mean I want to talk to Peter Brant. This is Howard Cohen."

Another time I couldn't remember my new last name. "This is Howard . . . ," and while I was wracking my brain the secretary piped up, "Cohen?"

"Yeah," I said. "Thanks."

The job of sorting out what to do with the Clark account fell to Robert Krantz, Kidder's top in-house counsel and a senior partner. The stocky, gray-haired corporate lawyer had been with the firm nearly twenty years. He had a habit of rambling when he talked and, in public at least, professed only a fuzzy understanding of the more complicated securities laws. Krantz, aware of Peter's clout, sent for reinforcements. He asked Kidder's outside law firm, Sullivan & Cromwell, to draft a memorandum outlining the possible legal consequences if Clark had a source at the *Journal*. The thirty-one-page memo, delivered to Krantz in early November, outlined a scenario under which Mr. W., a reporter at *The Wall Street Journal*, was tipping off Mr. C., a Kidder client, about stories scheduled to appear in the paper. The memo concluded a crime may have been committed.

Krantz asked Peter to set up a meeting with Clark. Late in the morning a day or two later, Krantz arrived at Clark's Madison Avenue office. Krantz checked Clark's account before he left for the meeting and discovered trades the day before in Coleco Industries, a company whose stock I had profiled negatively that morning in the "Heard."

"I assume you know why I'm here," he told Clark. "It's about the series of trades in your account coincident with *Wall Street Journal* articles. It's become so frequent that I can almost guess at your trades by looking to see what's in the "Heard" each morning. I wouldn't be surprised to find out, for example, that you had a transaction in Coleco Industries yesterday."

"That's right," Clark said.

"And I'll bet you were short."

"That's right. I covered my short position this morning."

"I'm a little concerned that a trier of fact [a jury or a judge] might conclude that you have a link with *The Wall Street Journal*," Krantz continued. It was impossible that anyone could come to any other conclusion. But Krantz was not about to level an accusation. They were both lawyers. In spite of Sullivan & Cromwell's opinion about possible criminal liability, Krantz had his doubts. He had no way of knowing Clark's expertise in the area. He didn't want to offend a fellow lawyer and a client.

Clark denied knowing anyone at the *Journal*. "Besides, if I was getting my information from the paper, I would be crazy to concentrate all of my trading with one firm." Crazy indeed! "Maybe the time has come to move my account to another firm anyway."

Clark described his loyalty to Peter, saying it was based on the huge profits Peter had made for him in Digital Switch.

"But Peter hasn't given me any reliable or useful help recently, and, as a matter of fact, I get my information from traders at two other firms, and I think I'll move my trading elsewhere. I'll leave my three hundred thousand shares of Digital Switch with Peter, but I'll plan to do my trading elsewhere."

Krantz was uneasy. Peter would scream bloody murder if Krantz chased Clark away.

"I didn't come up here to ask you to close your account at Kidder," he said. "I'm just concerned about how this would appear to a trier of fact. I asked our outside counsel to look into the matter and while it is unclear that there is any civil liability, there are more serious questions of criminal liability."

"Yeah," said Clark. "I'm concerned about how it looks, too."

Krantz found a phone booth in the Helmsley Palace Hotel after he left Clark's office and he called Bob Goldhammer, the head of national sales at Kidder and Peter's biggest ally and booster. Goldhammer told Krantz he ought to go talk to Peter, possibly soothe him about the chance that Clark might pick up his marbles and take his lucrative game elsewhere.

By the time Krantz got to Peter's office, Clark had already called his partner to discuss moving the *Journal* trading elsewhere.

"You know Clark's account is significant. It's somewhere around a hundred thousand a month in commissions," Peter told Krantz, adding, "But I understand why you're concerned. Have we done anything wrong?"

"I don't think so," Krantz said. "But it looks bad for the firm. The statistical frequency has got to stop. I don't want to see it anymore."

"What you're saying then," Peter said, "is that we can keep trading as long as it isn't every day." He had traded a dozen times around *Journal* articles in about a month.

"I don't want to see the statistical frequency anymore," Krantz repeated. Ken and Peter thought Kidder's top lawyer was being cagey, trying to say something without really saying it.

"Suppose," Ken said, "Clark did have a source at the *Journal*? Would that be illegal or insider trading?"

"To the best of our knowledge, in light of recent Supreme Court decisions, it's unclear to me that Clark would have done anything wrong," Krantz replied.

"Is it necessary to report this to anyone?" Peter said.

"No," Krantz said. "If all we have are unsolicited orders, I don't see any reason to report this to the SEC."

When Krantz left, Peter and Ken were in a state of euphoria, pounding each other on the back. They laughed as hard as college kids dropping water bombs out the dormitory window. Peter had misled Krantz, but somehow he managed to rationalize that minor detail out of existence. Instead, he focused on Krantz's final statements. They hadn't done anything wrong and Kidder wouldn't turn them in. It was all perfectly legal.

After seeing Krantz out, Peter returned to his outer office, where the two secretaries worked. "See," Peter shouted jubilantly to Diane Hackett, "Krantz says it's not illegal. All he told us was to do it less frequently."

Diane had complained to Peter about the trading. She knew who I was from my frequent telephone calls and from reading the *Journal* each morning. And she saw the trade slips and she knew the heavy options activity was beginning to attract attention. She had warned him the trading might cause trouble and that it was wrong. Now, Peter razzed her unmercifully.

"You're such a worrywart, so *moral* and high and mighty."

A few days later, Ken was waiting for the elevator when he ran into Evan Collins.

"You know," Collins began, "you guys told Bill Kennedy that the trades in your account were just copies of the trades in Clark's account. Well, I did some checking and you did some trades around *Journal* articles that were never made in Clark's account." A knowing smile creased his face. "Don't think we don't know the truth."

If Peter was worried about the dust he'd stirred up, he managed to conceal it from me. He never mentioned any of the warning signs that had popped up, telling me only that because of the statistical frequency he had to "cool it." He searched for a better way. First he told me that a "lawyer friend" was helping him out. He never mentioned Clark or the trading in Clark's account. I continued to feed him stock tips and he only showed concern over losses. On one of them, a column Gary wrote about a possible takeover of Getty Oil, Peter said he suffered a major loss, so big as to reverse much of the earlier gains.

The Getty column was one of Gary's best. A source had tipped him off that a peace treaty between Getty and a potential buyer of the company contained language suggesting a takeover was more, not less, likely. But he pointed out that the stock price already reflected high expectations for a takeover and might not have a lot of potential left in it.

Peter complained later, "You know it really holds the stock price back when you put in that 'however' stuff."

"I told you that we call them as we see them," I said. "I would have written that column the same way. If there are 'howevers' they belong in the column. I told you I wouldn't tamper with the journalistic integrity of the column."

He talked about fine-tuning the system.

"Instead of doing every single story, we've got to just take the ones that are really strong. We've got to try and hit a few of them big," he said. "We've got to find us a big kahuna."

Peter decided in early November to open a Swiss bank account through which the *Journal* trades could be funneled. This way, he said, if anybody asked he could deny knowledge of the source of his trading ideas, pointing to the Swiss veil of secrecy. He phoned a small Zurich bank that handled a trading account for two clients, the Greek shipping brothers. The bankers told him to send a U.S. bank check so Peter wouldn't have to wait longer for it to clear. Ken was just about to take a vacation to Spain and Milan to go hunting with some friends. The timing was perfect. Peter arranged for Ken to take a bank check drawn on Morgan Guaranty for $275,000 to Zurich where he would open an account under the name Western Hemisphere Trading Corp. Account Two. The Greek shipping account was called Western Hemisphere Trading Corp. Account One.

Paul Barber, Peter's contact at Morgan Guaranty, arranged for the check. Barber was a client of Peter's and they had talked about going into business together. As a personal account manager at Morgan, Barber had great contacts among the superrich. They had discussed opening up a small brokerage firm and pooling their resources.

David decided at the beginning of November to take a vacation to London. We had a mutual friend, an artist, who had been to Europe and was going to go with him. Together they would bum around London for a week or two, and maybe make a side trip to Paris. David had no idea where to stay when they got to London and I worried they'd end up blowing their budget in some over-priced hotel. I remembered Peter had contacts there.

"David's going to London for a vacation," I told him. "You've been over there. Can you recommend a decent hotel that isn't outrageously expensive?"

"Sure," he said. "I can't remember the name but it's in the

diplomatic area of the city. A nice quiet place. He'd like it there. I'll get the name and call you back."

Diplomatic we couldn't afford. This is a waste of time, I thought, but I let him follow through just in case and not to hurt his feelings.

He called me back at the office an hour or so later.

"I've got the name of that hotel. It's 39 Hill Street. That's the address, too. I'll have my secretary call and make the reservations. And I've got some English pounds for him to take along."

It was another example of the generosity I associated with him. I hadn't asked for money. He just offered it. So far I had gotten just the $15,000 and I was pretty sure, based on Peter's comments, that the trading profits had paid him back for that advance. But the offer of traveling money for David fell into a different category, like his suggestion that we come to live on his property on Long Island.

We met that night at the Oak Bar in the Plaza Hotel, a watering hole that has been characterized as a place where real men make real deals over real drinks. The Oak Bar was one of Peter's after-work hangouts. The entire Plaza Hotel is an institution devoted to the rich, with its huge European-style dining room, grand lobby, and, I imagined, extraordinary rooms with sweeping views of Central Park. Limousines usually cluttered the street at the hotel's front steps, which have appeared in countless films and commercials.

We couldn't find a table so we sat at the bar. Peter pointed at a large mural at one end of the room.

"See that," he said. "Cary Grant sat in front of it in a scene from Hitchcock's movie *North by Northwest*." He handed me the bank note—750 pounds' worth, equal to about $1,000 or so—in a plain envelope.

"Thanks," I said. "That was unnecessary but very thoughtful."

"Don't mention it," he said.

We talked about Ken's planned trip to Europe and the Swiss account until David joined us. Peter and I never discussed business in front of David, just as we hadn't in front of Lynn. We planned to have dinner. It was a cold, rainy, miserable night in the city. Ricardo was outside, but this time he was driving a beige station wagon. The Cadillac was in the shop for repairs. We stopped at one restaurant while Peter ran inside to see if he could get a table. The place was packed so Ricardo drove us to the Sherry-Netherland Hotel, where we had dinner at Doubles, the members-only supper and dance club in the basement on the spot where Peter's hero had splattered the men's room walls more than forty years earlier with his brains. The entire place was red—the walls, the floors, and the ceilings. The tables were covered with pink cloths.

"Frank Sinatra comes here," Peter said. We talked about London. This was to be David's first trip, so Peter wrote down the names of some restaurants. They were all good restaurants, I was sure, and all very expensive. The pounds would go a long way toward defraying the cost of the trip. But it wasn't the kind of money that allowed fancy eating or shopping.

At about the same time, Ken was on his way to Spain. After the shoot, he and his friends flew to Milan, where they picked up a rented car and headed north for the two and one-half hour drive into the mountains and across the Swiss border to Zurich. He had the check, an address, and some vague instructions Peter had written down for him about what to do when he got there.

He had a complete image of what he'd find at the Bank Institute of Zurich: a marble building with high ceilings, chandeliers and gold fixtures, vaults and dark wood paneling. But he found the address on the second floor of a side street in a small office building. The "bank" itself was no more than a professional office, just some Swiss businessman with a bank charter. Ken was uncomfortable. He didn't speak any other languages and was unfamiliar with European manners. There was no small talk. No "How's the kids and wife" or "Is this your first visit to our country?" The man in the suit on the other side of the desk was all business and no questions. It felt like another Peter Brant dress-up caper, but this time Peter wasn't along to share the laughs. Ken wanted it to be over so he could get the hell out. The whole thing had a creepy feel to it.

The man in the suit pushed a bunch of papers toward him and pointed to the spot where he was to sign. Peter had set the appointment up by telephone. When it came time to hand over the Morgan Guaranty check, Ken hesitated. The place didn't look like a bank and he had no way of knowing that the guy wouldn't walk away with the money.

"What happens if I die?" Ken asked. The way things were going, Ken could have been out of there without exchanging more than a dozen words with the guy.

The man in the suit started explaining in a German accent how the account was set up but Ken didn't understand and just shook his head.

"But if I die, no one will know that the account exists," he said. Peter had arranged it so no account statements would be sent. It was all very tidy. In fact, it was a rented corporation with a rented board of directors. This was the way some of Peter's clients hid their identities from prying eyes.

"Do you wish to record a beneficiary?" the banker asked.

"Yeah," Ken said. "Put down my wife."

Peter had told Ken to negotiate a monthly fee. "Try to get it for a thousand dollars a month but go to fifteen hundred if you have to," he'd said. Ken wasn't interested in haggling. He offered the guy $1,500 right off the bat and the deal was done. It was all over and he was back out on the street within twenty minutes.

In fact, Western Hemisphere was an empty shell whose directors—with German names like Blumenkamp, Meier, and Kreich—Peter and Ken had never met. What they bought for the monthly fee was a name and a legal cover. Western Hemisphere was legally based in San José, Costa Rica. But it was a safe bet the "directors" had never been there.

By November I had arranged for David to transfer his stock account to Charles Schwab from Merrill Lynch. We had bought and sold a few stocks, mostly losers, with the profits from American Surgery and Institutional Investor. I was learning something about the brokerage business. The big brokerage firms—called wire houses to distinguish them from one-office operations—hosed their clients coming and going. I had a Quotron on my desk so I could see the action in prices of stocks David bought and sold. Invariably Merrill charged his account a higher price when he bought and a lower price when he sold than the prices I saw on my Quotron. It really ticked me off. Then they added on a healthy commission that, in many cases, equalled 5% of the original investment. It seemed like stealing to me. Unless a client was dealing in huge amounts, those $100 charges really added up. We were only making trades worth maybe $1,000. In November I asked David to make his first trade in the Schwab account: he bought another 400 shares of American Surgery. The stock had skidded to $6 a share from its $20 high. I thought the worst was over and it might perk up again.

I was curious to see if I could duplicate Peter's trading and show a profit. In a way, my arrangement with him was making me a better columnist. It encouraged me to look aggressively for good stories, instead of lying back and picking easy topics. Now I wanted to see how it worked for real.

In the beginning of December, Gary and I found ourselves working on the same negative column idea about Rolm Corp., a maker of telephone equipment. Gary ended up doing the column, but I called David at home and asked him to buy some puts in his account.

"David, I want you to call Schwab and buy some put options in Rolm."

"Some Rome what?"

"Put options on Rolm. It's a company: R-O-L-M. Rolm."

"Okay, Rolm option puts. What's a put?"

"No, David, it's Rolm put options. Listen, get a piece of paper and I'll tell you what to say."

David had a way, at times, of murdering the language.

"Okay, now listen. Write this down. Call them up and say, 'I want to buy 20 December 50 puts on Rolm.' "

"Put what on Rolm?"

"No, no, no! Just write it down like I tell you. 20 December 50 Rolm puts. You got that?"

"Yeah, I think so." I had this momentary nightmare that he'd end up buying something completely off the wall or the order taker wouldn't understand a word he was saying.

The puts ended up costing us $690. The next day Rolm fell $1.25 per share and the value of the puts rose. We sold, ending up with a profit of about $775.

My brother, Chris, came to work for the *Journal* as an editor at the beginning of December. We had worked together once before, in Trenton, and we were both excited about a reunion. But he was saddled with debt from a house he'd recently bought in Pennsylvania where he was working. When the *Journal* offered him a job, he told me he didn't think he could afford to move to New York. He was married and planned to have a family. No way was I going to let him pass up a chance like that because of money. David and I borrowed about $3,500 from our loan account and lent it to him so he could pay the apartment fees, security, and other expenses. To quiet his curiosity, we told him that David had received an inheritance from the estate of his father, who had died a couple of years earlier.

About the same time, we lent $1,000 to a friend who was in deep financial trouble. After making these loans, Peter advanced us another $5,000 from the trading profits which we used to pay off the bank loan.

"Do you want cash?" he asked.

"Nah," I said. "Just a check, like before."

The Western Hemisphere account was in business by the beginning of December. But since the "cool it" period, things were going badly. On the first trade, Peter lost $16,000. The next trade netted a profit of only $7,000. Then, inexplicably, he used the Western Hemisphere account to take another big plunge in American Surgery. He bought 30,000 shares at about $7.50 a share, tying up nearly all the assets in the account. He ended up selling a week or two later at $5.50, losing some $60,000.

Peter next hit a whopper of a loser. Another reporter on the paper wrote a "Heard" column on Greyhound that I thought contained a compelling thesis. I helped the reporter out with some of the research. Greyhound, it developed, owned most of the real estate under its bus stations. The company was in the throes of a drivers' strike that had clipped the stock price. But Greyhound was talking about doing something with the real estate—building office towers and moving the stations out into the suburbs. The land was on the company's books at cost: the price it paid perhaps thirty to fifty years earlier. The appreciation in real estate over that time was a hidden asset that investors had overlooked. It was a powerful investment thesis and I told Peter so. He bought nearly $60,000 worth of call options on Greyhound, equivalent to more than 50,000 shares of stock.

The day the column appeared, the stock rose just 50 cents a share. The calls more than doubled in value. David had bought some and I told him to sell the day the column appeared. We made about $1,400.

Western Hemisphere had a paper profit of $82,000. Peter thought he'd finally found his big kahuna. The stock inched up for the next several days.

"We're going to hold on to this one," he said. "I really think this could keep going and we could make a bundle."

Instead, the shares stalled and began to sink. The big profit in the more volatile call options quickly dissipated. Peter stubbornly refused to sell and ended up losing nearly his entire stake—about $50,000. Next he bought 5,000 shares, or $170,000, of Digital Switch in the account. The price promptly sank two points.

One of the ironies of my arrangement with Peter was that—as much of a sure thing as he thought it was in the beginning—it was easy to get whipsawed. He'd said he lost a bundle on Getty Oil and complained about balancing language in the column. Yet, not a month later, a bid for Getty did develop and the stock and options soared. Getty could have been his big kahuna. On the other hand, he had a fat profit in Greyhound but he got greedy and ended up giving it all back and then some. The time was long gone when Ken Felis rushed off to work in the morning wondering how much money they'd make that day. Peter was choking, like a top-seeded tennis player who gets sloppy and lets a challenger sneak up on him. Peter was losing control.

Some columns he passed up. I'd tell him my investment thesis and he'd disagree with it. We discussed these stocks much the same as any two market players. We debated the market's direction, and the fundamentals of the companies I and others at the paper were writing about. Some columns I felt strongly about—"This ought to knock the stock right off its feet"—and on others I was less confident. We clashed once over a column I was preparing to write on Boeing. I told Peter that some analysts were guessing that Boeing could be hurt by competition from a European aircraft manufacturer. I thought the thesis was sound.

"Oh, no!" he cried out on the phone. "You can't do that. I own the stock. Besides, the company's doing great. Most of the airline fleets are getting old and they'll all be coming back to buy new planes. And the bookings are way up for next year."

"I know all that," I said. "But I still think the stock could weaken. I have to call them the way I see them." The negative Boeing column appeared the next day.

But he was never as forceful—even angry—as he was in mid-

December when another reporter, working with me while Gary was on temporary assignment on the foreign desk, wrote a bearish tail-end piece for the "Heard" on Digital Switch. The price plunged more than $4 a share to $32.50 one day when an influential analyst told his clients he thought the company's torrid earnings growth was slowing. The last sentence of the item quoted the analyst as saying the stock should sell around $25 a share.

I never thought about Peter's stock positions. I had no inclination to run interference for him. I told him the same thing I told the readers of the *Journal*. He had no influence over what went into the column. It was the only way I could continue doing my job and live with my sin. I had whored myself. But I wasn't prepared to whore my writing as well.

The morning that the Digital Switch item appeared, the stock sank another couple of dollars. Peter called and he was in a fury.

"Hey, pal, what the fuck are you doing to me?" he hissed into the phone.

"What are you talking about?"

"You see the goddamned column this morning? Look what the hell's happening to Digital Switch. They're killing me."

I hadn't looked but when I punched it up on my Quotron I saw why he was in a panic.

"At least you got to tell me about these things."

Now I was angry, too. Who the hell did Peter think he was? I didn't have time to call him every day there was a story in the paper that might affect him. And besides, Digital Switch had nothing to do with our arrangement. What good would it have done him to know anyway?

Peter got another round of visits from the boys upstairs. The elves had spotted correlations in a new account, Western Hemisphere Trading Corp. Account Two. Krantz, the firm's legal counsel, called Peter after someone at Kidder noticed a correlation between a trade in Western Hemisphere and a column I had written in the *Journal*. Krantz wanted to know whose account it was. Peter told him it belonged to David Clark.

A few days later Peter had lunch with Bill Kennedy, the New York regional sales manager who'd been the first person to confront him about the amazing coincidences.

"I'm leaving tomorrow for a vacation in Florida," he told

Kennedy. "I haven't been able to reach Krantz. Could you give him a message for me?"

"Sure," Kennedy said. "What is it?"

"Tell him the trading in Western Hemisphere has ceased."

Nothing seemed to be working. Peter grew more frustrated and dispirited. The crushing decline in Digital Switch and in Surgery had taken a big slice out of his true net worth and his cash flow. Since Krantz's first visit in November, few of his trades seemed to be working out. Even his arrangement with me had turned into a money-loser. The walls closed in some more. His box got smaller.

David and I enjoyed a quiet Christmas with my family on Cape Cod. It had been a helluva year, between my problems with Dick Rustin, big changes at the *Journal*, and my deal with Peter. I had been running hard, trying to rescue my error-damaged credibility at the *Journal*. In doing so, I had pulled the plow more often than Gary. I wanted it that way. It made me feel good to know that I could produce the larger number of columns. I had even gotten a written compliment from Norm Pearlstine, the new managing editor. And, in November, Gary and I got our new boss, Paul Steiger, to whom I took an instant and strong liking. He backed us up on all fronts. He was sunshine to Rustin's moonless midnight.

I took off the week after Christmas. As the New Year approached, I dreaded going back to work. My adrenaline was spent. I was exhausted and I wanted to coast. I couldn't get my traction; it was like driving on ice.

A few days into the New Year, Peter called.

"Hi. It's me." It was his voice but not like I'd ever heard it. It sounded small and vulnerable.

"Hi," I said. "How're ya doing?"

"It's all over." Then silence.

"Whattaya mean, 'it's over.' "

"I've got a gun. I'm going to kill myself."

10

The Big Kahuna

Ambition destroys its possessor.

—The Talmud

Ken watched helplessly as the market turned progressively more vicious and Peter slipped deeper into depression. Ken again made plans with his label-business partner, Steven Spratt, to quit Kidder. He was out of Surgery and DIGI, and the deal with me wasn't making money anymore. Ken had had his fill of Wall Street, and he'd learned a few disturbing things about Kidder, Peabody.

Peter had convinced Ken that they couldn't trust the people they worked with at the firm. Everyone seemed to be copying their trades, the legal department had badgered them about the *Journal* correlations, and Peter encouraged a general attitude of disrespect for the firm's executives and Kidder's research department. Peter's office acquired a bunker mentality that was intensified by the punishing he'd taken in the market.

Ken passively accepted Peter's characterizations of Kidder, but one thing about the firm really irritated him. It was the way Kidder's trading desk systematically screwed them on their over-the-counter trades in stocks like DIGI and Surgery. It took him a while to figure it out, but when he did he was furious.

Peter did a tremendous business trading Digital Switch. When the stock was rising, sometimes as much as fifty cents or a dollar a share in a single day, Kidder was skimming an extra profit on their trades. The way it worked was diabolically simple. Peter would phone an order in to the Kidder trading desk for, say, 1,000 shares of DIGI. The traders would post the order to buy, called a bid, on a national computer network called Autex. On computer screens in the offices of other brokerage trading desks around the country, the bid for 1,000 shares would pop up next to Kidder's symbol. Kidder's trading desk would buy the stock but, in a rising market, sit on the confirmation. Twenty minutes or so might pass and the stock would kick up another fifty cents a share. Then the trading desk would call Peter back and announce that the order was filled at the higher price. Peter and his clients would pay the higher price and the trading desk would pocket the spread, or about $500 on a 1,000-share order.

When the stock was falling, the trading desk would sit on a buy order. When the stock had fallen, the order would be filled at the lower price but billed to Peter and his clients at the higher price.

The system worked equally well on sales. In a rising market, the traders would sit on the order hoping the stock would rise, then sell at the higher price and credit Peter's accounts at the lower price. In a falling market, the trading desk would sell short (a process of selling stock they didn't own). If the stock fell, they would fill in the order ticket at the lower price and, again, pocket the difference. On top of this profit, they added the firm's standard commission—roughly 5 percent of the value of the transaction.

Ken suspected Kidder was playing these games with orders but he wasn't positive. Peter didn't have the kind of computer that allowed him to see first-hand when the bids were placed on the national network, when they were filled, and at what price. Ken complained constantly to the office manager, Evan Collins, and to top executives of the company whenever they stopped by to see Peter. It became a kind of crusade for him. The scalping was costing them thousands of dollars in sloppy order filling. He decided it was the same as stealing. One way or another he was going to prove it and make them quit.

"Look, Ken, that's just the way it is," Peter said each time Ken whined. "There's nothing we can do about it. That's the system. You can't change it."

It was the kind of thing Peter could have pushed if he wanted to, using his clout with the firm. But he had a conflict of interest. He had become a stockholder in the firm and his profit-sharing in part depended on the profits the trading desk generated each year.

He'd only hurt his position with the senior partners by making a fuss over one of Kidder's major profit centers.

Finally Ken concocted a plan to beat the Kidder traders at their own game. One of his college buddies worked at another brokerage firm and had access to the more sophisticated computer that showed bids as they were listed and filled. One day Peter placed an order for 10,000 shares of a stock that was rising. Ken called his buddy and told him to let him know as soon as the bid was removed from the screen.

When he got the confirming call from his friend, Ken immediately called up Kidder's trading desk.

"Did you fill that order?"

"No," the trader at the other end of the wire said. "I couldn't get it done."

"Well, then, cancel it!"

Ken knew from his friend that the Kidder trader was lying. Now the trading desk was stuck with 10,000 shares of stock and no account to charge it to. Sure enough, a few minutes later, the trader called Ken back.

"Oh, gee, I must have made a mistake," he said. "Turns out we did fill that order."

Ken presented the evidence to senior Kidder partners and demanded that Peter get the more sophisticated computer so they could keep the traders honest. The firm relented early in 1984.

Ken and Peter went to the mat and won with Kidder on other issues as well. The firm instituted a new "service" that allowed clients to debit their stock accounts directly by means of a plastic card or checks. Clients could get cash advances against their portfolios. Of course, when a charge against a client account came through, Kidder reserved the right to sell stock out of the portfolio to raise cash to cover the debit. This, not coincidentally, generated commission revenue. It was just another way of separating clients from their money. Kidder's market research suggested that such card usage and check-writing increased trading activity in accounts seven times. It was all on the up and up but Ken saw it as just another lousy financial product that did the client no good whatsoever. He stood up at the sales meeting where the program was announced and said, "What are we, just a bunch of vacuum-cleaner salesmen?"

When Kidder prepared to send out application forms along

with monthly account statements, he put his foot down. He persuaded Peter that they shouldn't allow the firm to stuff statements going to their accounts with the application forms for the debit cards and checks. They told Evan Collins, "If a single stuffer goes out to any of our clients, we're out here."

Kidder again backed off.

Ken was ready to quit anyway, but the way Kidder played the brokerage game sealed his decision. His simplistic, idealized image of Wall Street brokers as financial professionals had been trampled and stained. In the beginning of January, he was about to tell Peter that he was quitting when Peter plunged into an emotional abyss.

When Peter reached me at the office, I couldn't tell whether he was at home or at his desk. His suicide threat startled me. This was the first sign I'd had, and it was a big one, that he was in emotional distress.

"I can't go on. My life is over," he said in a voice that was flat and dispirited, completely out of character with the enthusiasm and animation I had come to associate with him.

"What do you mean?" I said. "You've got everything to live for. You have a beautiful family, your wife just had a healthy baby girl, you're wealthier than most people ever dream of being."

"You don't understand," he said. "The market's lousy. My clients are talking about suing me. I can't take the pressure anymore. It just isn't worth it."

"You know better than I that people always talk about suing when they've lost money," I said. "Besides you've got your friends. They love you. I care about you. What else in life is more important, or so bad, that you would want to take your life?"

We went back and forth like this for close to thirty minutes. By the time Peter hung up, he sounded a little better. In my experience as a reporter, I'd talked to a few people who called newspapers threatening to kill themselves. I'd heard that people who advertise their suicidal feelings often just need someone to listen to them. I was puzzled by Peter's state of mind but I didn't expect him to try to off himself.

Ken, however, was frightened. Peter started taking Valium more regularly and he'd spend entire days in his office lying on the sofa with his eyes closed. He had crying fits. He talked often about killing himself and asked Ken the best way to do it. Ken started meeting Peter in Locust Valley in the morning and riding with him back and forth to work. Lynn was on the phone with Ken each night comparing notes of their observations of him. Ken even stayed over in Locust Valley for a three-day stretch when Peter finally hit bottom. They were all afraid he'd slip away and blow his brains out. Ken put his quitting plans on hold a second time.

I had quit all my freelance work long since and wasn't looking for any, when a money manager I had quoted several times in the column asked me, early in 1984, to help him write a book on stock market analysis. He had a contract with a sister company of the *Journal*—Dow Jones-Irwin Books. The project interested me on several levels. The money manager was a wizard at untangling financial statements and an insightful analyst. One of the chief benefits of working with him on such a project was the knowledge I would gain. He also agreed to pay me $5,000 for my work editing and rewriting the book.

I told my new boss, Paul Steiger, about the project and he seemed agreeable. "I can't see a problem with this," he said. "But I suppose I should run it by Stew Pinkerton." A shudder of anxiety rippled through me.

Many *Journal* reporters had written books. Tim Carrington, who covered the securities business, was in the process of writing a book about merger mania in the securities industry. Gary recently had landed a contract to write a book about investing in technology stocks. He used the *Journal*'s facilities to research his book, and our mail, more than a foot high in normal times, doubled when he started receiving piles and piles of annual reports and SEC filings by hundreds of high-tech companies. I figured I'd have no problem.

A few days later Steiger called me into his office.

"Stew and I talked about this book project and I'm sorry to say we both feel it would be inappropriate for you to be working for someone you've quoted in the paper."

"I don't understand," I said. "The book is being published by our company, it's basically a textbook, and all I'm doing is editing and rewriting. My name won't appear on it anywhere."

"Well, it's a difficult call. But Stew thinks that it's unwise to accept editing payments from a source you've used in the column."

I couldn't tell if Steiger agreed with Pinkerton or was just repeating the company line. I thought the ruling had Pinkerton's fingerprints all over it. It's bad form to argue your case on the basis that everybody else is doing it so I didn't. But I was pretty angry everytime I went through our mail and saw all this crap that Dow Jones was paying somebody to open and sort for the benefit of a book Gary was writing for another publisher.

I really wanted to work on that book. I offered to stop quoting the guy in the paper. But Steiger and Pinkerton wouldn't budge. I had a weird thought: It had been so easy to make extra money on the sly, and now that I wanted to do something perfectly legitimate and straightforward I was blocked.

Digital Switch hit another sinking spell in January and Peter got yet another round of margin calls. Ken begged him to unload some of the stock, but he resisted until the middle of January, when he finally accepted that he had no choice. He called me one day at work. DIGI, which had recovered smartly from its December plunge to about $34 a share, began to slide again toward $30 after the company announced that a major investor intended to unload a million shares of the stock.

"Boy, if I could just get rid of some of this DIGI I'd be in better shape," he said. His mood seemed improved. "If I could get off some of the stock maybe we could have a distribution, each of us could take a hundred thousand or so."

Peter must have forgotten that he hadn't told me he'd spent some $150,000 of the Western Hemisphere funds for 5,000 shares of Digital Switch, so I didn't connect the distribution talk to our trading arrangement. "If we could just get some good news on the stock," he said, "maybe it would tick up and I could unload some of it. There just isn't any liquidity in the market."

I never learned if he was making a veiled suggestion that I write a positive column on Digital Switch or whether he was just musing out loud. Either way, he'd made the statement and I remembered it a few days later when DIGI popped two bucks a share. And there was news. An analyst at Prudential-Bache Securities, a guy I'd talked to frequently about the telephone and telephone-equipment stocks, had told his clients he expected a rollback in the soaring cost structure the FCC had proposed for such long-distance competitors of AT&T as MCI. MCI jumped as well, and the time seemed ripe for a fresh look at the FCC decision and the outlook for MCI, its competitors, and Digital Switch. The other bit of information I uncovered in my research was that the million-share block that was up for sale would not be dumped on the market but instead would be dribbled out slowly. Thus the share price would be less affected. I didn't bother calling Peter, just as I hadn't bothered to call him about the negative DIGI story a few weeks earlier that had infuriated him.

DIGI inched up about 50 cents a share the day my "Heard" column appeared. A few days later, Peter and I talked on the phone.

"By the way," I said, "how are you doing on DIGI?"

"The market stinks. I haven't been able to sell much stock. That was amazing about the column. We talked about the stock and then, bang, it jumped and there was news."

But the news did him no good. The stock continued to burn. By the beginning of February, the price had sunk as low as $21 a share. There were more margin calls and Peter went through another fit of depression.

David and I, meanwhile, talked about finding a summer place we could rent cheaply out in the country. It is one of the ironies of New York that people who lust to live there start talking about how they don't get away enough soon after they arrive. Neither of us were beach people and it seemed foolish to spend thousands of dollars to bunk in with a bunch of strangers at some shore resort like Fire Island. The traffic in the summer was horrendous and we were both farm boys: we preferred to take long, poky drives through farm country near the Delaware River in New Jersey and Pennsylvania. We fantasized about finding a small studio apartment on a farm where David could plant a garden and we could hang out on the weekend and enjoy the peace and quiet.

We met a real-estate salesman that month at a party we attended in Easton, Pennsylvania, right on the river.

"Our ideal place is set back in the woods on an open bit of land, off the main road with enough ground to plant a garden," I told him.

Two days later, he called us in New York.

"I've got the perfect place. Do you feel like buying?"

We had wanted to rent but the place he described sounded perfect, the price was reasonable—$70,000—and, if nothing else, we'd get a day out in the country looking at houses. Of course, the house was perfect, better than we'd hoped. It was set on an alpine meadow on top of a wooded mountain with more than three acres of tillable land. The house was built right after the Second World War and it was as solid as a concrete bunker. The flooring had come out of a defunct munitions factory, and the older couple who owned it had kept it in immaculate condition. It was small, just like we wanted, and the couple was willing to negotiate for the sale of a garage full of gardening equipment. David saw a field full of flowers. I saw a great place to sit and read and relax. We made an offer and, quite impulsively, put down a small deposit.

I had grown a lot in my work and, with Steiger's encouragement, felt more confident about my career future. My arrangement with Peter made me feel very secure financially. We couldn't afford to support a house and an apartment that would soon be going co-op on just my *Journal* income. But I had grown bold and willing to take chances I wouldn't have entertained before. The next day I called Peter. If he couldn't help, we'd just write off the deposit as an expensive weekend in the country.

"David and I are thinking about buying a summer place out in the country," I told him. I didn't mention we'd made an offer since it might be rejected and I didn't want to pressure Peter without reason. I had no idea what monies I was entitled to.

"Are there any profits I can draw against to help make the down payment?" David and I thought we might just resell the apartment at a profit anyway and live permanently in the house in Pennsylvania. The city was accessible by express bus and I could commute if I had to. Maybe I could share an apartment in the city during the week and spend my weekends out in the sticks.

"Yeah, sure," Peter said. "I'll get you a check drawn up. I don't know how much we can give you. We got killed in the American Surgery deal. I know that's not your fault but it's cut our liquidity quite a bit."

"Fine," I said. "Whatever you can do."

Peter owed Ken $15,000 for some trading profits so he drew a check for $25,000 payable to Ken and asked Ken to write a check on his account for $10,000 payable to David.

"What the hell should I write on this thing?" Ken asked.

Peter had talked with David in October about decorating, the drapes that were on order for the house in Locust Valley, and the lawn-furniture store idea for his wife.

"I don't know. If you have to put something down, put down drapes."

Ken wrote the word *drapes* in the itemization box on the check and made it payable to David. Peter sent Ricardo to deliver the check to me at the apartment.

We put the $10,000 in David's savings account where it could draw interest until we were ready to make the bulk of the down payment on the house in Easton.

Peter's trading on *Journal* articles stopped in mid-December, as did the trading in David Carpenter's Schwab account. Not until the beginning of February did Peter again raise the subject of trying to trade again. He had recovered from his bout of depression and he had a new plan.

"The way to do this is we have to plan it way in advance. What we should do is give you tips on story ideas. We'll do the trading and if the idea makes sense, you'll write the column."

It was the most appealing idea he'd had. This way, our relationship almost mirrored the usual source-reporter link. Source buys stock, calls reporter, reporter writes story, source sells stock. If his ideas were no good, I wouldn't waste my time.

He floated a few ideas by me but the one that caught my attention was about Quotron Systems, the company that supplied the stock-quote services that everybody used on Wall Street. I had a Quotron on my desk and so did Peter.

"We know somebody, a software writer, who says Quotron's biggest customer, Merrill Lynch, is working on their own system. Merrill is something like 25% of Quotron's business. If Merrill dumps Quotron, that would be disastrous for the stock."

Peter's source proved useless. But in the following days and weeks, I poked around the idea. The more I heard, the more I came to believe that Quotron could be in for some hard times. In any event, other companies seemed to be closing in on Quotron's market. Peter had sold short 10,000 shares of the stock in early February. Clark, who in the meantime had opened up an account at another brokerage firm, continued to trade on the *Journal* tips Peter provided him. Clark sold short 40,000 shares of Quotron.

The column appeared February 14. Peter waited a day and closed out his transaction, netting a profit of $10,000. Quotron sank $1.25 during the two-day period. I considered the Quotron column one of my better pieces. Events unfolded much the way my sources predicted. Peter ended up leaving plenty of profit on the table. The stock sank another $3 or so a share. Clark sold the day the column appeared for a profit of $33,000.

My only regret about the Quotron column was that I had been unable to reach the company's president. I had met him the summer before at a technology conference in Maine. We had walked together, with his wife, along the coast examining the wildlife in the tidal ponds. I enjoyed meeting him and wanted to talk to him for this negative column. But I reported "Heard" columns in pyramid fashion—from the bottom up. I tried to learn as much about the company as I could from analysts, money managers, and research documents. When I felt I could hold my own in a conversation with a company executive, I put in a phone call. At noon the day I wrote the Quotron column I tried to reach Quotron's president. I left urgent messages with his secretary and badgered the company's public relations department. When I left work that night, no one had returned my call.

The next day he called.

"I just got a message to call you but I see from the paper that I'm a little late."

"Yeah," I said. "I felt bad about that. I enjoyed our talk last summer and looked forward to discussing these opinions about your business so I could include your thoughts in the column. Next time I'll try to give you more lead time."

"I was out of the office most of the day. It's a shame nobody reached me."

"You ought to have sombody in your organization who can speak in your absence," I offered. "That way you'll always have someone available to present your side of the story."

Peter's spirits stabilized in February. He recovered from his depression and wanted to express his thanks to those who had stuck by him.

"I'm going to have a dinner party," he told Ken one day. "I want to invite just the people who are important to me. We'll forget DIGI and go on with our deal with Foster." He had a born-again feeling. He'd been through the trial of his life and wanted to make a fresh start. He invited David and me, Ken and his wife Vicki, and Gary Lickle, a lawyer friend from Palm Beach.

The house felt warmer than it had the preceding October. The drapes Peter had ordered now hung on the big French doors in the den. David, who once sold and installed drapes for a living, noticed they were hanging crooked. Peter was in good spirits, happy to have his friends around him.

Late in the afternoon Peter drew Ken and me into his private study, a small room off the den, which was decorated in a more contemporary style than the rest of the house and was dominated by a huge elephant tusk set in a base. Like the rest of the house, the decor didn't quite work.

Peter was reenergized about our arrangement.

"This is much better. We'll do fewer trades on better ideas and we'll probably end up making more money," he said.

"By the way," I said. "David and I have found a summer place we want to buy in Pennsylvania."

"Geez," Peter said. "I wish you'd waited on that. We've got the money tied up over in Switzerland and we need all the capital we have to continue trading."

"If you can help, fine. If not, that's fine too," I said. "I really appreciate the $10,000."

"Hey!" Ken said with a chuckle. "It's your money. You deserve it."

I had asked Peter a few weeks earlier if he could recommend a lawyer who might be able to draw up fresh wills for David and me. Now that we contemplated buying a house, we felt we needed current wills to protect each other. Peter now pressed me to talk to Gary, his lawyer friend.

"Look, he's here and it's no problem. Just spend a few minutes with him in the den and let him see what he can do for you."

"I don't know, Peter. I don't know the guy and I don't want to bother him. Besides, David and I really haven't sat down to figure out how we want our wills to read."

"Come on. I'll talk to Gary and get him to sit down with you. It won't take long."

We ended up spending about ten minutes with Gary in Peter's den. He was easygoing but, just as I suspected, we didn't have our act together yet so little was accomplished. Gary, a member of the du Pont family and the Palm Beach jet set, was tall, slender, and good-looking in a Waspy sort of way.

"What kind of assets do you have?" he asked.

"Well, not a lot," I said. This seemed a little silly. Here's this guy, none of whose clients are probably worth less than a million or two, giving advice to a couple of low-rent types from the East Village. "We've got $10,000 in the bank but we expect to put that down on a house we want to buy. The house is the thing we're worried about if either of us should die. Then we've got a stock account that's worth a few thousand. That's about it, I guess."

The meeting ended inconclusively. We were supposed to get together a list of our assets and who we wanted to leave them to.

After dinner we played Trivial Pursuit in teams for a pot into which each team put up one dollar for each question. We rotated the questions and the first person to answer correctly got whatever money ended up in the pot. Gary ended up winning most of the money.

Later we watched "The Wall Street Journal Report," a half-hour weekly television program the *Journal* co-produced with a New York station. The show interviewed *Journal* reporters on different subjects. That week I was the resident genius on the stock market. I hated watching myself on any television, let alone Peter's huge screen suspended from the ceiling. And I hated giving my opinion of the market. It was one thing to write a column quoting the best and the brightest on Wall Street. It was quite another thing for me to be giving my personal opinion. What the hell did I know? I tried to waffle, attributing my opinions to Wall Street "experts." This time I was negative, which wasn't going to win me any awards because the market already was crashing.

I came away from the dinner party feeling closer to Peter than ever. Seeing him enjoy himself made me feel good. Everyone at least put on the appearance of accepting David and me as a couple. The chill I felt in that house in October had been replaced by a sense of warmth and family.

We had all been through a difficult period and the mood seemed to be lifting.

Peter gave me another idea that generated one of my best columns. Chicago Milwaukee Corp., a rail holding company that was going through a tangled bankruptcy similar to Penn Central's many years earlier, was scheduled to sell its rail lines. A group of bidders had lined up and, from my reporting, it became clear that the price they were willing to pay for the assets was far higher than the market thought. The stock had started to pop, jumping from

$100 a share to more than $115. Peter had said he wanted to buy two or three thousand shares but that was usually more than a day's volume in the thinly-traded stock. One day, before the column appeared, I phoned Peter to gossip. He was out so I talked to Ken.

"How's it going?"

"Okay," he said. "Peter's not here." Ken and I had talked maybe once or twice on the phone since I first met him. He always deferred to Peter.

"How you making out on Chicago Milwaukee?" I asked.

"Oh, I think we only got 600 shares. You know I don't do anything around here when Peter's away."

A few days later the column appeared and the stock jumped $7 a share. Peter phoned.

"Stock's doing great," he said. "It definitely looks like you hit the nail on the head. I haven't seen Kenny yet. I just got back."

"I talked to him a couple days ago. He said he had problems getting the stock. He said he only got 600 shares."

"What!" he exploded. "That stupid fucking asshole! I told him to keep buying. We should have had 2,000 shares by now. *Goddamn it!*"

In fact, they ended up with 800 shares in the Swiss account. Clark, meanwhile, had socked away 6,000 shares of the stock worth $700,000 in his account at another brokerage firm—Bear, Stearns. Peter decided this was a hold, like the Greyhound call options. Both Peter and Clark ended up selling a few weeks later at a loss. Six months later, the stock sprinted to more than $160 a share and, still later, traded as high as $200 a share: an extrapolated profit to Clark of roughly half a million and to us of more than $50,000.

The big waves Norm Pearlstine kicked up when he became managing editor started to lap at the "Heard." The day was approaching, Gary told me, when he finally would get the foreign assignment he'd been lobbying for for more than a year. His wife had been agitating to be closer to Israel so she could visit her family more often, especially now that she had a child. To get closer to the Middle East, he'd even considered jumping ship to work for the Paris-based *Herald Tribune*. Gary's handling of his *Herald Tribune* interview was masterful. He and his wife went to Paris together and made it a vacation. He practically announced he was going to the entire newsroom and then, when he returned, talked boldly about the interview with anyone who'd listen. He even had editors coming up to his desk saying things like, "I hope you'll stay," and he got a nice note from one of the really big guns in the eighth-floor executive offices. He used the interview as leverage.

Gary ultimately decided he didn't want to work for the *Trib* ("I got the impression they didn't know what the hell they wanted") but he also was talking to *The New York Times*, where Var-Var was still serving stock market leftovers to readers of the paper's "Marketplace" column.

By February 1984, the *Journal* was paying Gary about $55,000 a year. Steiger, my new boss, had won me a merit raise around Thanksgiving of $35 a week, bringing my weekly gross paycheck to $610.05, or about $31,000 a year. It sure was a raise, but the *Journal* hadn't exactly been throwing money at me. In spite of my deal with Peter Brant, I still considered myself a journalist who liked working for a prestigious company and learning something useful in my next career move. So when Standard & Poor's Corp., a division of McGraw-Hill, sent me a feeler about coming to work for them as a newsletter editor, I was real interested.

S&P, as Standard & Poor's has been known for decades by everyone in the financial community, maintained a stable of stock analysts who spent their time preparing dope sheets on a few thousand publicly-held companies. S&P published these sheets in three-ring binder form, the equivalent on Wall Street of an expanded *Yellow Pages* to the stock market, and sold it to users. The company also published periodic industry forecasts and stock market outlooks. It also owned a financial newsletter for individuals that generated some $6 million a year in revenue. The newsletter, called *The Outlook*, appealed mainly to conservative investors, especially the retirement crowd.

I knew the managing editor of *The Outlook*, Arnie Kaufman, and had quoted him from time to time in the "Heard" on the broader investment themes. I met Arnie at S&P's offices, which were just a few blocks south on Broadway from the *Journal* office.

"Obviously, we're familiar with your work and we like what we've seen," he said. "I've been running *The Outlook* for a long time now and it needs another person. I've got other responsibilities that take up an increasing amount of my time. We're interested in hiring someone as an editor who, if it works out, ultimately could take over my obligations."

The idea sounded intriguing. S&P wanted to liven up the publication so that it would appeal to the next generation of investors, who were partly responsible for the bull move. The job they described was a natural fit with what I was already doing. We talked for most of February until S&P finally made an offer of $40,000 to start, with a raise if, and when, I was deemed ready to assume the helm. The money was awesome, a third more than I was making. I'd have a chance to learn something about the analytical side of Wall Street while continuing to do the kind of market reporting I enjoyed on the "Heard." Many of the brightest money managers and analysts I knew had gotten their start as analyst trainees at S&P. But the daily pace would be less nerve-wracking because *The Outlook* was published once a week.

I was ambivalent about my job at the *Journal* at the time. Until something better came along, it was still the best job I'd ever had. But I sensed that something better, or at least different, was just around the corner. I had watched Gary—completely confident of his position with the *Journal*—play cat-and-mouse with our bosses when other publications tried to seduce him away. I tried to imitate his negotiating style. When S&P made a firm offer near the end of February, I went to Steiger.

"S&P has made me an offer of $40,000 to write and edit for *The Outlook*. I am disinclined to accept. But this raises again in my mind the issue of my salary here. I'm unhappy with it and I think I deserve more."

"I agree," he said. "Let me see what I can do."

A day or so later he came back to me.

"We can't do anything right now, but I can offer you a commitment that down the road your salary will be readjusted."

I liked Steiger but it was clear someone further up the line was pulling the strings.

"How far down the road?"

"In the summer."

It was the wrong response, but I decided to let the thing ride for a while. In fact, I hadn't told S&P that I would refuse. Gary, meanwhile, was offered a new post in London. The prospect of his leaving sent me into a depression. We had worked side by side, day after day for almost eighteen months. There were days when I felt closer to him than anyone else in my life. We had shared with each other the ups and downs of our home lives. I remember a day we talked after he arrived at work in tears over some misunderstanding he'd had with his wife. He had been my mentor, my supporter when I refused to believe in myself, and he had been unstintingly generous with his knowledge of the market. I wasn't sure that I even wanted to write the "Heard" without him. The only advantage to his leaving was that I would become the senior writer of the column. But that also meant I would be working with someone new whom I probably would have to train. That, in turn, meant another extended period of long hours.

March 1, 1984, a Wednesday, was shaping up as a dull but easy day. It was my turn to write one of the statistical fixtures we ran in the "Heard" every so often on things like investment returns among mutual funds. This one was an analysis of trading in specific stocks by major institutions. The figures suggested that the money managers had bought the stocks that subsequently fell and sold the stocks that rose. These miscalculations promised a fair amount of moaning when the final figures for investment returns for the first quarter of the year started to come in.

I was just past the halfway point in writing the column when the phone rang. It was Norm Pearlstine, the *Journal*'s new managing editor, and it wasn't social. Even before he was named managing editor, the gossip in the newsroom held that he was destined to become chairman of Dow Jones. It was a tradition that newsmen rose through the ranks to executive positions, and no one seemed as favored by the stars as Norm. He was tall, handsome, and poised, the ethnic twin of the company's chairman, Warren Phillips. They both had short black hair and mustaches. Unlike *Journal* people like Pinkerton, Norm radiated an engaging warmth and self-confidence. But his presence, enhanced by his reputation as a comer, was commanding. He was the capo di tutti capi of the entire news operation. Norm and I also had a small-world connection. Just a few months earlier I learned that when he was a young man growing up in Philadelphia he had dated my cousin.

"Foster, this is Norm Pearlstine," he said. "I need to see you in my office."

I noted the time. It was about 4:30 and getting dangerously close to deadline. Bad timing, but this was a big event.

"I'll be right up." What the hell could he want with me? I thought. Of course! Steiger told him about the S&P offer and he's reconsidered holding off a raise until the summer. Maybe it's a raise or a new assignment.

I threw on my blue blazer, the one I'd found in a seconds store—only $28 because of a misstitch in the collar—and took the elevator up to the executive offices on the eighth floor. I stood in the foyer for a few minutes and Pearlstine finally appeared. Someone was with him. I followed them into an inner office. Pearlstine shut the door and, still standing, he gestured toward his companion, a gray-haired man in a suit.

"This is Bob Sack. As you probably know, he's our general counsel."

Cripes, I thought. Somebody's suing us.

"In a few minutes John Fedders of the SEC will be calling us here. He has some questions he wants to ask you."

11
Sudden Impact

"You can buy him for a bag of salt."
—Gary Cooper, describing a journalist
in the film *The General Died at Dawn*

The American Stock Exchange investigation had inched forward in the weeks and months after the first computer tipoffs in October. Two exchange analysts assigned to the inquiry detected additional trades bracketing *Journal* stories. By February, they had identified eleven stories—most of them "Heard" columns—around which a customer of Kidder, Peabody had been trading. They picked up similar trading by a customer at another brokerage firm, Bear, Stearns. The customers turned out to be one and the same—David W. C. Clark, a New York lawyer.

The AMEX turned over its file to the Securities and Exchange Commission in Washington, which began to assemble the pieces of what sure as hell looked like a gusher of a leak at *The Wall Street Journal*. The evidence was circumstantial but overwhelming. On February 29, Joseph Cella, a serious young career SEC investigator with a round face, long straight hair combed helmet-like to his head, and the body of a linebacker, phoned David Clark's law firm, Appleton, Rice & Perrin. Cella worked out of the SEC's headquarters in a plain white office building in downtown Washington. Clark was out of the office. He left a cryptic message with Clark's secretary at the end of the day—only his name and his phone number.

The next morning, March 1, Clark returned the call.

"This is David Clark returning Mr. Cella's call. I'm afraid I don't recognize the name Cella," he told the male voice which answered the phone. "Can you tell me whose office this is?"

"This is just Mr. Cella's office," the voice said. "He'll call you back."

Ten minutes later, Cella dialed Clark's number from a speaker phone in the office of another SEC staff investigator. In front of them they had an outline of questions.

"Mr. Clark, I am Joseph Cella from the Securities and Exchange Commission. We are conducting an informal inquiry into trading in a series of securities to determine whether there have been violations of the federal securities laws." The disembodied voice, distorted by the speaker phone, echoed as though it came from inside a tunnel. Cella told Clark his cooperation was voluntary, that he faced potential criminal action if his answers proved to be deliberately false, that any information he gave could be turned over to the Justice Department for possible criminal action and also could be gotten by others through a Freedom of Information Act request. These were standard SEC warnings to possible targets or witnesses in an investigation.

The SEC for which Joe Cella toiled had come a long way from its beginnings in the wreckage of the 1929 Crash and the Depression that followed. Legislation creating the agency was the product of public anguish and anger over the financial collapse, which, in its most visible form, was triggered by rampant speculation and manipulation of stock prices during the roaring twenties. The public and Congress, in their search for scapegoats, laid blame for the nation's economic disaster on the doorstep of the New York Stock Exchange at Broad and Wall Streets. The hearings and revelations that led to enactment of laws creating the SEC were as widely followed and glamorous as the Watergate hearings more than forty years later. Franklin Roosevelt, in a twist of historic proportions, appointed as the SEC's first chairman Joseph P. Kennedy, an active speculator whose crafty and profitable plunges in the market Congress had declared illegal. The fox was sent to guard the chickens.

During the next thirty years, the SEC managed to avoid making much of a name for itself. During the 1930s, the markets were largely moribund and opportunities to rig stocks or scalp investors were limited. The war and postwar recovery years of the 1940s actually saw the SEC shipped off for a time to the boondocks of Philadelphia when space in Washington was dear. The agency saw little action during the Eisenhower years as well. Ike wasn't interested in the markets, self-regulation was thought to be working well, and years of neglect had left the agency to wander aimlessly. Not until the early 1960s and a strong bull market did the SEC begin to stir, inspired in part by a couple of famous scandals, including the De Angelis oil fraud.

The assassination of John Kennedy in 1963 sent the SEC back to sleep. Johnson was preoccupied with the struggle to hold the country together and, later, when he was under siege for his prosecution of the Vietnam War, Wall Street was one of the few places where he had support. The SEC seemed to lurch into action after a sharp market downturn at the start of the 1970s but focused mainly on the market as a system and particularly on commission rates, which had always been fixed.

The current character of the SEC was born in the mid-1970s. The man credited with injecting it with a fresh commitment to fight unfairness in the markets was Stanley Sporkin, an energetic young lawyer and a moralist who headed the agency's Enforcement Division. Sporkin was viewed by some as an unstinting and uncompromising reformer. Others saw in him an ambitious publicity hog, running roughshod over individual rights on the merest whim to create headlines and a favorable impression for himself and, in Congress, for the agency.

By March 1984, the SEC was in full cry on a crusade against insider trading. John Shad, chairman and an early appointee in President Reagan's first term, promised to come down hard—"with hobnail boots"—on those who attempted to make a quick buck by buying or selling in advance of the general dissemination of corporate information—such as takeover announcements. The SEC brought a large number of insider trading cases, at first losing a few major decisions in the Supreme Court on faulty legal theories. A spate of big mergers swept the markets in the early 1980s. Big money was being thrown around in the takeover game, and leaks were springing all over Wall Street—at law firms, printing houses, and investment banking departments.

The Enforcement Division, which investigated David Clark in 1984, was headed by another energetic fellow named John Fedders, a tall, charismatic lawyer who harbored a deep-seated suspicion that many reporters traded in advance of newspaper stories. His eyes must have lit up like a pinball machine when word reached his desk of a possible leak from *The Wall Street Journal*, the most respected newspaper in the country and *the* business publication.

David Clark tried to throw Joe Cella off the scent during the March 1 phone interview. Clark somehow dredged from his memory the investment theses of the stories Peter and he had traded on, recalling details of my columns and other stories that had appeared in the paper. When Cella asked Clark why he'd traded on TIE/Communications, Clark was able to regurgitate, chapter and verse, the essential thesis and facts of my "Heard" column. He claimed he got his trading ideas from various sources on Wall Street and talked to an investment advisor named Tony Adams with a money management firm called QSR Advisory. QSR had managed money for Clark's mother. He denied knowing in advance about *Journal* articles and said he knew no one at the *Journal* or at other Dow Jones publications such as *Barron's*. Peter Brant, he said, just executed orders for him.

Clark called Peter after the SEC call and gave him a blow-by-blow account, "I sent them up a blind alley."

Later that day, Ken was talking to Peter in his office, half-sitting on the edge of the credenza. He had planned to leave for months, but something always came up and Peter convinced him to stay. Now, he was ready to act. His decision was final. Ken had stuck by Peter through two bouts of depression and babysat with him through a false suicide alarm. Peter had stabilized and Ken wanted out while the getting was good.

Peter would plead with him to stay, but Ken was sure he could resist. He recalled his conversation with Peter that day because he was so shocked by what he heard.

"Peter," he began, "I've had it with this business. It's no fun anymore. I'm going back to my label business."

"Hold the fort, pal. We've got a problem."

"What do you mean, 'We've got a problem'? What kind of a problem?"

"Clark just heard from the SEC about trading on Foster's stories."

"Oh, great," Ken said. He thought a minute. The Kidder

lawyer had said in October that it wasn't illegal and he saw no reason to report it to the SEC. So why should the SEC care? Hell, it probably didn't amount to anything.

"Look, it's no big deal," he said. "We didn't kill anybody. Let's just tell them what happened. It's probably nothing. Besides, Kidder already told us it's legal."

Peter rolled his eyes and shook his head. "You don't understand, it's more than that."

"What do you mean?" Ken said it with a sarcastic edge to his voice. Here we go again, he thought. Peter's got some manuever up his sleeve to get me to stay. "More than what?"

"It just isn't that simple. I'm ruined."

Ken was startled and baffled. In his simplistic view of Wall Street, the trading on *Journal* stories was perfectly innocent and Kidder's scalping on trades was stealing. Big deal that the SEC called Clark. They hadn't done anything wrong.

"Ruined! Hell, you've still got some five million bucks or so. What's the big deal?"

"There are other things," Peter said.

"Oh, shit! What other things?"

Peter told Ken he was worried about some embezzlements being discovered. When Ken pressed him for details, he was vague.

"Look," Peter said, "you're better off not knowing. There are just other things that could come out. I'll be ruined."

Peter would later deny Ken's version of the conversation. He would testify only that he was worried about how certain transfers from Roger Wilson's account would look to the Securities and Exchange Commission. He denied, under oath, embezzling any money.

About four miles south of Peter's office, my breath grew shallow and quickened as I looked out the picture window of the office on the eighth floor at Dow Jones. I could see desks and people working at them in the offices in the World Trade Center across the street. I wondered what they were worried about right this second. The city looked miserable: gray and cold outside. My mouth was drying out faster than a wet griddle on a hot stove. I nervously licked my lips as I waited the long minutes for the call from the SEC. Pearlstine had given me no information as to what the call was about but I had a good guess. He talked quietly with Bob Sack, the company's lead attorney. I took a yellow pad from a table so I could take notes. Finally, the phone rang.

"I will signal you if the questions get into an area where I think you shouldn't answer," Pearlstine said. "I'm going to stay on the line." Sack lingered in the background as I picked up the receiver of a green phone on a table near the desk where Pearlstine simultaneously picked up a second phone.

A voice, hollow and disembodied as through a speakerphone said, "This is Joseph Cella."

"We've been here expecting your call," Pearlstine said. "Foster Winans and I are on the phone and Bob Sack, our counsel, is in the room."

My heart pounded in my temples and my chest. My leg muscles flexed nervously. My hands were wet with sweat and my face felt hot. My lips were starting to stick to each other.

"Mr. Winans, are you there?" It was Cella.

"Yes," I barely croaked. I doodled arrows across the top of the page of my pad. Pearlstine scribbled on his pad.

Cella ran down a list of preliminary statements. I barely heard him—Justice Department, Freedom of Information Act—the words ran together.

"Are you willing to proceed?"

I looked at Pearlstine and he looked back at me. "Well, you haven't asked me any questions yet," I said. I waited for some cue from Pearlstine. Should I answer, should I decline? The paper jealously guarded the identity of sources. I knew that was Pearlstine's primary concern.

"Are you willing to proceed?" Cella repeated.

"I don't know," I said. "You haven't asked me any questions." I was confused, my mind a kind of video film playing at high speed. I was boxed in. Pearlstine, whom I respected and who was my ultimate boss, had summoned me to this phone call with the thinnest explanation. I had been plucked from my daily routine and dropped into an interrogation. I was more afraid of Pearlstine than anyone else.

Cella began ticking down his list: he asked my date of birth, address, how long I'd been at the *Journal*, education.

"Are there any common sources for your articles?"

I looked at Pearlstine and he shook his head sideways.

"I have to talk to counsel before I can answer that question," I said.

"Do you maintain any brokerage accounts?"

"No." The Schwab account was in David's name.

"Do you know a person by the name of David . . ." My mind supplied the last name—Carpenter.

". . . Clark?" A wave of relief.

"No." Who the hell is David Clark?

"Do you know a law firm by the name of Appleton, Rice & Perrin?"

"No." Who the fuck is David Clark?

"Have you disclosed to anyone prior to publication the subject of your articles."

Pearlstine shook his head.

"I can't answer that until I have a chance to discuss it with counsel." I sipped coffee from a Styrofoam cup but I couldn't get that dry feeling out of my mouth.

"Do you know an individual named Peter Brant?" My heart pounded harder.

"He's a broker at Kidder, Peabody," I said. I could feel my voice cracking. Could they hear it too?

"Have you ever spoken to him."

"Yes."

"Do you know any of his customers?"

"No."

"Do you recall the last time you spoke to him?"

"No. I was going to do a feature story about him last year but it didn't come to pass."

"Have you ever told Peter Brant about articles that you were writing?"

I looked at Pearlstine.

"I can't answer that until I have a chance to discuss it with counsel."

"Do you know someone named Scott Muller?"

"No."

"Anthony Adams?"

"No."

"QSR Broadcast?" Broadcast? Who are these guys anyway? Who *is* this guy Clark?

"No."

My mood swung wildly with every question. I cringed as I expected a direct accusation. But with each question, Cella seemed to get further away from the trouble spot. These questions about people and things I'd never heard of were kind of reassuring. It was like when I was a child hiding in a bush in a game of hide-and-seek and listening to the voices growing distant and thinking I had escaped detection. Then, suddenly, a voice booms right next to my ear.

"Have you ever received money from Mr. Brant."

I didn't hesitate and I didn't look at Norm Pearlstine for direction.

"No."

"Have you ever received money for writing a story?"

"No. Other than my salary." It was true. I shared profits with Peter. He didn't pay me to write stories.

My whole body vibrated as waves of adrenaline poured into my bloodstream. How could I tell the truth with Pearlstine sitting next to me on the phone? The guy was a godhead at the paper and probably the single person most responsible for my coming to work for the *Journal*. I couldn't tell him the truth. And I couldn't refuse to answer Cella's questions.

Cella asked about a few columns, including the one I wrote on Chicago Milwaukee. Christ, I thought. That story appeared just a few days ago! These guys must be following me around!

"I might know people who bought Chicago Milwaukee," I said, looking at Pearlstine. "But I can't answer because of source problems."

"You're sure you've never heard of David Clark?"

"I'm certain," I said, wanting to babble on all afternoon and all night about the people I *didn't* know. "I talk to hundreds and hundreds of people in the preparation of hundreds of stories. I may have spoken to him but the name doesn't register."

Who the *fuck* is David Clark?

The phone call lasted just a few minutes. When it was over, Pearlstine asked me to hang back after I'd finished the "Heard" to go over with Sack the columns that Cella had mentioned, including TIE, Key, and Chicago Milwaukee. Could they see how shaken I was?

"If you feel at some point that you would be more comfortable with your own attorney, just let me know," Sack said. How could I? If I said I needed my own lawyer, I might as well admit what I'd done. All I could think about was getting the hell out of the building.

As I left, Pearlstine tried to calm me. "It happens eventually to everybody." I assumed he meant that reporters who cover Wall Street eventually get dragged into investigations of their sources.

"Well, this is a first for me," I said, and walked as steadily as I could to the elevator. My mind whirled like in an acid trip. Things looked unreal, dreamlike. My shirt was wet, my hands freezing and damp. My throat was constricted. When the elevator doors closed, I was alone and I heaved an audible sigh. It was a relief to be off the eighth floor.

When I got back down to the fourth floor, I fell into my chair, hunched over and stared at the piece of paper rolled into the typewriter where I'd left it some twenty minutes earlier. Deadline was fast approaching. My thoughts were hazy. The letters on the page looked like black dots instead of words. I lit a cigarette and realized I had a fresh one burning in the ashtray. It took me a few minutes to pull myself together and then, very slowly, I sifted through the notes on my desk and composed the next sentence. By 5:30 I finished the last piece and turned it in.

I was supposed to attend a high school alumni meeting in midtown that night at six o'clock. An hour earlier I had looked forward to hearing the gossip about the kids I went to school with and maybe surprising a few people with how well I'd done. In a few minutes it had all turned to ash. I grabbed my coat and left. I wanted to get away from the *Journal*. A poison was coursing through my veins. I took the subway home. David was out. I threw off my coat and lay down on the sofa. My stomach had a hollow, churning feeling to it. I lay there and smoked one cigarette after another.

The phone rang and I nervously sprang from the sofa.

"This is Norm. I thought we agreed you would stay after work to talk to Sack about those articles." He was irritated.

"Oh, jeez. I'm sorry. I forgot. I had this high school reunion thing. I was running late and completely forgot. I'm sorry."

"Well, I want you to get together with Sack tomorrow. He'll call you to set up a convenient time. You should locate your notes on those columns so he can review them with you."

I hung up and fell back on the sofa, shivering with the effect of the prolonged flood of adrenaline. I pulled an afghan over me. Anxiety began to merge with depression. I couldn't get warm. I listened to the sounds of the street traffic below, sirens, car horns, and the drug dealers arguing over something. My brain replayed the telephone interview over and over. Some of it made no sense at all: ". . . David Clark?"; ". . . Tony Adams?"; ". . . QSR?" Some of it left me trembling with recognition: ". . . Peter Brant?" ". . . receive any money . . . ?" I had the strongest urge to pick up the phone and dial Peter's number but I now was paranoid because Cella had asked about a column that ran just days earlier. The phones must be tapped. I had to make some decisions. But about what? I hadn't been accused of anything. Maybe I never would be. I decided to review my options.

One thought kept popping into my head and it finally lodged there like a fish bone in my throat. Suicide seemed the only answer. I would leave a detailed tape-recording of my relationship with Peter. As I lay on the sofa shivering, I conjured mental images of the George Washington Bridge and tried to imagine falling all that distance to the river surface. I wondered if I might survive. I debated other methods. It was a way of avoiding the real problem.

Finally I settled on a plan. I wouldn't kill myself unless David did too. We would drive in our station wagon to the country, I would tape one end of a hose to the exhaust, the other end I would poke through a partially opened window and seal the window with more tape. I'd leave the heater running so we'd be warm. In my imagination I watched someone discover our bodies and saw a state trooper listening to this bizarre tape-recording he'd found. It was like making a movie in my head.

The phone rang and I bolted from the sofa.

"Hi, it's me," David said.

"Wherever you are, you *must* come home right now," I said, my voice grim and unsteady.

"Why? What's wrong?"

"Just come home," I pleaded. "I can't say." I was on the verge of crying. "I'll explain when you get here. *Please* just come home."

I flopped back on the sofa. Where? We'd have to park the car so we wouldn't be discovered until it was over. How long does it take? Do you just go to sleep or does it make you sick? Headache? Vomiting?

It seemed to take David forever to get home. He had been drinking.

"The SEC called me at work today," I told him. "They're

investigating Peter's trading. I was telling him about stories in the paper. Pearlstine dragged me into his office and they asked me a bunch of questions on the phone. It's all over. They even know about a trade just a few days ago. They must be following us or something. I can't go on living if this is going to come out. The only answer is to kill ourselves."

Suddenly the shelter I'd built of all my rationalizations in the past six months caved in on top of me. I thought about Gary Putka. We had talked about not investing in the market. But this was worse. This was unthinkable. Just about the grossest ethical violation I could think of. Not only would the *Journal* learn about Peter and our arrangement but the government would be involved. I couldn't even focus on the government. I never wanted to step inside the *Journal* offices again. In an instant, like a nuclear blast, my career had been vaporized.

"I'm not killing myself," David said. "Besides you're probably overreacting. What's the big deal? So you get fired. So what? You're good at what you do and you can always find another job."

"Maybe you're right. But if it comes out, I can't live with the shame. If we don't kill ourselves, they'll do it for us! It'll be headline news." I was shouting. How could he not see that the world might be just about to fall on us? I felt like a prophet of doom nobody believes.

Finally my anxiety was temporarily spent. We sat next to each other on the sofa.

"Look, we probably should get in touch with Peter," I said. "At least we should know who these other people are. I don't know whether he's heard from the SEC but maybe he'll know what to do. All of a sudden, I don't know what the fuck is going on."

"The SEC didn't ask about you so I think you should call Peter from a pay phone, just in case our phone is being tapped. For all I know, they've got this apartment wired and I'm being followed. Call him from a pay phone and meet him somewhere. I'll give you a message to take to him. Don't use your name, just in case his phone is tapped or something. And say something besides 'the SEC.' "

We scrounged up some change and David left for the phone booth on the corner. I sat on the sofa smoking cigarettes and listening for the elevator motor to start up. It seemed as if he had been gone forever when he finally got back.

"Well, what did he say?"

"I told him the drapes weren't hanging right. He said, 'I know. Call me tomorrow at the office,' and hung up."

"That's all?"

"Yeah. I don't think he knew what I was talking about. Maybe he was asleep."

"That's ridiculous. Go back and call him again. Tell him it's you. I've gotta find out what this is all about."

This time David got the reaction I expected.

"He's on his way into the city." It was now close to midnight.

I sat down at my typewriter and banged out a cryptic note to Peter describing the call from the SEC:

> Know Peter Brant?
> A: Yes.
> Tell about stories
> A: Can't answer.
> Get money?
> A: No.

And so forth. I listed the names they'd asked me about.

> Know David Clark?
> A: No. (Who the hell is David Clark?).

When I finished I folded it up and gave it to David.

"Read it to Peter. Bring it back. Do not leave it with Peter." Monsters of intrigue and mystery were marching around in my head.

David left and I flopped back on the sofa. I was still shivering and hadn't eaten.

Peter lived about thirty miles from the city, but somehow he managed to arrive at his co-op on the East Side, forty blocks away from us, ahead of David. The apartment was in a posh new high-rise overlooking the East River. As he rode up in the elevator, David wondered what he would find. He was both baffled and terrified by my emotional state. What would Peter say? What would his reaction be? The whole atmosphere, riding in the empty elevator in the middle of the night, gave him the creeps.

The apartment was sparsely decorated with a few good pieces—a sofa and coffee table. There were a marble table and four

chairs in the dining room. The walls were painted a light gray. The
place looked like a lot of money had been thrown at it, but it had
the same cold feel of the house in Locust Valley. Peter was dressed
in slacks, loafers, and a sweater. He paced back and forth as though
in deep thought. "You want a beer or something?"

"Yeah."

"I'm sorry I didn't recognize your voice the first time."

David pulled out the note I'd written and read it to Peter.

"Foster wants to know who these other people are. So do I,"
David said.

"Ah, it doesn't matter." He jumped up from his chair and
started pacing again with his hands in his pockets.

"Who is David Clark?"

"Doesn't matter. Doesn't matter," Peter said, his voice trailing
off into unintelligible mumbling. David couldn't tell whether Peter
was telling the truth or not. Peter sat down again.

"At least the checks were in your name and not Foster's," he
said.

"Yeah, but we put them in our joint account."

"What do you mean?"

"Foster and I have a joint account. It has both our names on it.
We put the checks in the account."

"Holy shit!" Peter threw his head back as though he'd been
hit. "Holy shit! How could you be so fucking stupid?"

"Well, it was a check, right? You put checks in the bank, right?
Why not? What did you think we'd do with them?"

"Oh my God! How could you be so *stupid*?"

"Also, I have a stock account," David said.

"Did you trade in it?"

"Sure. I mean, Foster told me things to buy and stuff. He said
it was like the stuff you were doing."

Peter paced in front of the sofa. He couldn't sit still more than
a few minutes at a time.

"Peter, who is David Clark? What else are you involved in?"
Peter was scaring David and David was growing paranoid. Was
Clark a mobster? Were we going to be gunned down on a street
corner or something? Are these guys in the Mafia?

"Look," Peter said, "I want you to take some notes to take back
to Foster." He found a piece of paper and a pen, handed them to

David, and started dictating. But David couldn't make sense of what he was saying. Peter rambled and then stopped in mid-sentence and started another thought. David scribbled some words but none of it made any sense.

"Just tell Foster that everything will be all right. Tell him not to worry." Finally, they left. Peter drove his BMW down to 14th Street and dropped David off at the corner.

I pounced on David as soon as he returned. "What did he say?"

"He freaked out when I told him about our checking account and my stock account."

"But what did he say about the SEC, about Clark? Did he tell you who Clark is?"

"No. He just said 'you don't want to know.' He said not to worry, everything will be all right."

I took back the note, reread it, and cut it into confetti which I flushed down the toilet. I fantasized that an axe blade wielded by a Federal agent would come punching through our door any second.

"I can't do that," David said, when I asked him again what he thought about suicide. "I just can't. Besides, we don't even know what's going on. Peter said it's going to be all right."

12

Descent into Hell

Wall Street has more leaks than a cheap apartment's plumbing.
                —*The Wall Street Journal*, March 1, 1984

Sleep that night was fitful and I awoke the next morning with a
pounding in my chest. I had to go to work and had to put on a face
of confidence and normalcy. Bob Sack expected to meet with me to
go over the six columns mentioned by the SEC's Cella. When I got
to work I scrounged through my files to find the folders of notes
and research materials relating to each of the columns.

When I was done, I scanned the day's paper. A few days
earlier one of the *Journal*'s Washington reporters had written a piece
about trading in put options on G. D. Searle by employees of CBS
News in advance of a broadcast listing health concerns about
Searle's hot-selling artificial sweetener.

Now the paper had run a whole collection of articles covering
nearly every angle of insider trading and the SEC's efforts to stop
it. The headline read:

Illegal Insider Trading
Seems to Be on Rise;
Ethics Issues Muddled

---

*Difficulty of Tracking Tips
And Courts Hobble SEC;
Whom Does Law Cover?*

The second paragraph read: "Whether trading on hot information ahead of the crowd makes you a shrewd investor or a federal lawbreaker depends on where the information came from and how you got it. As a practical matter, it also depends on whether you get caught."

I read every word in the package of stories, especially the one with the headline:

*Media Policies Vary on Preventing Employees and Others
from Profiting on Knowledge of Future Business Stories*

The day was beginning just as strangely as the day before had ended. Gary was sitting at his desk reading the same story on media policies when he suddenly sat upright and burst out, "Hey, Foster, you see here where it says the *Journal* has a three and a half page conflict-of-interest policy?"

"Yeah." I read that paragraph several times.

"Have you seen it?"

"Nope."

"Well, it sure the hell is news to me," he said, laughing.

There was another paragraph I found more interesting—and upsetting. Somehow Pearlstine had managed to insert a mention of the SEC investigation into the story in time for deadline, two paragraphs below the mention of the *Journal*'s conflicts policy:

"It was learned yesterday, for example, that the SEC is informally investigating allegations that a stock trader had advance knowledge of certain articles that have appeared in *The Wall Street Journal*."

"I wonder what the hell that's about," Gary said. "Do you know?"

"Could have fooled me," I said. I was quivering and tried to say as little as possible to keep from showing my nervousness.

The other articles described how difficult it is for the SEC to win insider trading cases. They are built on circumstantial evidence, John Fedders, SEC enforcement chief, was quoted as saying. "No one writes a memorandum about insider trading. You're linking together the circumstantial evidence of whispers."

But I still felt like a condemned man waiting for the firing squad order. The phone rang. It was Bob Sack. I gathered my files and, as inconspicuously as I could, made my way up to the eighth floor. We spent about thirty minutes going over my notes and names of sources for each of the columns. I told Sack that the idea for the Chicago Milwaukee "Heard" came from Peter Brant and named a few of my other sources on the other columns. I studied Sack to see if he was playing cat and mouse but he didn't show it. He never let on that anything was amiss. He took some notes and I returned to my desk. No one had seen me. No one asked me any questions. No one acted strangely toward me. My boss, Paul Steiger, was silent. I had this bizarre feeling that no one wanted to know the truth. I wondered whether maybe the whole thing might blow over.

Pearlstine and Steiger had decided, meanwhile, that I should steer clear of the punchier, heavier-hitting columns until the investigation sorted itself out. Gary, without knowing that an investigation was under way, picked up the slack with help from other reporters on the paper submitting guest columns.

That night, Friday, I sent David down to the phone booth at the corner to call Peter again. I wanted Peter to know about my meeting with Sack. David was back in a few minutes.

"Peter wants me to come out to the house this weekend," he said. "I'm going to take the train out."

"Why? Why not meet in the city?"

"I don't know," he said. "He just wants me to come out to the house."

"Well, maybe we'll get some answers about who these other guys are."

David and I had just gotten approval from a bank in Pennsylvania for the mortgage we needed to buy the house in Easton and we had put down a $7,000 deposit.

"David, I really think we ought to back out of this deal. We have seventy-two hours from the time we made the deal, which means we've still got time."

"*No!*" he shouted angrily. "I've waited all my life to have my own house. This thing with Peter probably won't amount to anything. Besides, even if you get fired, we could give up the apartment and move out there."

Gary, meanwhile, had gotten official word that he was to be transferred to London at the end of March. The prospect of his departure increased my desire to get the hell out of the *Journal*. Dean Rotbart, a reporter I had spoken to on the phone from the Dallas bureau, was to take Gary's place. I liked Dean but he knew nothing about the stock market. He admitted as much, and I dreaded the thought of having to show him the ropes. At least I'd had experience on the ticker. Gary's leaving and Dean's arriving only meant more work for me. I would have to cover the column every day just in case Dean couldn't fill the bill. He would struggle even more than I did in the beginning.

Meanwhile, something at the *Journal* was dying. Norm Pearlstine had hired a hundred or so new employees in the months since his ascendancy the preceding September. New layers of editors were assigned to coordinate different industry groups. The markets writers got their own extra layer in the form of a former *Journal* reporter and editor who had just completed a stint on a new Dow Jones radio service that fell flat on its face. And he knew little or nothing about the markets. Gary and I viewed these changes with suspicion and dismay. Overnight, the individualized effort that had made the *Journal* a fun place to work was being replaced by a bureaucracy. More editors with their own biases and knowledge gaps were gaining control over and trying to homogenize individual reporting efforts. Infighting between the bureaus and the departments of the paper grew. The atmosphere was changing. The old *Journal*, which operated more like a metropolitan daily, was being turned out to pasture. In its place grew a collection of city-states, each with its own goals and aspirations.

All of these changes—Gary's leaving, the SEC investigation and the "new" *Journal*—persuaded me to take a harder look at the offer from Standard & Poor's. I had told Steiger I would turn down the S&P offer but really hadn't. It was still there for the taking.

As I contemplated the future that weekend, I thought that just maybe Peter was right that all of this would not be a problem. I knew only that I now wanted out of the *Journal* and that S&P might be a graceful way to make that possible. I was beginning to feel more optimistic. A few of my better sources had gotten their start at S&P, so I called them and asked what they thought. The opinion was unanimous. If I wanted to get experience on the analyst side of Wall Street, and make better money doing it, S&P would be the perfect place, they told me. At the time Gary Putka was earning more than $50,000 a year and I was earning $31,000.

Peter came unraveled after Clark was interviewed by the SEC, and once more Ken put his plans to quit on hold. He tried to talk Peter into putting back whatever money Peter thought might have been embezzled.

"Just put it back," Ken said.

"I don't have enough," Peter said.

"Well, then sell the New York apartment." The co-op had cost nearly two million.

"It isn't enough," Peter said. "Besides, if I have to sell it I might as well be dead."

He oscillated widely between lying comatose on the sofa in his office popping Valiums, and hyperactivity. Ken was baffled and disturbed, especially because Peter kept deflecting his questions.

In his panic, Peter descended from the millionaire Wasp into a new role—millionaire desperado. Reality and fantasy began to merge. He told Ken he was going to drive his Aston-Martin off a bridge or blow his brains out. Then he said he and David Clark were going to flee to Switzerland. It was the perfect plan because they'd be protected by Swiss law from extradition, they could live in luxury, and Peter could still trade in the stock market from behind the veil of one of those rent-a-corporations.

David Carpenter took the Long Island Rail Road out to Peter's house the Saturday after the day I was interviewed by the SEC. It was a cool early-spring day. I gave David another typewritten note describing my meeting with Bob Sack the day before. Peter met David at the train station in his BMW.

The mood in the house was somber. Lynn was there with her son Todd who looked worried and paced nervously at the doorway to the big den trying to overhear the conversation. After a time he disappeared. Lynn stood at the French doors, her arms folded in front of her. She stared pensively out the windows at the pool and the backyard.

"How serious do you think this is?" she asked David. She looked dazed, like someone had died unexpectedly.

"I don't know," he said. "Maybe it's not that serious. Maybe it's just checking on what they were doing."

She sighed. "I could do without all this. Peter did very well and didn't need to do these other things. But he wanted more and more."

David gave Peter the note I had written. He read it and handed it back. David couldn't figure out why the hell he'd made the trip. It seemed a waste of time. They sat in the den and had tea.

"We'll have to get some good lawyers," Peter said. His mind seemed to be someplace else.

"I'm really worried about Foster. He's in bad shape. This thing is driving him crazy. This kind of thing doesn't just happen by itself. We both need some answers." David didn't want to make Peter angry but he asked him again about David Clark.

"He's a lawyer." David felt a small rush of reassurance. Well, if he's a lawyer it can't be too bad. Lawyers know everything.

"It's no big deal," Peter kept saying. "It's just harassment. Tell Foster not to worry. But we have to explain these payments to you."

Peter took David around the house again, showing him some of the pieces he'd bought, like the Stubbs eighteenth-century painting and the draperies. He'd just taken delivery on a hand-woven rug for the formal living room.

"You'll make up invoices for all this stuff. Do it on your stationery. Put down that the payments were for services." He rambled on and on and then, suddenly, waved his hand.

"No. That's no good. Just make up bills for consulting work. Like I hired you and Ken hired you to keep tabs on our decorators to make sure they weren't ripping us off. That way we don't need a bunch of invoices for goods."

Ken showed up partway through David's visit, which lasted about an hour.

"Do *you* know what the hell is going on?" David asked him.

Ken shrugged his shoulders. David realized for the first time that Ken was just Peter's pal and not really his business partner, that he did as he was told. Peter was keeping them both in the dark. David decided he wasn't going to make up invoices, but he listened as Peter described an elaborate plan to explain the two checks he'd written to David and the third check written by Ken. It was a confused meeting that seemed to bear little fruit. Peter drove David back to the train station.

When he got home that evening I was as confused as ever. David hadn't learned anything to shed light on who Clark was, except that the guy was a lawyer. The questions seemed to multiply. Peter had given David a handful of five-milligram Valium tablets. I hadn't stopped shaking, at least emotionally, since the phone call from the SEC. David and I both took a pill. Within thirty minutes I could feel the iron grasp of anxiety finally loosen its grip and a wave of relief pass through my body. The monsters in my head took a break. I remembered how good the little yellow pills were at killing mental pain.

The SEC finally caught up with Peter that Monday. In a long telephone interrogation, Peter told some real whoppers, hewing to the line David Clark had taken in his interview. But more than simply sending the G-men on a wild goose chase, Peter was stalling for time: he and Clark had decided to flee to Brazil. He had an elaborate plan all worked out. Lynn and the baby were going to live with Ken in the guesthouse on his property in Connecticut. Her older kids, Todd and Stephanie, would live with their father in Boston.

Ken didn't think of himself as having any problems. Peter and Clark were fleeing their own problems. His label business was still spitting out a six-figure income, so he could just go back to his life before Kidder, Peabody. Kidder had told them back in the fall that the *Journal* trades were legal. He felt bad for Peter but saw himself as a spectator at someone else's tragedy.

Peter went to Morgan Guaranty where he withdrew about $20,000 in hundred-dollar bills. Peter later described his movements that week, including activities in which he claimed Clark participated. Peter said he met Clark on Tuesday. They both had their passports and Ricardo drove them to Rockefeller Center, where, in the black-marble shopping arcade on the first floor, they each bought one-way tickets from Kennedy Airport to Rio. Then they went upstairs to the Brazilian Consulate where they got in line to wait their turn to get entry visas stamped into their passports. Clark, who had been drinking, handed his passport to Peter and excused himself to go to the bathroom. The line inched forward and the minutes ticked away. Peter kept looking for Clark to return as he got closer to the window. He was growing impatient. Finally, Peter reached the window, got his passport stamped, and returned to his office. Clark had disappeared.

Peter stormed into Ken's office waving his hands. "You wouldn't fucking believe what just happened! You won't believe it! We're standing in line to get our visas. Clark goes to the bathroom and never comes back! Just like that!"

Peter had Clark's passport in his hand. He threw it as hard as he could, swearing a blue streak, into the trash can next to Ken's chair. Ken reached over, picked it out, and placed it on the corner of his desk. "C'mon, Peter. This is the guy's passport for Christ's sake. You can't do that."

The next morning when Ken arrived the passport was still sitting on the edge of his desk. He took it in to Peter's office.

"Have you thought about this?" he said as he handed it to him.

"Yeah," Peter said, laughing derisively. "I've thought about it," and flung it into *his* trash can. Ken shrugged his shoulders and walked out.

He never intended to flee to Brazil, Clark later told the Securities and Exchange Commission. He testified that he only accompanied Peter to the consulate to try to talk him out of fleeing. Peter was distraught and, Clark claimed, he finally gave up and walked out on Peter in disgust when he couldn't reason with him.

Peter next planned to go to Brazil by himself and live in a hut on the beach, fishing for his food. The idea was laughable, especially for Peter with his highly cultivated taste for fine cigars, English-tailored suits, and alligator wallets. Fantasy had replaced reality. He had assumed a new identity and was playing the role of the fugitive financier.

"I'm telling you what you should do," Ken pleaded. "Just sell *everything*. The stocks, the house, the apartment, the art. Sell it all and put the money back."

"I can't," Peter said. "There isn't enough." Of course there was. But from childhood Peter had never walked out of his front

door without a hefty wad of cash in his pocket. He had made
certain promises to himself: that he would never be so poor he
couldn't afford the best medical care, for instance. Money was the
yardstick he used to measure his place in the world. He had worked
too hard to get where he was to just toss it away. Peter contemplated giving up everything else—his wife, his newborn child, his
social position, cars, house, horses, the dog, his best friend—for
money. He wasn't about to give that money to Roger Wilson, or
anybody else for that matter, without a struggle.

"What do you mean, 'not enough'?" Ken said. "Money is
money. You can always make more. We both started with nothing.
You'll just do it all over again." Ken was growing more nervous
about this "other" problem of Peter's. Peter wouldn't come clean. If
his best friend had suffered ordinary business reversals, Ken would
have taken him into his label business in a second. But this sounded
like a major problem that could end up getting them both in a lot of
trouble.

Peter toyed with the idea of taking a friend, a woman with
Brazilian citizenship, with him to Rio. They would marry there,
giving Peter complete protection from extradition. That didn't jell
either. He talked about dragging Ricardo with him as his inter-
preter. Never mind that Ricardo spoke Spanish and the language of
Brazil is Portuguese. Either way, Peter was going to "flee the
jurisdiction." Lynn would live with Ken's family and they would
sneak visits now and again.

Ken drove across the Whitestone Bridge to Locust Valley at
four o'clock in the morning the day after Clark disappeared from
the consulate. (He turned up later in a fancy detox hospital in
Pennsylvania.) Ricardo drove Peter and Ken in to the office.
During the day, Lynn loaded Ken's car with what clothing she
could fit into it and the baby's things—all the stuff they would need
to live in Ken's guesthouse. That night when Ken and Peter got
back from the office, Ken drove his packed car home. Everything
was set. Then, at the last minute when it was time for him to leave,
Peter balked. He had to come up with a new plan: wait and watch.
Maybe the SEC thing would blow over and the bad stuff would
never come out.

Ken was fed up. This wasn't his thing and it was beginning to
make him and his wife crazy. A bunch of his friends were going
skiing. He went home, packed and left for Vail, Colorado, where
for ten glorious days he forgot the whole mess. He didn't call Peter

once and Peter couldn't reach him. He thought about Peter and his problems, but never thought that he himself was in trouble. The crooks were the guys at Kidder, Peabody. What Peter had been doing with *Journal* stories was nothing compared with the institutionalized stealing that had been going on around them long before Ken ever entered the picture, he told himself.

The Monday that Peter got his call from the SEC, I went back to Standard & Poor's about their job offer. I told Arnie Kaufman that $40,000 a year wasn't quite enough to make me jump ship. I was beginning to think maybe this would really all blow over. I hadn't heard a peep from anyone, Pearlstine or Sack or Steiger, about the SEC inquiry. S&P came back with $45,000 to start and a virtual guarantee that I would be promoted in about six months to the managing editor's job at *The Outlook* with a big pay increase.

I told Paul Steiger that I intended to leave the *Journal* for S&P.

"They've sweetened their offer. I've talked to a number of sources I respect and asked their opinion about whether I should take the job. They all said yes."

"Would it make any difference if we were able to bring forward a raise for you?" Steiger asked.

"It might," I said. This was getting so complicated. If I told Steiger that I was leaving no matter what, he and Pearlstine would smell a rat. I'd just been interviewed by the SEC and all of a sudden I couldn't wait to leave the paper? I had to play it cagey. I couldn't say for sure how the SEC investigation was going to unwind. It might blow over and everything come out all right. Maybe I would end up staying at the *Journal* after all.

"We're prepared to raise you to $40,000," Steiger said when he got back to me a short time later. Amazing, I thought. I worked my butt off all this time and all I got for my trouble was a $35 raise. A week ago all I could muster was a promise of a raise in the summer. Now that I was under federal investigation, they suddenly want to throw $10,000 at me. I didn't hold it against Steiger. He was the new boy and I suspected that he was acting as a messenger for Pinkerton and, maybe, Pearlstine. They were making it tough for me to quit but I knew, finally, that I had no other choice. My career probably was over in any event. I only wanted to work with Gary but he was leaving and the S&P job, if I ever got there, was right up my alley.

"I don't think so, Paul. I appreciate your efforts and apologize if it causes you any embarrassment with the boys upstairs. But I think the money and the potential responsibility at Standard & Poor's is what I want." Then, for some reason, I said the most arrogant thing I would say all month, although Steiger had no way of knowing it.

"Besides, at S&P I can trade in the market. Here I can't. Maybe I'm a lousy stock-picker but I'd like to find out." I didn't intend it as arrogance. I wanted to give Steiger a long and compelling list of reasons for leaving, reasons that had nothing to do with an SEC investigation. But, under the circumstances, it was a perfectly outrageous thing to say.

Steiger didn't ask me about the investigation, or whether it affected my decision. But I'll bet his stomach did a little flip-flop as he wondered whether, in fact, I had done something stupid with this guy Peter Brant.

The days passed in relative quiet, but I kept an emergency tablet of Peter's Valium in my jacket pocket. I broke it in two and made sure I always knew where it was in case I needed it on short notice. It was my insurance policy against complete hysteria. The dam could burst anytime and I wanted to be ready. March 30 was to be my last day. Gary's last day was to be a week earlier. I told almost no one else that I was leaving. My nightmare was a going-away party spoiled by the disclosures of my relationship with Peter. I didn't want anybody slapping me on the back or telling me how sorry they were that I was leaving. I just wanted out, and the feeling grew stronger with every hour. The job I'd loved better than any other had become my recurring nightmare.

As the week wore on, I remembered all the long hours, the many Sundays I had worked with no compensation. I could build a solid case for taking the last week of my remaining days off as time owed. That would get me out of the place earlier. I wrote Steiger a memo to that effect and he granted the early termination. Now Gary and I would "graduate" the same day. If I were going to S&P, I would have an extra week to take my notes home and sort them in such a way that I could use them as resource materials for the work I would be doing at the new job. I oscillated between genuine excitement and dread that my career, and maybe even my life, would soon be over.

That week I wrote one "Heard" column, one of my worst. It was about Commodore International, the computer manufacturer, and it was one of those pieces that had no spine to it: I couldn't conclude whether the stock was a buy or a sell. During the next weekend, away from the strain of work, I fantasized about the job at S&P. They were so excited to have me when I called to accept. I was excited to be going. I sat down with a calculator and tried to see where we'd stand financially with my new salary. The prospects looked good. We could carry the house as well as the apartment rent. It was a way to avoid dealing with the gathering storm. I wondered what Peter was up to.

The following week started slowly. Twelve more days at the *Journal*. I interviewed a money manager and wrote a column on bank stocks. A month or so earlier I had written a rip-roaring bear column on a tiny oil company whose stock had gotten way out of line. The company's president told its shareholders, after the stock sank, that I was "bought and paid for" by a money manager for a religious cult—Scientologists. It was pretty funny, actually, and I took a sheet of paper and wrote on it "Bought and Paid For" and hung it as a sign on the outside of my desk. Nobody mentioned it. I was cracking up.

I was starting to think about the awesome task of packing up my files, two cabinets full, when Stew Pinkerton phoned and asked me to come to his office. He had recently been promoted to associate publisher and, a few months earlier, had passed the bar to practice law in New York State. The smell of disaster was in the air. I popped a half a Valium and lingered as long as I dared. When I finally got to Stew's office, Steiger was sitting with him. Neither of them smiled when I walked in.

"The SEC has voted to make this a formal investigation," Pinkerton said. He had a pained look on his face. Steiger's brow was slightly furrowed. They both looked kind of sad, searching my face for clues. I felt like I was on stage. "I think the best thing to do, since you're leaving soon anyway, is to take you off the column altogether. You can help Dean Rotbart out until you leave. The SEC assures us you are not a target of the investigation but we think you should have your own attorney. If you don't know an attorney, Bob Sack will get you a list of recommendations and you can pick one."

I felt like I'd just heard the ten-minute warning siren for the nuclear holocaust.

When Steiger got back downstairs to his office he called me in and finally asked me the tough questions. But he did so in an oblique fashion. He asked me a few vague questions about Peter Brant. No one at the *Journal* had put the *big* question to me yet. Steiger, visibly uncomfortable, took a stab at it.

"Are you sure you haven't taken anything from these guys or done anything that might embarrass the *Journal*?"

I had nine days to go until I had to turn in my ID card. I wasn't about to push the plunger and blow myself up now.

"Yes. I'm sure."

Steiger dropped the subject and never asked me again.

I used an empty office with a door on it to call a lawyer I had known when I worked in Trenton. He was a nice guy but he wasn't the person I was prepared to confide in. He was all excited. This was going to be his big break-through case. A juicy First Amendment fight between the nation's largest newspaper and the SEC.

Gary, meanwhile, had picked up the seismic tremors going through my life.

"Foster, is there something going on here that I'm missing?" he said with a conspiratorial smile on his face. I motioned him into the empty office and gave him a thumbnail sketch.

"The SEC is investigating one of my sources. They say I'm not a target. I have to get my own lawyer. Don't ask me any more questions. I really can't discuss it." Of all the people I had worked with at the *Journal*, the person I cared most about was Gary. I couldn't tell him the truth. He probably would have strangled me right there on the spot. I had grown to love him as a mentor. So it was excruciatingly painful to hear the next words out of his mouth: "Well, I'm sure your ethical standards are just as high as mine." I managed a weak smile.

Whether the storm would break before my last day I couldn't tell. That night when I got home was a repeat of March 1. I was flying apart inside. David wasn't home and I dusted off the suicide plans. There was no going back. I laid on the sofa chain-smoking cigarettes. The Valium took some of the jangle out of my hysteria as did the knowledge of my impending death. I had spoken to no one besides David about my plans.

When he got home we walked downstairs to the pay phone so David could call Peter. I stood next to him as he placed the call. It was chilly and I shivered both from the temperature and the adrenaline surges.

"It's David," he said. "We have a problem with the draperies and I think you should see them."

"I know," Peter said. "Don't worry about it."

"It's serious. Something's come up. I need to see you in the workroom."

David's level of paranoia had surpassed mine. More than two weeks of watching me come unglued had taken its toll on him. Somebody had parked a sparkling clean van on our filthy street and he was convinced it was packed with federal agents snapping pictures and listening to us.

Peter relented and agreed to meet David at the apartment on East 52nd Street in the wee hours of the morning. And as before, David returned with no new information. He didn't say that Peter had been asking for invoices and that he'd asked again. David was even more frightened than before. He was almost positive that Peter was a dangerous man and he tried to protect me by telling me little about their meetings. David was making less sense to me each day as a result. He imagined Clark was in the Mafia and we were going to be kidnapped and buried in cement.

He didn't want to give Peter anything in writing but he also was afraid not to. I asked him why he was so upset but he wouldn't articulate it.

"I can't explain it," he said. "I'll just bet he cheated you and did something really bad that you don't know about with that Clark guy."

"Like what," I said.

"I don't know. Peter won't tell me who Clark is. I just feel it in my bones that he's up to something."

Each time we talked I ended up more confused and rattled. I looked like hell, bags under my eyes, and David worried that, on my way to work, I might throw myself in front of a subway train. We sat together on the sofa that night, after he returned from his second visit to Peter's apartment.

"When this gets out our lives will be ruined," I said. "We won't have any friends, our families won't talk to us," I rambled. "The life we know will be over." Neither of us had ever dreaded the future as much. David hugged me and we huddled like that for a long time in stunned silence.

Going to work became harder each day, softened only by the knowledge that, in my fragile state, at least I wouldn't have to write any more columns. I rationed the half-tablets of Valium so I wouldn't run out before my last day. The next weekend we drove out to the country to visit some relatives of mine in Pennsylvania and drove by the house we were supposed to buy. It was a sad day. We had both fallen in love with the place and I knew how much David was looking forward to planting a garden. We didn't say it to each other but we both knew we were going to lose it.

Sunday I managed to keep an appointment to have breakfast with Dan Dorfman, the *Daily News* stock market columnist. He congratulated me on the move to Standard & Poor's and we talked about the market.

On Monday of my last week at *The Wall Street Journal* I started sorting and packing up my files. I planned to take them home but before I could, the lawyer from Trenton told me to store them at the *Journal* so no one could later claim I had tampered with evidence. I put them in a storage closet and got a signed receipt from Steiger.

Ken flew home from his ski trip to Vail to find Peter still in a state of high anxiety mixed with depression. He was still scheming. He was going to use influence somehow to short-circuit the SEC investigation. He still wasn't making any sense.

At about noon on Wednesday of my last week, David answered the telephone at home.

"Hi. It's Peter," the voice said. David felt a rush of fear. What was wrong? he thought. Peter was more paranoid than anyone. Why was he using the phone and calling on our home phone?

Peter's voice was curt, businesslike. "I want you to meet me at the apartment at one o'clock. And make *sure* you bring your paperwork." David knew what he meant. He wanted those invoices. But now David was more frightened than ever. Was this it? Would he get there and be kidnapped or murdered?

He took snap-apart memo forms, threw them in the typewriter and banged out three "invoices" in message form. Peter had told him how to write them.

Dear Peter,

Thank you for the opportunity to be of service to you, and I appreciate the introduction to Mr. Felis. As I discussed with you, my fees are based on the amount of time I spend on research and a percent-

age of what you actually spend on the total of
interior design. Again, please understand that I will
only advise. Please forward a check for $15,000.

Peter,

I hope you liked the book with the art photos in it.
And I think you own one. [Peter had shown David
an art book containing his eighteenth-century
Stubbs when he wanted David to make up invoices
for the goods.] What is better then to see that you
have indeed made a wise art investment. I am
finding your project(s) taking more of my time then
I expected. Please send me a check for $5,000. I will
at a later date look into your draperies, I know you
aren't happy with it. I'll see what can be done.

Dear Ken,

Thank you for the opportunity to be of service
to you. Please forward a check payable to me in the
amount of $10,000. A review of your purchases
indicate you might do better to slow down for the
time being, while I take a closer look at the invoices
and see if you are getting your moneys worth. This
process takes a great deal of time. I will be in touch
soon.

David deliberately omitted his signature and the date. The
invoices were a joke, and he hoped he had rendered them essentially useless. He wasn't going to give them up unless Peter
demanded them. He decided this was going to be the last time he
saw Peter.

He got to the apartment house first. Ken showed up and they
waited for Peter in the courtyard.

"Is this really serious?" he asked Ken.

"Yeah. I think so."

"Well, what's inside information? I mean, isn't that like corporation stuff?"

Ken shrugged his shoulders. He seemed awed by what was
happening. "I don't know either."

Peter arrived a few minutes later with delicatessen sandwiches. Upstairs he and Ken ate at the marble dining table. David opened the wrapping on his sandwich but he couldn't eat. We were both losing our appetites and he had begun vomiting after each time he ate. David squeezed Peter again about David Clark.

"Who is David Clark? What's he got to do with all this?" He kept badgering until Peter finally exploded.

"Just *shut up*, all right? Shut the fuck up about this Clark stuff!" Then, more calmly, "Look, I told you. You're better off not knowing."

"I'm worried about Foster. We don't know what to do and he's getting worse every day. I think he's about to do something, like jump in front of a subway train or something. We have no one to turn to."

"I've gotten advice from my attorney," he said. "It's no big deal. But we've got to meet with Foster. I want you to set it up. You call Foster at work and have him meet us."

This is *definitely* it, David thought. They'll get us together and the Clark people will kill us.

"There's no way I'm going to let you meet with Foster unless it's in a place where there's a lot of people," he said.

"Maybe we can all buy tickets and fly on different flights to Atlanta or some place like that," Peter said. "We could meet there."

"That's crazy, Peter," Ken said. "That's just plain stupid."

Peter badgered David all afternoon about meeting face to face with me. David wondered, Are they stalling for somebody else to show up? He was certain that Peter was dangerous.

"Did you bring the paperwork?" Peter finally asked. David's heart fluttered. He'd hoped Peter would forget. Now he worried he would notice what a sloppy job he'd done of the invoices.

"Yeah." David pulled out an envelope containing the snap-apart forms. He handed it to Peter who stuck it in his jacket pocket unopened. Thank God! David thought. His mind isn't on them so he won't notice they aren't signed and dated. He'll probably just throw them away when he sees them.

The three of them finally left the apartment but had no destination, so Ricardo randomly drove around the city. They decided to stop and have a drink. They sat for a time in a coffee shop on First Avenue. They all had strong drinks. The alcohol mingled with David's adrenaline and created a potent mixture. He was freaking out.

"Look," Peter said. "You call Foster and have him meet us at

Trader Vic's in the Plaza Hotel. It's in the basement. We'll meet there at six o'clock."

David finally gave in, just to get rid of them.

"Take the car and have Ricardo drive you anywhere you want, all right?" Peter said patronizingly. He and Ken got out at the Racquet Club. David told Ricardo to drive him down to the Village.

"Do you think Peter's in a lot of trouble?" Ricardo asked as he drove. Ricardo knew more than anybody. He drove Peter everywhere and often ferried Clark with Peter or by himself when Peter lent his car.

David didn't know what to say. The guy was making his thirty grand a year, plus the $5,000 bonus Peter gave him at Christmas. He was worried about his job.

"I don't know, Ricardo. I don't think so."

David had Ricardo wait for him while he stopped in a restaurant that was a customer of his advertising business. He had a couple of drinks. When he came out, he decided he was going to go back to Peter's apartment and tell him no deal, no meeting. It seemed too risky. But Peter wasn't home. David sent Ricardo away and waited for a while. Then he walked to a nearby bar and had another drink. He was now functionally drunk and emotionally over the cliff.

I was sitting at my desk at the *Journal* when David phoned. He sounded hysterical and made no sense.

"It's all over. We're finished. We're dead. It's all over."

"What are you talking about? What's happened?"

"It's all over. We're dead." He hung up.

A young guy, probably a hustler, sat down next to David at the bar. David got an inebriated idea. He would pay this guy to go to the Plaza and rent a room. He would give David the key. David would give me the key and I would go up to the room. David would collect Peter from Trader Vic's downstairs and come up to the room. That way, he would know if anyone was following us and no one could knock us off.

I was lying on the sofa, wondering about David's bizarre phone call that day at work, when David got home. I could tell instantly that he had been drinking. A young guy, looking like a street hustler, walked in the door behind him—a thin, pasty-faced kid in jeans and a sweater. Now what? David talked in disjointed riddles.

"Look, there isn't much time. Don't ask me any questions." He turned to the kid, who looked pretty bewildered. "Now you're going to go rent the room, right?"

I pulled David into the bedroom and closed the door. "What the hell is going on? Who is this guy?"

He tried to pull away and I tightened my grip. "He's just some kid I met. Peter's waiting to meet you at Trader Vic's. The kid is going to rent a room. They're waiting to kill us."

It still didn't make sense. We came out of the bedroom. The kid was picking up the vibes and getting nervous. "What is this, some kind of murder plot? I don't do murders, you know."

I decided to go along, if for no other reason than to find out what the truth was. I knew David had snapped and didn't believe a word of what he was saying.

After considerable confusion, the kid and I left in a drizzle for the Plaza. David had given him some cash to rent the room. The kid was supposed to pay for the room, and then bring the key to me in the Oak Bar, Peter's old hangout at the other side of the lobby.

On the ride uptown, the kid was complaining and I tried to reassure him that no one was going to be hurt, let alone killed. When we got out of the cab, the kid went in the front door and I ducked in the side. I found a seat at the bar and ordered a drink. Fifteen minutes went by and David showed up. He sat next to me but we pretended at first that we didn't know each other. I was starting to play the game myself! Finally I said, "The kid's gone. He probably took the money and split."

"Peter's supposed to be waiting downstairs in Trader Vic's. You go down. I'll be down in a few minutes."

I found Peter and Ken sitting in a table tucked in the farthest corner of the restaurant hidden behind a pillar. They both stood up. Peter looked taller than I remembered. Instinctively we hugged each other. I had never hugged him. I almost burst out crying. I shook Ken's hand.

"Where's David?"

"He's upstairs. He's got some crazy idea we're being followed or something. He's out of his mind."

"No kidding," Peter said.

They looked worried but not hysterical.

"I'm about ready to blow my brains out," I said.

"Tell me about it," Peter said.

Ken nodded his head and said, "No shit!"

"Look, you're okay," Peter said. "I talked to a lawyer." He fished in his pocket and withdrew a small piece of folded paper with some writing on it and shoved it toward me. We ordered drinks.

"He says there are three big cases that prove we didn't do anything wrong. There's this case about the printer." I looked at the piece of paper but it was just a few words and didn't mean anything.

"Are you getting any heat from the *Journal*?"

"No. They say they're going to fight any subpoenas on a First Amendment basis. Besides, I'm going to a new job in two weeks."

"Good, good," Peter said. "Look, when I get rid of my apartment in the city, I'll give you guys fifty or sixty thousand. I'm just real tied up right now."

David arrived looking as wild as I had ever seen him.

"They followed us!" he hissed.

Peter craned his neck, his eyes widened, and he stood up. "What do you mean? What do you mean? Who followed us?"

I took David's arm. "Look, just sit down. You're making a ruckus." The tables on all sides were occupied.

David mumbled something about the room and the kid. I stayed just a few minutes more. I was jumpy, David was still freaking out, and this whole dramatic meeting was a big waste of time.

"We'll just stick with the story," Peter said. "We hired David to do decorating. It'll all work out fine. When it's all over, we'll move to Florida and go into business and become millionaires."

It was clear that none of us knew what to do. I had avoided meeting with Peter all month and this meeting, with its chaos, made me even more paranoid than before. I wanted to leave.

"This isn't solving anything," I said. "I'd better go. We'll just have to see how things develop. I'll go first. David should wait a few minutes and then leave." I shook hands with Peter and Ken and left.

Then David finally peaked.

Peter pulled a card out of his jacket without turning it over. "This lawyer told me it's no big deal."

"If it isn't such a big deal why is everyone in such bad shape?" David yelled.

"*Look*," Peter said sternly, "you got to be on the team to play!"

They were shouting at each other now.

"I can't play if I don't know the game!"

"You don't want to know!"

"I think you're a fucking liar! You're destroying Foster because of your fucking *greed*! You're just a goddamned asshole! I know some things about people at the *Journal*. They all trade on this stuff. And I know some things about you guys too." David was completely out of control, his imagination working overtime. "If Foster gets hurt I'll make sure you guys hang, too! I know where you live and I know you have families! I know some things, too!"

Peter's face grew red. There *were* things to know. David didn't know them, but Peter couldn't be sure.

"What do you know?" He pressed the attack. "You gotta tell me. You gotta tell me. We gotta stick together! If you don't tell me, we'll never be able to stick together! You gotta tell me! If they ever question me, I gotta know what you know!

David mumbled and blustered until Peter realized he didn't know anything else.

He eased up. "Look, I'll give you guys some money, fifty thousand, sixty thousand, as soon as I sell my apartment. Nobody's going to do time."

"You just said it's no big deal. Now you're saying nobody's gonna do *time*! I don't want any of your fucking money! I want you out of my life and Foster's life! I don't know how to do that but I want it *now*!" He jumped up and left the table. He headed for the stairs up to the main lobby and the exit. Halfway up the stairs, he burst into tears and sagged against the banister.

"Hey, Peter. You can't let him leave angry like that," Ken said. He was ready to wring David's neck for making threats against him but he couldn't stand to see him being the wreck that he was.

Peter jumped up and strode across the room, past the bar and up the stairs to where David was slumped, sobbing. He grabbed David's arm.

"Come on back," he said quietly. He towered over David. "Let's talk this out."

"No!"

Peter pulled him by the arm and walked him down the stairs over near the bar. "Have another drink. It'll calm you down. You can't leave till you're calmed down."

"I said leave me the fuck alone!" David shouted.

"Have another drink!" Peter pinned David to the wall and said slowly and deliberately, "Everything's going to be all right. Nothing's going to happen to Foster. No good guys, no bad guys, right?"

Ken had come over. "C'mon, Peter. Leave him alone. Keep your voice down."

"Ah, those fuckin' gooks don't even speak English!" Peter said it loud enough that everyone sitting at the bar, including the Oriental bartender, could hear.

Then, as if somebody had unplugged him, Peter gave up. He sagged in defeat.

"I want to go," David said quietly.

"No problem," Peter said backing away. David left and took a cab home.

13
Ground Zero

They didn't want me to know any more than that.
You know, it was only because I kept, you know,
asking that they finally, like a kid, you know, your
mommie finally gives you a cookie, you know, so
he gave me a little bit to keep me satisfied.
                    —David Carpenter, SEC testimony

My life had become a fiction. The next morning I had my picture taken at Standard & Poor's for its employee newsletter. It looked like I might actually make it through my last day at the *Journal* before the apocalypse. The last sentences I would ever write as a reporter for *The Wall Street Journal* had appeared that morning in the form of an unbylined statistical item about short-selling which was buried inside the paper.

Bob Sack phoned me with the names of three lawyers in New York who could represent me. I phoned the lawyer in Trenton who did a quick check and called me back, suggesting Don D. Buchwald of Buchwald & Kaufman.

"They are two former United States prosecutors," he explained, "who are highly thought of among some big-gun securities lawyers." The enormity of what could happen hit home again. I even had a couple of ex-federal crimestoppers representing me. Bob Sack had said the *Journal* would help with the cost, which made me an attractive client: I had a deep-pockets boss willing to pay the bills.

I still hadn't come clean with the lawyer from Trenton. He

was an eager beaver but I couldn't trust him to be sympathetic. Besides, he knew people in my old stomping ground. I was worried that he couldn't resist the urge to use my juicy New York gossip as cocktail fodder back in River City.

That night in the mail I found a notice from New York Telephone: records of all my calls from June 1983 to February 1984 had been subpoenaed by the SEC's Joe Cella and would be turned over the following Monday. I took another half-Valium.

I made my first call to Don Buchwald on the morning of my last day at the *Journal*, Friday, March 23, 1984. Don sounded cheery (these lawyers were just delighted to be associated with a case that showed the promise of becoming the news industry's legal event of the year). We agreed to meet Saturday, the next day, at his office in the Chrysler Building. In the meantime, I had a clerk photocopy all of my bylined stories, about 200 of them, and messenger the package up to him.

Every second of the last day at work was filled with some kind of pain. Paul Steiger and his junior editor took me to lunch. It was mostly small talk, some discussion about what I would be doing in my new job, and no mention of the SEC investigation.

I had a long cup of coffee with another reporter, John Andrew, who'd just moved east from the Los Angeles bureau. He was interested in writing the "Heard" and the fact that there now was another opening. In the process of discussing the work I'd been doing, John remembered a story he'd heard about a previous "Heard" writer. Seems this person was quietly but vigorously pressured to resign: something to do with the SEC. John couldn't have known why I pumped him so hard for details.

Only a handful of people knew I was leaving. My efforts to keep the thing quiet had worked out the way I'd planned. I just wanted to slink away into the darkness. I threw a few things, some papers and some phone numbers that I hadn't stored, into my shoulder bag. My desk was bare. I sat in the chair for a few minutes, listening to the ticker grinding away and watching the Quotron screen blinking its green numbers. It was Friday and deadline for the next edition wasn't until Sunday so the place was kind of quiet. Gary was beginning to pack up some of his things and sorting through the crap on his desk. He had decided not to help Dean Rotbart out with sources, as he'd helped me.

"I might need them some day," he told me. "Why should I give up something I've worked hard to build?" I thought Gary maybe was thinking about going to work someday on Wall Street. He'd hinted at it, anyway.

I would never sit here again, I thought. I would never identify myself again as a reporter for *The Wall Street Journal*, a label that had meant so much to me once and now I was so eager to shed.

I stood and extended my hand to Gary. This was his last day as well.

"Well, it's been real," I said, at a loss for anything more profound.

He stood up and we shook hands. I wanted to hug him but we were separated by desks and a low divider.

"I want to say that the last eighteen months," I hesitated. My throat tightened and I swallowed hard. I took a deep breath. "That the last eighteen months have been the best of my professional life. I have you to thank for that."

A sad look passed over Gary's face but he smiled wanly.

"Thanks, Foster. It's been great."

I turned, hoisted my briefcase to my shoulder and trudged down the aisle one last time, trying to sop up as much as I could of the sounds—the ringing phones, snippets of conversation as I passed by the rows of desks, typewriters clacking. It was like leaving an apartment for the last time, after all the furniture has been removed, the floors swept, and the lights turned out. I stopped for a moment, took one last look, like a snapshot that I might be able to preserve in my memory. I nodded in recognition at someone walking past me who didn't even know this was my last day.

Then I turned and walked out.

I slept hard that night and awoke late. The weather, which had been rainy and chilly most of the week, yielded finally to a warm, sunny spring day. I showered and dressed slowly. I felt better than I had in weeks, just knowing I never had to go back to that place again. Nothing could have been worse than that. Yet I still didn't know what we were going to do.

Don Buchwald had sent his partner, Alan Kaufman, in his stead for our first meeting that afternoon. The lawyer from Trenton was there as well, with his blow-dried hair and salon tan, dressed in pastel pants and white shoes. For some reason his

Florida golf-course outfit clinched my decision: I knew for sure I didn't want to confide in someone who dressed like a pool accessory. Alan, on the other hand, looked like a real New York lawyer and ex-federal prosecutor. He was dressed in dark suit pants, white shirt, conservative tie and dress shoes. He was slender and handsome with a chiseled chin. He was young (about my age, thirty-six) and he didn't have a tan, which meant he took his work seriously. He was smiling but I could see that just beneath the surface beat the heart of a tough and skeptical lawman. That was the one I wanted going to battle for me. Not the balloon-head in the clown suit. The office was on the 55th floor of the Chrysler Building. The view of the city laid out below was incredible, especially under the strong clear sun.

We talked about legal strategies, First Amendment defenses against the telephone subpoena, and the role Dow Jones would play in the battle that loomed just ahead. The SEC was moving now to subpoena my other records, like bank and brokerage accounts. Dow Jones had promised to pay my bills at least through my last day on the payroll, a week away because of the extra week I'd wangled out of Steiger to compensate for overtime. Steiger and the lawyer from Trenton had been the only ones, other than the SEC, who had asked me all month whether I had done anything wrong. Now, the Trenton lawyer asked me again.

"Now, you're sure you haven't done anything improper here?"

I looked at him but there was no way I could tell him the truth. "Yes, I'm sure."

We made plans to touch base on Monday.

When I got home I decided it was time to act. Things were moving rapidly to a head. David and I sat on the sofa smoking cigarettes.

"David, I don't see another way out. This is going to come crashing down around us and I just don't want to be alive when it happens."

"I know. I know." He paused in thought. "How would we do it?" It was the first time he'd asked and I found it difficult to describe out loud my plan—the hose and the tape.

David looked like he was thinking—when he burst without warning into deep, wracking sobs.

"I can't do it, Foster. I just can't. I know how you feel and I really do understand why. I wish I could but I can't. Please, please don't ask me anymore. I can't take it. I'm so scared you're going to do something. You've got to promise me you won't leave me alone."

Now I started crying. "I promise. I promise." I pulled him to me and we wept hard in each other's arms. I was ashamed of myself for tormenting him.

After a time I got up and made us some more coffee.

"Well, if we aren't going to do it, then there's only one other solution," I said. "We have to tell somebody the truth. I can't live with this inside of me anymore. It's killing me." I looked out the window at the shoppers and drug dealers on 14th Street. The warm weather had brought everyone out. I wondered what normal people were doing today, how they felt, where they were going, if they were happy.

I found the business card that Alan Kaufman gave me with his partner's home phone number on it. I hunched over the phone, lit a cigarette, and looked at David.

"Well, here we go."

I dialed and Don answered the phone.

"Don, it's Foster Winans." Anxiety, fear, and even a tinge of relief surged through my body. My voice broke and tears began to flood my eyes. "I'm calling you as the only alternative to suicide. I have a long story to tell you."

"Okay," he said slowly. "Do you want to meet this afternoon?"

"Yeah," I said, sniffling and wiping back the tears.

"Do you feel as though you are in some danger?"

"I can't tell. David, he's my lover, we're gay, thinks we might be. I can't tell whether that makes any sense at all."

Two hours later we drove out to the suburbs to meet with Don and Alan at Don's house. Don had sent his wife and children out for an hour or two just in case we were in physical danger and being followed. We sat in his living room and told them in fractured fashion the basic story as we knew it. A broker at Kidder, Peabody had traded in advance of stories. We got about $30,000 from him.

David was cooler than he'd been all month. Now I was falling apart, teary-eyed and full of piercing shame. I felt as dead as if we had killed ourselves. I hated the sound of my voice telling this sordid story, but the unburdening was the first respite from pressure I'd had in four weeks. Don seemed especially sensitive to our emotional state. He accepted our relationship and kept saying as we were leaving and for weeks afterward:

"Now, don't hesitate to call for any reason. You're upset but we'll work this out together. Call me for *any* reason," and he looked me straight in the eye and I knew I would do just that if I had to.

The next day, Sunday, I spent about twelve hours with Don in his office going over all the sordid details. He was about the same age as Alan, close to forty, but his face was naturally ruddy and he was prematurely graying, which gave him a distinguished look. Don wasn't classically handsome like his partner but he had a warm, inviting face. I found him easy to be around. He had a good sense of humor but I could see he was tough when he had to be. His big thing was honesty and I was ready for that. When I told him something that didn't make sense or sounded like rationalization, he'd bore right in:

"Now, Foster," he'd say. "Think about that for a second. Does that really make any sense?"

He understood the stock market. I was impressed that I didn't have to explain options and short-selling to him. He also was anticipating reactions all the way down the line to the inevitable revelation of my deal with Peter. I sat on the sill in front of an open window in his office so the smoke from my cigarettes would be drawn out. Don was an ex-smoker and rarely so tolerant. This would be the last time I was allowed to smoke inside his private office. He kept looking at the window and finally said with a mischievous grin on his face, "Ah, now you aren't going to do something like fall out of that window sort of on purpose are you? I mean I'd hate to lose this nice case on the first day." I burst out laughing and it felt so good. I'd found a soulmate with a sense of humor as demented as mine. The honesty washed over me like a hot, relaxing bath.

The biggest problem we faced was how to get the *Journal* off the hook. The paper was marshaling its resources to fight the SEC on the grounds that it had no right to subpoena any of my records. *Journal* lawyers, operating on the presumption of my innocence, were preparing to duke it out with Uncle Sam using as their primary weapon the hallowed right to a free and unfettered press. The paper wanted to guard its confidential sources and would wrap itself in the American flag for a good, old-fashioned constitutional slugfest.

But I was not innocent. When I had to testify, a certainty at this stage of the game, I couldn't in honesty plead First Amendment protection. I would either have to hide behind the Fifth Amendment or tell the truth. In either event, the press and public would question whether the *Journal* had been trying to sweep its filth under the Constitution.

The longer I remained silent, the greater the likelihood that the cloud of suspicion would grow and cover other *Journal* employees as well. The guessing game as to where the leak had sprung and how far it reached would spread like a cancer and implicate or entangle people I cared about—people like Gary.

As unethical as my behavior had been, I couldn't see what laws I had broken. But I knew that wouldn't stop the SEC from pushing its investigation. I had been a reporter for too many years, watched too many trials, and seen too many government prosecutors at work to delude myself into believing the SEC would look the other way. I was a big target—working for the largest business publication in the country cowriting the best-read stock market column in the world. What I had done confirmed the suspicions of many investors about stock market writers—that they take personal advantage of the information they gather.

Realizing this hit me pretty hard. I had begun to think of Peter as the bad guy. After all, I reasoned, he was rich and I was not. But I temporarily forgot that I worked for the *Journal*, which conferred its celebrity status on its employees: I was not just a journalist on a daily newspaper.

My long session with Don, followed by similar sessions on Monday and Tuesday, worked as a balm for my anxiety. At last I was able to unburden myself of the truth. But the old fears were being replaced by new ones: how the *Journal* would react to my revelations, what our friends and family would say and think, legal entanglements, attorneys' fees, and the firestorm of publicity I expected.

On Monday, David and I cashed in all of our chips so we could pay Don a $15,000 retainer. We sold what stocks we still owned, borrowed what we could from our loan account, and withdrew the remaining funds from the $10,000 check from Peter. It would be a week before we would have a chance to decide about the house in Pennsylvania. But this was only the beginning. The only person I thought I knew well enough to borrow money from was a friend from my old days working on a newspaper in the state of Washington. Her career had taken her to Moscow, where she worked for an international wire service. We had lived together from time to time, and David and I considered her to be our closest friend. Reaching her was a hassle. Mail had to be sent to Helsinki where it was transferred to diplomatic pouch. Otherwise, the Russians opened it or, in the case of magazines, stole it. There was no time to write, so I put an order in with the international operator early in the evening and went to bed.

The phone rang about 3 o'clock in the morning and we were connected. She sounded like I woke her up or like she had been drinking. She was an alcoholic who'd recently fallen off the wagon after more than a year sober. Moscow was a tough and lonely beat. I knew she held strong moral beliefs and it was a difficult task to try to explain, without being specific, that I had done something unethical.

"I'm in a lot of trouble. I can't explain but it has something to do with my work on the *Journal*. David and I have had to hire a lawyer and it's wiped us out. Can you lend us any money?" Her living expenses were mostly paid for and she had once explained that she had lots of extra cash because, working abroad, her income taxes were low.

"Yeah, I guess so. I think I can spare $3,000. What's it about?"

"I can't say but it's serious enough that my lawyer sees his main job to keep me from going to prison."

"What happened? What did you do?"

"Please don't make me go into it. I can't. All I can say is I got some money I shouldn't have."

"Did you sell the column?"

"No," I said. She was being a reporter and I was getting irritated although I recognized that if the roles had been reversed I would have bored in on her the way she was grilling me. "But it will look that way."

We had decided against pleading the Fifth. The only other alternative was to come clean. Tuesday morning David and I gave Don the go-ahead to start the process of "bringing us in." We were approaching the point of no return. Don called a lawyer at the SEC on Tuesday just before lunch to arrange an urgent meeting. He didn't say why it was urgent, but the SEC lawyer sensed things were coming to a head. The two attorneys agreed to meet in Washington Wednesday morning at 10 o'clock.

Then Don called Bob Sack, the *Journal* lawyer, and met with him Tuesday afternoon to give him the bad news that I had unclean hands and would be admitting what I'd done to the government. We wanted to give Sack enough of a warning so he could bring a halt to the paper's plans to fight subpoenas. But we hoped Sack would be able to restrain himself from telling the news staff at the *Journal* as well and triggering premature press coverage. We wanted the SEC to hear it from us before reading about it in the papers. The timing was so tight.

Don gave us a final phone call of encouragement at our apartment and caught an early-morning shuttle flight to Washington on Wednesday. He gave the SEC staff people a taste of our story. David and I were eager by now to unburden ourselves and we told Don we'd agree to testify without grants of immunity or special considerations. Don left the SEC meeting with only a promise that they would call him when he got back to New York.

Don called his office for messages when he arrived back at New York's La Guardia Airport early in the afternoon. The SEC had called while he was in flight. They wanted David and me to testify right away. The SEC had learned that the *Journal* planned to run a story in its next edition, Thursday. The paper was refusing the agency's pleas to hold off publication lest Peter Brant and David Clark have enough warning of our cooperation to flee.

We agreed with the SEC to fly that night to Washington, where, the next morning, I would begin testifying in a private session with Joe Cella and his buddies. We had no idea what Peter was up to but we were pretty well convinced that he would bolt, or blow his brains out, as soon as he realized that David and I had quit his team.

In fact, the weekend that I unburdened myself to Don, Peter was preparing again to flee. After the chaotic meeting at Trader Vic's, Peter's new plan was to take the 52-foot *Finesse* out of port from West Palm Beach and spend a few years living in the islands of the Bahamas while Lynn lived with Ken and his family. They'd sneak occasional visits. Peter flew off with Lynn and the baby to his apartment in Wellington, one of those instant towns that sprang up in the 1970s from the Florida swamps west of Palm Beach, where the truly rich spent their winters. The apartment stood at the edge of the playing fields at the Palm Beach Polo Club, an exclusive enclave where the cognoscenti of the sport of kings played in the winter months. The apartment was just across a small canal from two huge expanses of grass where folks like Prince Charles had whacked around the wooden ball.

Peter called Ken from Wellington and begged him to come down to Florida.

"I have to see you. It's important."

Ken resisted but finally gave in. He flew in to West Palm Beach airport, where Peter met him in a rented powder-blue Cadillac.

"Boy, am I glad to see you," Peter said on the twenty-mile trip to Wellington. "Thanks for coming." By now he was over the edge. Peter had metamorphosed into his new role. He was a desperado, and he had Lynn convinced as well that his only salvation lay in fleeing in the boat and living in the islands. He now existed in his own fantasy world.

Back at the apartment, Peter showed Ken the equipment he had started to assemble, laid out on the bed, for his journey—marine gear of all sorts and rust-proof stainless steel automatic rifles for protection against drug pirates. Peter talked a mile a minute about how he'd move from island to island, spearing fish for his meals and living in the sun. He talked about cocaine deals he said David Clark was arranging. They'd make a ton of money and fix the embezzlement thing. There was just one small problem. The boat was drydocked at a yard on the mainland across the inland waterway from Palm Beach, awaiting the refitting he had put off since the summer before, when he first bought the *Finesse*. Peter couldn't just jump on the boat and sail off into the sunset.

"Peter, this is ridiculous," Ken said. "Why don't you just face the music and take your medicine? This isn't the end of your life."

"Suppose it meant spending fifteen years in prison?" Peter asked. "What would you do then?" Ken wasn't worried about having stolen money from clients so the question was moot. But he thought about it a second and said, "I guess I'd be down there with you at the visa office."

Peter continued to skip from one plan to another, downing Valiums all the while. He heard that Frank Sinatra was in Palm Beach and would attend a party thrown by someone Peter knew. He wanted to wangle an invitation and talk to Sinatra to see if he could pull strings with the Reagan administration to short-circuit the SEC investigation. It was just another crazy idea that never went anywhere. The party was canceled at the last minute anyway.

Peter didn't have the guts to run and he had exhausted all his other workable options. He and Ken were sitting in the apartment.

"You know, the SEC can't prove anything," he said.

"What do you mean?" Ken said.

"Well, think about it. They can't connect me with the thing. The trading was in your account."

Ken looked into Peter's eyes and what he saw there raised a lump in his throat. He had known Peter for nearly twelve years. They had shared the same room, worn each other's clothes, shared their secrets, their dreams, and their fears. Ken had befriended Peter because he'd felt sorry for the overdressed boy from Buffalo. They had laughed and played as hard as Ken ever had or thought he ever would. He protected Peter the summer they worked issuing credit memos for Bowmar. Ken's family had taken Peter in when Peter rejected his own. They'd spent hours, like old ladies, talking on the boat in Long Island Sound or on the telephone. The two men had trusted and loved each other in a deep abiding way that men sometimes do, even more than brothers. Now, as Ken gazed into Peter's eyes, a silent but powerful metaphysical communication took place. A sick feeling twisted his gut. Ken couldn't speak. But he knew, with the suddenness of a slap in the face, that Peter was going to try to pin the whole thing on him. The umbilical cord that had linked them all those years, badly frayed from the strain and stress of the past few months, soundlessly snapped.

Ken left Florida the next morning. For the first time he felt alone and isolated. On the way home and over the next several days he added and re-added the damages. Peter had insisted on trading in Ken's account. He arranged for Ken to take the money to Switzerland. He told Ken to write a $10,000 check to David. It was almost as if Peter had planned from the beginning to dump the thing in Ken's lap. He wanted to cry. Then he was scared. How could he prove that this was Peter's deal? Had Peter been conning him all along? Suddenly Peter's every gesture and word took on sinister meaning.

They talked one last time. Ken was in the office. Peter called from Florida and gave Ken the name of a lawyer he could hire.

"What about the rest of the money in Switzerland?" Ken

asked. "I checked like you asked me and there's still a few thousand left in the Western Hemisphere account."

"Oh, that's all right. I don't want it." Another denial, Ken thought. First he said he needed the money. Now he could deny it was half his.

The weather on Wednesday, March 28, turned vicious as a powerful winter storm moved up the Atlantic coast dumping snow along the way. From Buchwald's office I could see the storm clouds darken and the snow begin. Within an hour the city far below was hidden by a curtain of wet snow, sleet, and rain. The weather nicely fit the mood inside. Don had already tipped the *Journal* that I was going to the SEC to testify. We were scheduled to start the next morning in the SEC's Washington headquarters. Earlier that afternoon David and I packed overnight bags and set the apartment straight. We put a new tape in the telephone answering machine, took out the garbage, and locked the place tight.

We brought with us file folders full of papers—checking account records, brokerage statements, telephone bills—anything we could find to document where the money came from, where it went, and our movements.

At the *Journal*, Sack filled Pearlstine in on the gory details, as much as he knew them. A battle group of editors and reporters were assembled and assigned to cover the various aspects of the story for Thursday's edition. These included the people with whom I had worked most closely—Dick Rustin and Gary Putka among them. Late Wednesday, Paul Steiger called Don for comment. Don read to Steiger my statement, a statement I couldn't read without weeping. We had worked on it together, trying to capture how I felt without giving out details the SEC didn't yet have directly from us:

> I deeply regret the anguish which I have caused. Most particularly, I apologize to the talented and highly professional people with whom and for whom I worked at the *Journal*. That the reputation of any of these fine people or of the newspaper itself may be harmed in even the slightest measure by my conduct is my greatest shame.

At the SEC's offices, arrangements were being made for tape-recording equipment to be set up in a private examining room deep inside the agency's headquarters. Couriers were to pick the tapes up as they were recorded, take them to the stenographic pool, and return the transcripts as soon as they were completed. SEC lawyers geared up to issue a new wave of subpoenas and to file motions to lock up assets and keep people from fleeing the country.

The orchestra was tuning up, the players were fixing their makeup, and the curtain was just about to rise.

The weather turned so fierce the New York airports were starting to shut down. At the other end, Washington National was already closed. So David, Don, and I grabbed a cab to Pennsylvania Station to catch a rush-hour Metroliner to Washington. We now were traveling incognito. We didn't want to run into any reporters. The *Journal* was going to press, in spite of pleas from the SEC to hold off for a day or so in case they needed to put the bite on Peter and Clark. By Thursday morning, the whole world would know. We found seats in a non-smoking car. But soon after the train pulled out of the station, Don spotted a newscaster, Ralph Penza, from a New York television station. We packed up and moved to a different car. Don, from his days as a prosecutor with the government, knew a lot of lawyers who regularly made this trip back and forth between D.C. and New York.

"If I accidentally run into anyone I know, I won't introduce you," he explained. When he remembered something he wanted to say, he whispered almost inaudibly into our ears. The train was full of people with business in Washington and New York. Any one of them could have been a lawyer with connections to the case or a good idea of what was going on.

David and I were nervous as hell. We had no idea what to expect the next morning. We stood on the platform between two cars to smoke our cigarettes and talk.

"This is like a fucking spy movie," David said.

"Yeah. It's about the weirdest thing I've ever been through. We may not be able to stay at home when we get back. The press will be all over this thing by then and they'll be hanging around outside the apartment house, TV cameras and all. We'll work it out."

Neither of us had eaten much of anything for close to two weeks. David vomited anything solid he tried to get down. I didn't even try to eat solids. Mostly we drank milk and coffee. We had each lost ten pounds or so and joked that our old clothes had started to fit again.

"At least we're getting *something* out of all this," I said as the train sped south through the blizzard.

The worst of the storm was past Washington when we arrived. A cab negotiated the snowy streets to a motel a few blocks away from the SEC offices. The SEC was paying for the room David and I stayed in, our transportation, and witness fees of $60 a day. We had no promises of immunity from suits or criminal prosecution. Don had a room down the hall. We stayed in our room and ordered our food from room service. That way we wouldn't be spotted by some enterprising reporter. David and I watched some television and fell into a fitful sleep. When we awoke, everyone in the world would know my secret.

At about ten o'clock that night, Dick Rustin called our home phone and left a message on our answering machine:

"Foster Winans, this is Dick Rustin. All I've got to say to you is I think you are the scum of the earth."

The next morning we ordered in breakfast but all we could do was pick at it. I munched on toast and drank a glass of milk. Don went down and got a copy of *The Wall Street Journal*. The story appeared on page three, the equivalent of the front page in any other newspaper, where the front page isn't devoted to features. A short synopsis on the front page headed the list of the day's stories inside the paper.

> The SEC is investigating allegations that a ring of
> securities traders made illicit profits using informa-
> tion leaked to them by a *Wall Street Journal* reporter
> about articles published in this paper.

At least my name isn't on the front page, I thought.

The article inside took up all the space on page three not devoted to advertising. I had worked for years as a reporter writing about the misconduct and misfortunes of others. Now, for the first time, I read a story about my own misconduct. Strangely enough, it was as though it was happening to someone else. I cringed as I read the words but I still wasn't quite connected to them.

The *Journal* reported I had been fired the day before. My last day on the payroll was two days away anyway but it hurt just as much to read it.

Those bums, I thought. Even cops get suspended with pay pending the outcome of misconduct cases. The story quoted the chairman of Dow Jones, Warren Phillips: "When an individual breaks faith and casts a blot on the paper's reputation, it can only inspire a deep sense of hurt and outrage. . . ." It also quoted Norm Pearlstine: "'For anyone to use this kind of knowledge for his own benefit is worse than theft."

The *Journal* revealed that it had been working on an earlier article about the investigation but stopped when it learned that I was coming in out of the cold. I was amazed that Peter's name appeared nowhere in the story. Neither did Ken's. We did learn that the mysterious David Clark had traded on the tips I was giving Peter. He had been interviewed, saying he'd never talked to anyone at the *Journal* and claiming he got his investment ideas from "various sources" on Wall Street. At least one piece of the puzzle found its place.

The article contained a fair amount of anguished breastbeating and some inspired nonsense: "To make sure unprinted information doesn't inadvertently leak, the ["Heard"] column isn't put into type until shortly before deadline." The deadline was about 5:30 or 6 P.M., nearly two hours after the stock markets had shut down for the night and no one could trade. Well, maybe when Gary wrote the column, I thought with a chuckle, but only because he often got his stories in *so* shortly before deadline they risked *never* being set in type. The statement was just plain baloney. A bunch of composing room editors and typesetters up in Chicopee must have been scratching their heads that morning when they read it.

And this one: "On occasion, the *Journal* has killed columns when it feared word of an impending column might have slipped out." Well, there were plenty of times when sources guessed from our questions what we were working on and the stock jumped or sank. But no editor killed a column while I cowrote the "Heard" and Gary only knew of one occasion before my tour when a "Heard" was killed for such a reason.

But I expected this kind of self-exculpatory coverage from the

Journal. The paper had two primary goals: to make damn sure it didn't get scooped on its own story, which meant printing everything it knew and some things it could only speculate about; and to make equally sure that the authenticity of my stories hadn't been compromised. The only thing worse than my transgressions hitting the open air would have been for some other news organization to break the story or dig up juicy details the *Journal* didn't have first. The paper had to be aggressive or risk raising the odor of cover-up.

The *Journal* also needed to reassure readers, as well as it could, that the accuracy of its stories was intact. The *Journal*, for all the information it printed that day, really wasn't sure what it was dealing with. It had two protagonists, one who traded on leaked stories (Clark) and one who leaked them (me). Each claimed, correctly, that they'd never met the other. How did the leak get from one to the other? And why did I do it? The paper had no clue—money, sex, drugs? How extensive was the leak? How much money was made? All the possibilities must have run through the minds of the reporters working on the story. The *Journal* also didn't know where David and I were.

Don called my brother, Chris, to let him know that I was all right. I had a nightmare that he would have to quit the *Journal*, where he worked as an editor. I knew the *Journal* people would have blood in their eyes, and I worried that his shame and their anger would make it impossible for him to stay.

As David and I showered and dressed for our debut at the SEC, I wondered what was going on in a dozen different locations: my mother's house, my brother's apartment, the *Journal* newsroom, Pearlstine's office, Gary's desk. What, I wondered, were these people thinking and doing?

The newsroom was strangely silent that morning as everyone in the place read and reread the story. Gary told a fellow reporter, "I feel like a piece of dead dogmeat."

Don and I left the motel that morning by cab. It was a sure bet I'd be testifying all day so we left David, with instructions not to leave the room, back in the motel where he'd be more comfortable. An SEC lawyer met us at a side entrance to the building and hustled us inside through the employee door.

"Lots of reporters out front?" Don asked.

"Yeah," the lawyer said. "A whole bunch of them in the lobby. I guess everybody reads the *Journal*."

At 10:30 in the morning I finally was sitting in front of a microphone in a small, windowless room across a Formica table from Joe Cella and a couple of other SEC staffers. Don sat next to me with a stack of yellow legal pads. Everyone looked so serious. One of them took out a pack of cigarettes and struck a match. Don raised his hand.

"Sorry, fellas, but I can't deal with smoke in this tiny room. If you smoke," he kidded, "you'll be violating my client's right to counsel."

The room was just big enough to hold a large table and some molded-plastic chairs. I was nervous but anxious to tell the truth. My goal, if I had one, was to renovate my credibility with the SEC and prove that the content of my columns had not been corrupted by my arrangement with Peter. But I couldn't get dates straight to save my life and I kept apologizing:

"I'm sorry, I'm trying—I'm really trying, I'm trying to be helpful, but it's a blur to me. Some of these things are a blur. Um."

Cella finally told me to stop apologizing.

I realized for the first time that all of my notes, now at the *Journal*, contained the information I needed to set these guys straight. My first meeting with Peter I put in the summer or fall instead of in late spring. But I had the substance of what happened in fairly good form and order. I called David at the motel during the breaks.

"How's it going?" he asked.

"Oh, pretty good, I guess. I can't tell. I can't seem to remember anything, like dates and stuff. I wish I had my notes. But they aren't beating me up or anything. They're just asking a bunch of questions and I'm trying like hell to answer them. Anything on TV?"

"No. I've been watching all day but no news yet."

We had agreed not to discuss facts of the case so that if we were asked we could honestly say we hadn't. Otherwise, the SEC could imply that we had tried to make our stories consistent. It was strange because we were so used to talking about everything. Now it was as though even our conversation was out of our control.

I was drained when I got back to the motel that night. I had testified until 8 P.M. David had seen a brief mention of the developments on one of the network news shows. I phoned our answering machine for the first time since we'd locked up the apartment. There were fifty messages, beginning with a call at 9:30 Wednesday night, after we'd arrived in Washington, from *USA Today*. They were already on the story before the *Journal* hit the newsstands. The second one was the "scum-of-the-earth" call from Dick Rustin.

And then a long list of news organizations, worried friends, and family. I had a pad and tried to jot them all down as I sat on the edge of the bed, the receiver cradled on my shoulder. Some of them made me choke with shame:

"This is, uh, Joe. I just wanted Foster to know that, uh, I'm thinking of him and, uh, I'm a friend."

Beep.

"This is Mike Jensen from NBC News. We're doing a story for 'Nightly News' this evening on Foster Winans and the events at *The Wall Street Journal* involving the SEC and divulging information. I am interested in talking to Mr. Winans for an interview."

Beep.

"This is the Associated Press. We're interested in getting a photograph of you if it's possible."

Beep.

"This is Eleanor Randolph with the *Washington Post*. I'm in New York and trying to get in touch with Foster Winans."

Beep.

"Please call John Henry at the *Daily News*."

Beep.

"Mr. Winans, this is Brian Demain with *Fortune* magazine. We'd like a comment on the *Journal* story."

Beep.

"This is Larry. I'm just calling as a friend. I really feel for you. If there's anything I can help you with, please call me."

Beep.

"Gary Putka looking for Foster Winans."

Beep.

"This is the *Miami Herald*."

Beep.

"Foster, it's Tucker. I read the article and just called to let you know that we still think fondly of you here. I know you're going through a hard time. Good luck and call if you get a chance."

Beep.

"This is Judy Lynch. I am an attorney for the Reporters' Committee for a Free Press."

Beep.

"Foster, it's me, Dan Dorfman. You're terrific. If there's any way I can help, please let me know. It won't be bad. You'll soon be back. Give me a call and good luck, buddy."

Beep.

"Rick Bruns, *Time* magazine. Please call me back."

Beep.

"Gary Putka here. Looking for Foster or David."

Beep.

"This is Mark. I just wanted to call and tell you I couldn't give a fuck what they wrote in the *Journal* today. If you need help, call me."

Beep.

"This is Nancy Stanton of *Newsweek*."

Beep.

"Hi, it's Mom. If you're not there, I'd like to think you're monitoring this. I love you. I'm with you and I'd like to know if there's something I can do."

Beep.

"This is your old friend calling just to give you a message of cheer and to condemn a certain newspaper for a very shoddy job of reporting."

Beep.

"Hello, this is Lucia. Just wanted to call and say howdy and hope it's not too bad a time. Call me sometime. I've been thinking a lot about you."

Beep.

"It's Mom again. I just wanted you to know that I'm here for you. Please get in touch with me."

Beep.

"Just heard the news on TV. If there's anything I can do, please call on me."

Beep.

"Just wanted to let you know I was thinking about you."

Beep.

"This is Gary looking for Foster. I'm home. Please give me a call. This is affecting my life too."

Beep.

"Hi. It's Chris [my brother]. I love you very much. If you want to talk to me . . . I love you and I'll give you all the moral support I can."

Beep.

"It's Chris again. Everyone at work has been very supportive of me and they express nothing but positive feelings for you. I'm talking about a lot of people. I wanted you to know it's not causing me any problems at work. I understand if you can't call me back."

Beep.

"This is Doug Magill of *The New York Times*. I'm standing right outside your building at 234 East 14th Street and I'd like to talk to Mr. Winans. If you're there could you pick up or call me at this pay phone?"

Beep.

"Hi. Doug Magill from *The New York Times*. It's 9:15 Thursday night. If you can't call me could you call Alex Jones at the paper?"

14

Firestorm

Some of the old newspaper traditions, of course,
we maintain. Our self-righteousness, I can assure
you, is undiminished. Our capacity to criticize
everybody and our imperviousness to criticism
ourselves, are still, I believe, unmatched by novel-
ists, poets or anybody else.

—James Reston, *Columbia Journalism Review*, 1966

My mother was sitting on the edge of her bed early the night of my
SEC testimony. The television was on but it couldn't drown out
the howling winds of a particularly violent nor'easter that was
raking Cape Cod and rattling the windows in her Victorian house.
Her mail, including a copy of that day's *Wall Street Journal*, lay
unread next to her on the bed. The phone rang.

"Hi! It's Baum" (her cousin who lives in Florida).

"Hi!" she said in her usual cheery voice. She rarely heard from
her relatives and she was delighted.

"I just wanted to let you know how sorry I am and how much
we hope things work out all right."

My mother was puzzled. She assumed he was talking about
the weather, which was bad but not so bad that it warranted
condolences from Florida. She started mumbling about how they
were used to the weather up there in New England.

"Haven't you read *The Wall Street Journal*?" her cousin asked in
disbelief.

"No," my mother said. A feeling of dread began to dawn in

her. She reached for the paper and began to read. When she was done, she called and left a message on my answering machine. She next called my brother and then phoned my father in Connecticut. She caught him just in time, before he sat down to watch "The NBC Nightly News."

Everyone on the *Journal*'s national news desk, including my brother, put down their pencils just after 7 P.M. when Tom Brokaw's face and the NBC News logo appeared on the television screen suspended from the newsroom ceiling.

Brokaw began the segment something like, *The Wall Street Journal*'s "Heard on the Street" columnist, R. Foster Winans, is now *on* the street." All of a sudden all of the cute lead-ins to crime stories my brother had ever written, read, or heard seemed unnecessarily flippant.

The morning after my testimony we bought the *Journal* and *The New York Times*. The *Times* had a story, under the byline of Alex Jones, which contained this incredible statement: ". . . a man identifying himself as Mr. Winans, reached at his home in Manhattan, told *The New York Times* last night: "I did not give information to outsiders. The *Journal* article is not accurate."

Every major news organization in the country chased the *Journal*'s first story on Thursday. The Friday morning papers all had items quoting the *Journal* story. But Alex Jones, the reporter for *The New York Times*, managed to come up with a quote that in every respect I could not have uttered. Even if he misdialed my phone number, the probability approached zero that someone answering a random wrong-number call would come close to uttering the words, "The *Journal* story is inaccurate." Reporters are always being accused, rightly and wrongly, of misquoting people. But this was different. The answering machine tape proved he couldn't have reached me in New York. His colleague, Doug Magill, had called from the pay phone at the corner. That was a fact. It was on tape. David and I were some 300 miles away in Washington, D.C., not in New York and not in our apartment. Those were concrete facts as well. Besides, the *Journal* got its story from me, via Don Buchwald. The probability was nil that I would deny on Thursday facts I supplied to the *Journal* on Tuesday.

The day Jones's story appeared, Friday, David was scheduled to testify. I asked Don to call my mother to reassure her that we were all right. He wouldn't tell her where we were, so she gave him a lecture.

"If you won't let me talk to my son or David, I'm holding you personally responsible for the safety of those boys," she said.

We checked out of our motel rooms. When the three of us arrived at the SEC that morning, Don talked to John Fedders, chief of the SEC's Enforcement Division and Cella's boss, about the possibility that someone had broken into our apartment and answered the phone. It made no sense, of course, but Jones's story with its impossible quote raised that as the most likely answer other than his having imagined the whole thing.

The *Times* story caused us infinite grief. The *Journal* reacted like a beehive that had been whacked with a stick. First I gave them the scoop, and then, the way it looked, I tried to make them out to be liars. It took Don a little while on the phone to get everyone calmed down again. We couldn't tell Jones why I couldn't possibly have been home. Our location was still supposed to be a secret until the SEC had decided what to do about Peter Brant and David Clark.

Jones interviewed my brother, Chris, ending up writing a short item for the next edition, Saturday. But he refused to admit an error, a typical way for newspapers to deal with mistakes. The *Times* had covered itself by saying "a man identifying himself as Mr. Winans." But that didn't explain away the answering machine tape.

The *Journal* battle group of reporters and editors, meanwhile, was hitting the beaches. "We've got so many reporters working on this story it looks like D-Day at Normandy," one editor observed. The *Journal* seized the nine cartons of my notes which had been locked up for safekeeping. A group of editors sorted through every box, page by page, looking for clues to what I'd done. In the process, they found a wire basket of telephone messages I had saved for the phone numbers. The paper also pulled my personnel file, which listed personal friends as references, and dug out telephone company bills showing numbers I had called.

Gary's planned transfer to London was put on hold. He had already rented his co-op apartment in Brooklyn to someone else and he had to move into a hotel with his wife and child. George

Anders, the London editor whom I was friendly with and who preceded me on the "Heard," joined the task force to try to dig up what dirt he could. A full-scale assault, fast shaping up as a witch hunt, was under way.

The reaction of individuals at the *Journal* ran the gamut from fury at my traitorous behavior to concern that I would take my life. As a community, the *Journal* advanced through the predictable stages of mourning beginning with shock, disbelief, and denial. Some of the people I had worked with on the ticker and at the *Journal* refused at first to accept the truth of what I'd done. A similar reaction seized sources of mine on Wall Street. One of them, a money manager I knew well, thought, I'd never believe this of Foster.

The *Journal*'s relationship with Wall Street has been compared to the Catholic Church's influence on Christianity. The *Journal* reacted to my transgressions just as pious Catholics might if I had made an attempt on the Pope's life. No treatment of me would be harsh enough to compensate for what I'd done. In its evangelical zeal to cleanse itself, the *Journal* went temporarily berserk.

Gary, a personal friend, and Dick Rustin, a personal enemy, were among those with axes to grind who were assigned to cover the story. It was like assigning a cuckolded husband to sit in judgment on his own divorce suit. Neither Gary nor Rustin was capable of objectivity. Both had left emotional messages on my answering machine. It was the kind of conflict of interest that has gotten reporters fired. The difference in this case was that the conflict was institutionalized and sanctioned by the *Journal*. There was more.

The *Journal* personnel department supplied the news staff with information from my personnel file, a file the confidentiality of which is supposed to be guaranteed. The paper also allowed its staff to paw through 24,000 pages of my notes and papers. It was the same kind of conduct the *Journal* and every other newspaper in the country would have condemned if indulged in by a government agency. But the *Journal* had the power to bend the rules to fit its anger and hurt. Things would get worse in the days to come.

I waited in another small, windowless examining room while David spent about five hours testifying. I slept fitfully on a row of chairs and smoked a lot of cigarettes.

When he was done, David and I waited together in the room for Don to huddle on legal points with the investigating team.

"I think they want to send someone back with us to New York to pick up the invoices," David said.

"What invoices?"

"The ones I gave Peter."

"You gave him invoices?"

"Yeah. For the checks. I gave them to him the day we met at Trader Vic's. They want to send someone to get them from the apartment."

A few minutes later, a tall, balding man with bright, piercing eyes opened the door and came in.

"I'm John Fedders. How are you guys doing?"

"We've been better," I said.

"I just wanted you to know that I realize how difficult it must have been for you to come down here like this. You've made our case and we won't forget that."

Cella and the boys were setting up for another round of interviews, this time with *Journal* people, including Dick Rustin, who had been whisked down to Washington to help the SEC. The *Journal* was now feeding the SEC every scrap of negative information about me that it could get its hands on and some wild rumors as well. No effort was spared, short of divulging confidential sources. The *Journal* agreed to provide the SEC with a set of photocopies of my 24,000 pages of notes, with names of sources removed. George Anders read to the SEC over the phone from London, and then telecopied, three personal letters I had written him, none of which had anything to do with my transgressions.

Everyone wanted a hand in braiding the hangman's noose.

David and I waited until arrangements were made to sneak us out of the building along with an SEC gumshoe named Vincent DiCarlo who was to accompany us on the flight back to New York. DiCarlo was to go with Don to our apartment to collect copies of the invoices David had given to Peter a week earlier.

An investigator drove us out of the employee parking lot to a nearby hotel where we could catch a cab to the airport unnoticed. We kept our distance from DiCarlo in public places. The press was on to the story now and the need to avoid reporters and lawyers representing other people in the case was more important than ever. David and I were jumpy in public. A man in a suit recognized

Don in the airport and came over to chat. Don artfully separated himself from us and managed to deflect the guy.

When we arrived at La Guardia, DiCarlo took a separate cab and we all met at Buchwald's office about 6:30 or 7 o'clock. DiCarlo was quite the wise guy, a young attorney who bragged about his days in the Brooklyn district attorney's office. He marched right in to Don's office and casually perused the papers lying on top of Don's desk until we chased him out. Don and David prepared to go down to the apartment on 14th Street. David was going to pick up a change of clothes for us, the invoices, and the answering machine tape.

"There probably will be some reporters out front so we don't say anything to anyone, right?" Don said.

"Oh, yeah?" DiCarlo said. "This must be a big deal, huh? Maybe I'll get my picture in the paper." I wasn't feeling very charitable at the moment and the guy made me sick to my stomach. For all I knew, the feeling was mutual.

The three of them left and I waited in Don's office, copying some documents we needed and taking cigarette breaks to stare out the window at the city below.

The sidewalk in front of our apartment house was empty when they got there. The door to our apartment had a note taped on it to call one of the neighbors about a tenants' committee matter. The door was secure. No one had broken in. Alex Jones's story was looking more foolish all the time. David opened the door and his foot kicked an envelope that had been pushed through the opening of the sill. It was a letter that had been hand-delivered Wednesday night.

> This letter is to notify you that your employment with Dow Jones & Company is terminated, effective immediately.
>
> The cause of your termination is gross violation of the Dow Jones Conflicts of Interest Policy.
>
> Yours truly,
> Norm Pearlstine

The doorbells for our building were inside a locked entryway. The only way strangers or delivery people could get into the building was by calling first from a pay phone on the corner or catching the door as someone else entered or left. David wondered how the letter got under our door. Even ordinary events assumed elements of mystery.

The apartment was dark and, under the circumstances, had an eerie feel to it. David still didn't know if someone had broken in, maybe through a window. But everything was just as it had been when we locked up Wednesday afternoon. Piles of laundry waiting to be loaded into the washing machine lay on the floor where David had left them when we packed in a rush to leave.

He found the copies of the invoices he'd given Peter and gave one set to DiCarlo, who initialed them. DiCarlo also initialed the answering machine tape which David removed from the machine. David installed a fresh tape and reset the machine. The telephone rang several times and someone rang the door buzzer. David filled a suitcase with clothing. We were going into hiding that night at a friend's apartment a few blocks away where we wouldn't be hounded by the ringing phone and by reporters and TV cameramen hanging around in front of the house.

When the three of them reached the lobby on the way out, the superintendent, an older Italian guy named Nick, emerged from his apartment.

"David, I got some mail for you. A whole buncha reporters and televisions been hanging around here. What's going on?"

"Nothing, Nick. No problem."

Through the glass door David could see Gary Putka and two other people waiting on the sidewalk. David lugged the suitcase, and a portable typewriter I asked him to bring, through the door and they headed east toward Third Avenue to find a cab. Gary trotted beside David and the two other people, also reporters, tagged behind.

"David, I know you're in a lot of pain right now but this is affecting my life, too," Gary said as they walked. "I'm entitled to some answers."

"I can't say anything."

"David, what's going on?" Gary asked. David and Don walked on in silence with the three reporters tagging behind.

"You know if there's a pay phone around here?" DiCarlo said. "Long as I'm in town I might as well get together with my girlfriend and tie one on."

At Third Avenue a cab rescued Don and David.

*   *   *

That night we moved in with our friend and hunkered down for the weekend and the next wave of publicity.

David and I left Washington feeling we'd done the right thing. Fedders had made us feel good about telling the truth. I was so guilt-ridden, and so confused about the timing of events of the preceding six months, that I would have confessed to the assassination attempt on the Pope if they'd asked me.

But after taking Rustin's testimony, and after trading information and rumors with the *Journal*, Fedders changed his mind. By Saturday, he decided that we weren't telling the whole truth. Our efforts to be honest and provide the SEC with all the documents we could find, including some it hadn't asked for, and the incredible pain we had been through, suddenly turned to naught with the eager assistance of the *Journal*. I began to doubt the wisdom of our decisions to live and to tell the truth. How could we ever compete with the credibility of an organization like the *Journal*?

The *Journal* reporters were dreaming up all kinds of wild fantasies. Gary, torn between his feelings for me as a friend and his anger at my having misled him, guessed the suitcase he'd just seen David lugging down 14th Street was full of cash and David was on his way to the airport to flee the country. At least that's what he was saying early Friday night. "If you repeat this," he told one source, "I'll deny I ever said it." I was growing sick about Gary; sick that he got sucked into my nightmare, and sick about how I had hurt him and violated his trust in me. But there was no way I could call and tell him that, as much as I wanted to. He was a reporter and, having been a reporter myself, I knew that his first instinct would be to report everything I said, even if it hurt me. I didn't want to put him in the position of having to make that decision. And there was nothing I could tell him at that point that wouldn't prove harmful to our credibility with the SEC.

Monica Langley, a *Journal* reporter assigned to its "Fostergate" S.W.A.T. team, spent her weekend dialing up every telephone number the *Journal* could find in my files and elsewhere. Instead of identifying herself, she started her phone conversations off by barking, "Do you know Foster Winans?" She called friends in New Jersey. The adults weren't home, so she interviewed their nine-year-old son.

She called a friend in New York who had just learned his father was dying of cancer and correctly suspected that he himself was dying of AIDS.

"Do you know Foster Winans?"

"Yes. Who is this?"

"This is Monica Langley with *The Wall Street Journal.* We're doing a nice story on Foster Winans."

"Look, I have nothing to say. I've just learned that my father is dying and I don't feel like talking."

"There's another man living at your address whom Foster listed as a reference on his application. Do you live together?"

Some people she was more blunt with: "Are you gay?"

My friend hung up on her but his phone, and the phone of a neighbor and another friend of mine, rang all weekend.

I began to get reports back from these friends during that "scorched-earth" weekend. The *Journal* doesn't publish on Saturday or Sunday. The next edition would appear on Monday and the *Journal* was going full-bore on a major story that I imagined would dredge up every speck of dust from my background. We got reports that the *Journal* thought the trading was run by a ring of homosexuals. All kinds of crazy speculation was going on. By Sunday evening I was a mess.

"We should have killed ourselves, David. Tomorrow the *Journal* will probably have a front-page story in which we'll read everything negative that anyone has ever said about us. And then every other newspaper will reprint what the *Journal* runs. We might as well be dead." But now I was all talk. It was too late, we'd gone too far to end it now. We sweated out the hours until Monday morning. I couldn't sleep. We had lost control over our lives. Our future lay in the hands of our lawyer, the SEC, and a handful of angry, injured news people at the most powerful newspaper in the country.

I got up at about six o'clock Monday morning with my heart in my throat. We had not been out of our friend's apartment in daylight all weekend. We would wait until two o'clock in the morning to sneak back to the apartment to get fresh clothes and pick up the mail. We were afraid of being spotted. Now I prepared to make my first foray in sunlight. I put on a pair of jeans, a sweater, and my coat. I wrapped a scarf around my face, pulled on a wool cap low over my forehead, and donned a pair of sunglasses. When I got down to the front door I looked up and down the street. My heart was pounding. New York, for its massive size and teeming population, can sometimes seem like a small town. It's common to run into familiar faces in just about any neighborhood.

I stepped out onto the sidewalk and stayed on the shadowy side of the street, my head bent down. The pain and anxiety were excruciating and my eyes welled up. At the newsstand, I grabbed the paper without looking at it, threw down the fifty cents I had ready in the palm of my hand and dashed back to the apartment.

There it was, on page one, the far right column with drawings of David and me.

Stock Scandal

SEC's Inquiry Widens as It Questions Broker, Others in Journal Case

It Studies Reporter's Links, Professional and Personal, in Insider-Trading Probe

Role of a Journal News Clerk

NEW YORK - Last spring R. Foster Winans, then one of the two principal writers of this newspaper's Heard on the Street column, proposed doing a favorable story on Peter N. Brant, a successful young broker at Kidder, Peabody & Co.

The story was almost, but not quite, as bad as I expected. It contained the first public mention of Peter's role. Some of it made me wince, reminding me of George Anders's comment about being encouraged to write stories that make subjects "embarrassed to go home to their families." Most places where it touched on my contact with Dick Rustin, the facts were recalled in a way unflattering to me. Because I wasn't talking to the press, I had to accept this one-sided treatment. All I could do was sit at the table and shake my head as I read the story.

Someone (George Anders, as it turned out) had interviewed my reporter friend in Moscow and she had recounted my tearful 3 A.M. phone conversation with her a week earlier. Her comments were reported anonymously. I was devastated that someone I considered a close friend, also a seasoned journalist, would have been so stupid as to grant an interview in the first place. She was a reporter, I thought. She, better than anyone, should have known. David and I decided with grief that she had turned against us. We realized we couldn't trust anyone to still be a friend. Everyone was a potential enemy. We were alone.

The *Journal* reported a distorted and negative picture of my proposed superbroker story on Peter and made a big deal about its being rejected. This again had Rustin's angry fingerprints all over it. "Mr. Winans argued that the idea was a good one because, in his view, Mr. Brant was unusual. . . . Pressed for more detail and justification, Mr. Winans could offer no more support and dropped the idea."

The story treated my American Surgery articles the same way. Rustin was quoted saying he'd told me not to trade in stocks. The issue was immaterial, but I had never had such a conversation with him. The *Journal* even speculated that some of my columns had been planted to benefit sources. The story explained my relationship with David, down to nitty-gritty details like the wedding band David had given me, and went on at length about our financial problems. It stated incorrectly that I thought I was being discriminated against at the *Journal* because of my homosexuality. That was *Gary's* speculation, not mine!

But there were a few balancing statements as well:

"Foster could be tough, going for the jugular, when writing a story . . . but he also could be very naive and trusting in his dealings with friends and acquaintances.

"Reporters and editors at the *Journal* remember Mr. Winans as a personable, unpretentious man with a ready smile and an infectious laugh. When the news broke . . . reaction among colleagues was one of shock and incredulity . . . that Mr. Winans . . . would do anything unethical."

Everett Groseclose, my boss at the ticker, remembered me as a "standout" employee.

I learned more details, although sketchy ones, about David Clark. The *Journal* had glommed on to Peter, but it could only speculate on exactly what part he'd played. Clark, I learned, had been chased out of Kidder, Peabody because his trades correlated with *Journal* stories. Finally, we learned who the guy was and our suspicions that Peter had been lying to us were confirmed.

We stayed in hiding for about two weeks as the press continued to report on the *Journal's* stories and what additional scraps of information could be dug up. It was weird sitting in an apartment

of an old drafty building, listening to the sounds of the city outside
and wondering what the rest of the world was up to. We watched
television, read, and ventured out once a day to shop and buy the
morning papers. On the mornings I came back from the newsstand
and there was nothing in the papers about us, we joked that it was
our "day off."

A week after the big front-page story in the *Journal*, Peter
resigned from Kidder, Peabody. The firm issued a short statement
to the press that said he was quitting because of the "time-
consuming distraction" of the SEC investigation. I burst out
laughing when I read that line. It sounded formal, as Peter could,
and it was so obviously crafted to make him out to be the innocent
victim. But the news also saddened me because I knew how much
Peter relished his prestige and position. David and I, knowing that
Peter had been suicidal over less embarrassing matters, expected
any day to hear that he'd blown his brains out.

Some of the papers continued to dig into our background.

The *Washington Post:* "Friends said that they had difficulty
determining a motive for Winans. . . . He was ambitious and
diligent about his work, but one friend said he 'wore socks with
holes in them and a coat that looked like it came out of a rescue
mission.' "

The *Philadelphia Daily News:* "A former editor . . . said,
'Winans was a good reporter and a good human being—and he still
is."

The *Washington Post* again: "Friends and former colleagues of
Winans said he might have yearned for [the wealthy] lifestyle but
was mostly broke. One *Journal* employee said, 'He worked most of
the time, and he ran around wearing sweaters with holes in them.
My most vivid image of him is running around the *Journal* in his
socks with his headset on—the cord just dangling off behind
him."

NBC News: "The paper and the SEC have been investigating
a kind of soap opera of high finance. . . . Peter Brant and his wife
Lynn were fast-rising socialites until . . . Peter Brant was hit by
scandal . . . one of the biggest financial scandals in years. Federal
investigators [said] Clark may have made well over a million dollars
. . . from Brant's information from inside *The Wall Street Journal*.
Clark . . . says he has no intention of giving back any of the money

he made just because his broker happened to have a spy in the newsroom of *The Wall Street Journal*."

Holy Moses! Could it be? Could Clark have made a million bucks off my tips? David and I were fast becoming spectators in what clearly was a much larger soap opera. We now learned as much from the press as anyone else.

Ken Felis sat in the living room of his guesthouse watching television the night of the NBC report about Clark and his million dollars. The room was dark, lit only by the bluish glow from the TV screen. He watched in growing horror as the screen flashed images from his life—a photograph the network obtained of Peter and Lynn at a Palm Beach social event, a copy of the advertisement featuring Peter in *Avenue* magazine. He saw the film clip of David Clark walking down a New York street and stepping into a taxicab. He braced to hear his name but it wasn't mentioned.

Kidder had managed to keep Ken's name out of the investigation through most of March. He got calls from Kidder saying, "They haven't asked and we aren't offering your name." After David and I testified, though, Ken was interviewed by the SEC.

"I'm just a small-fry in this thing," he told an investigator. He was anxious to tell what he knew.

Many messages were passed on to us by family, former co-workers, and friends.

April 3: *USA Today* has information from my Dow Jones personnel file. Is the *Journal* giving out information to other newspapers?

April 4: The Dow Jones employee union is questioning the *Journal*'s use of my personnel file. There is a battle going on between those in the union who want to go to the mat with the company over violation of confidential files and those who'd like to see me hung from the rafters. The union also discusses the legality of the conflict of interest policy since it was never negotiated with the employees or made a condition of employment.

April 5: The *Journal*'s conflict of interest policy, which neither Gary nor I had seen, was handed out to all employees the day before I was officially fired.

April 6: A *Journal* friend reports Gary and another *Journal* reporter covering the case, Tim Metz, "have blood in their eyes" for me.

April 8: A friend says he knows a woman at a national monthly business magazine who works in the art department and claims artists have traded "dozens" of times around stories for which they were assigned to produce artwork.

April 9: There is a report out by a Florida-based newsletter publisher that analyzes how well stocks did after they were mentioned in the "Heard" and concludes that Gary and I were "stock-pickers extraordinaire."

April 10: Some people I used to work with at Dow Jones want to donate money toward our legal expenses.

April 11: My brother relays messages of cheer from several *Journal* reporters.

April 14: Awoke with a raging anxiety attack from a bad dream that my father was involved in the case somehow and I had lied to the SEC. My brother's wife shows early signs of labor. David saw a *Journal* reporter on the subway. He thought he escaped detection.

April 19: Some reporters at the *Journal* are outraged by statements attributed to David Clark on NBC that he had done nothing wrong and wouldn't give up any of his profits. Friends worry that if Clark can't be prosecuted, the authorities will come down harder on us.

Phone messages:

"David, it's your sister. Please call me. Hope you guys are all right."

Beep.

"This is *New Statesman* of London, Washington bureau."

Beep.

"Hey, Foster baby, it's Gary. Things are rapidly moving toward a major story here and I just called to let you know it would be a good idea if you called me."

Beep.

"Just calling to say, sorry about all this. Don't let the bastards get you down."

Beep.

"Eleanor Randolph of the *Washington Post* for David Carpenter."

Beep.

"Alex Jones, *New York Times*."

Beep.

"Foster, it's Gary, Still trying to get through."

Beep.

"Hi, guys. Hope we can go out for a drink soon or have dinner at my place. You know. Give me a buzz. Thanks for letting me know you're all right. Jesus, I want to see you."

Beep.

"I wish I could do something for you guys. Anything I could do?"

Beep.

"*USA Today*. Wanted to talk about your freelance activities."

Beep.

"*Columbia Journalism Review*. Please call."

Beep.

"Jack Roberts, *Philadelphia Daily News*. Calling about articles in the *Journal* and statements made by *Trentonian* editors."

Beep.

"Brian Ross, NBC News."

And on and on.

The hysteria triggered by my admissions and the *Journal*'s coverage finally began to subside after a week or so. The number of calls from newspeople on the machine tapered off as they realized we weren't going to return them. Meanwhile, the SEC slowly was coming back around to its earlier view that David and I were telling the truth during our testimony. It seemed the agency had gotten caught up in the same hysteria. But it was clear that the SEC intended to sue us. We put our energy into convincing them that David wasn't part of the thing and shouldn't be sued along with me. We faced the possibility of being asked to pay a fine that our lawyers estimated might reach a third or so of all the money Peter and his buddies made. If Clark made a million dollars, well, oh boy! We waited for a decision with little hope.

The *Journal* assembled, bit by bit, evidence that corroborated our testimony. A backlash from its page-one story developed, including mail to its editorial page criticizing the detailed description of my relationship with David. The *Village Voice* labeled it a "lavender herring."

We moved back home in the middle of April, stocking up food in case the press decided to lay siege again. It was on a flawless spring day, warm, dry and sunny, that we repossessed our home, and it felt great to be around familiar things.

Later I went for a long walk, retrieving from the post office a certified letter informing me that Standard & Poor's had withdrawn the job offer. I felt lousy for having had to string them along right up until the end but I had no choice. I wandered around our East Village neighborhood and stopped in a park where I watched a basketball game and listened to an African drum group. The neighborhood, populated mostly be Eastern Europeans, university students, artists, and musicians, proved calming. I knew I wouldn't run into anyone from the world of finance. It was the first day since before March 1 when it felt good to be alive.

The next day *Time* and *Newsweek* came out with full-page articles rehashing all the facts as presented by the *Journal* in its stories that week. I met Don Buchwald and we visited Bob Sack, the *Journal's* counsel, in his office at Rockefeller Center where we looked through a set of photocopies of my notes, with source names cut out. Sack said he had a dream—that he was going into battle armed only with a pair of scissors. The *Journal* copied everything in my files, even making a picture of a tube of toothpaste and a bottle of mouthwash I kept in my drawer. I felt like my privacy had been violated.

But the saddest thing about this period was giving up the cottage in Pennsylvania. It had meant so much to David, but we agreed that we just couldn't handle it financially. I called the real estate agent.

"Yeah," he said with a big sigh. "I saw the news."

The bank canceled its mortgage commitment but the seller's attorney decided to sit on our $7,000 deposit until they found another buyer. Every detail of our lives was in someone else's control.

Rustin was reassigned from his foreign-desk job back to the "Heard" to "restore credibility" to the column. To some it looked like a demotion, maybe tied to his ill-timed "scum of the earth" message on my answering machine. The fact that he left such a message had somehow gotten back to the *Journal*. Rustin's enemies at the paper speculated that he was being punished for his unseemly enthusiasm. It sounded to me like he was the only one with any "Heard" experience in the joint and this was a rescue mission.

Gary was off the column and headed for London. All the *Journal* had to write the column was a handful of stock market neophytes.

Gary stopped by the news desk from time to time to talk with my brother.

"I hear Foster was in Bob Sack's office the other day. I hear he looks terrible. Hasn't shaved in two weeks." (I was growing a beard and looked like hell.)

Another time: "Just between you and me: were Foster and David buying a house in Pennsylvania?"

"Just between you and me?" my brother said.

"Yeah."

"I don't know."

Norm Pearlstine, to his enduring credit, went out of his way to assure my brother that my sins would not be visited upon him. But Chris was torn between his loyalty to the *Journal* and his loyalty to me. He couldn't help but hear the occasional snide remark around the office. And he was especially queasy when he learned that the money David and I had lent him and his wife—so he could accept the *Journal* job and move to New York—had come from Peter Brant. We'd told him David had inherited some money. He sat in his apartment in Brooklyn one night and looked around at the space this tainted money had allowed him to rent, and thought about the job the tainted money had allowed him to accept. The feeling of good luck now was sullied by my misdeeds. He went through a kind of mourning period. We talked about it one night on the phone.

"I'm at work at the *Journal*," he said, "and I stop and think, 'I just can't believe this has happened.' It's like a sudden, unexpected death in the family—I just can't believe you're gone from here. You went to the top and wham. When I hear a witty lead-in to a television news item about somebody getting caught with their hand in the till, I have a lot of sympathy for them.

"When I saw your picture on television, I saw everything I liked about you. I thought of us as kids—there's my mischievous brother.

"What's going on doesn't affect how people feel about you. Your friends at the *Journal*, even Pearlstine, still respect your abilities and like you. They don't change their opinions overnight because you made a mistake. People remember your personality—who you are, not what you did. You fucked up, but you're not a fuckup."

I needed these pep talks. I was wallowing in my own filth, feeling guilty, ashamed and hurting for those I had hurt.

Meanwhile, the SEC was gearing up to sue us.

15

The Road to Room 1306

Prosecutors are supposed to be interested in justice: the motto on the wall of the Justice Department proclaims that the government "wins its
point whenever Justice is done." But in real life,
many prosecutors reverse the motto and believe
that justice is done whenever the government wins
its point.

—Alan M. Dershowitz, *The Best Defense*

By the end of April I was having dreams about the bizarre turn my
life had taken. In one of these dreams, David and I went out to eat.
At the restaurant we ran into Gary Putka, who was waiting for a
table and had his left arm in an L-shaped cast. I stuttered. I helped
him into the restaurant and we sat down at a table. There was a
piece of paper on the table. I wanted to talk to Gary and sort of
stumbled around the subject a few moments. He started to pick the
paper up, and I got nervous that he was going to take notes. I
excused myself and, in trying to find the table where David was
sitting, realized that the restaurant was full of *Journal* newspeople.
They tried to talk to me as I walked between the tables.

The press, especially the *Journal*, was still puzzling over my
disclosures at the end of April, a month after the first *Journal* story.

Most of the essential facts were out except for the big one: what had been my payoff? Pinkerton speculated that if it was money, it wasn't much. Otherwise, he reasoned, I wouldn't have been so forthcoming. He told another editor, "It's my observation that crooked businessmen who have made a lot of dirty money and get caught don't mind going to jail. White-collar crooks just sit in prison waiting for the day when they get out and can go get the hoard they stashed."

Some *Journal* people still couldn't accept the notion of my guilt, theorizing I was the victim of some enormous hoax or mistake, or that I had accidentally let slip the content of the column in the process of interviewing people. Or that I was just trading information for tips I could use in the column.

"Winans had the bad luck of being under formal investigation and . . . he quite properly kept his mouth shut," Tom Goldstein, a journalism professor at the University of California in Berkeley and a former *Journal* reporter, later observed. "This worked to his severe detriment." The *Journal* felt it owed its readers a complete airing of its dirty laundry. "That is a fine and proper sentiment for a paper that has a long tradition of exposing insider trading and of exposing journalistic lapses," Goldstein wrote in his book *The News at Any Cost*. "But this same sentiment led to the exoneration of the editors and unfair treatment of Winans. At the time of the [April 2, page one] story, he was only a target of an investigation, nothing more, but the *Journal* treated him as if he were a convicted freak."

The *Journal* reacted as an institution that had been betrayed. But it was made up of human beings who were just plain angry, afraid, and even paranoid. Despite my public assertions that no one else at the paper was involved, *Journal* employees found themselves casting furtive glances at their neighbors and coworkers and wondering about their private financial affairs. Gary probably suffered more of this than anyone. We had worked closely together and we had been friendly. There were those who wondered whether maybe I was taking the fall for others. Conspiracy theories multiplied in the poisoned atmosphere.

Journal reporters, whipped on by their own feelings or the institutionalized anger, indulged in some journalistic excess. For the first time in my life, I got a chance to really watch a news organization at work from the outside. It was not a pretty sight.

David and I knew a young man who'd just moved to New

York from a small town out West and was naive and innocent. He'd landed a good job on the trading desk of a small securities firm. His phone number was in my notes. Monica Langley, the reporter who liked to bark "Do you know Foster Winans?" got this guy on the telephone the weekend before the big April 2 story.

"Yeah, I know Foster," he said. She had spent a few minutes with him on the phone. He thought he was mostly unhelpful. He didn't know us all that well.

Two weeks later, Gary phoned him. The guy didn't want to talk until Gary employed an old reporter's trick—the negative response threat.

"Look, you said some things to Monica that wouldn't look very good in print the way they stand. I think we'd better meet and talk about these things and get them straightened out. We know where you work."

Our friend fell for this malarkey and met with Gary in a Horn & Hardart in midtown. He didn't know me that well and had little to offer Gary. But the *Journal* followed up with calls to his boss and three days later, the guy was out of a job.

People like Gary and George Anders were stuck in a bad place, wearing two hats and having to choose between their personal feelings and their professional responsibilities. I couldn't fault them for making mistakes. Like George's decision to read to the SEC my personal letters to him. It was just plain wrong, the way I looked at it. But I doubt I could have told Pearlstine to take a leap if he'd called me and said, "We're trying to protect the reputation of the paper. These letters may be important."

I was ambivalent about the *Journal*'s efforts to bury me. In a weird way, it felt good to be punished by those I had let down. All the garbage was out in the open all at once. The public whipping helped round out my guilt feelings.

Pearlstine later wondered whether the page-one piece seemed ill-advised, but concluded that it was not. He even wondered aloud whether he bore some responsibility for what I'd done. After all, he knew that I was unhappy with my salary and he knew I was having problems with Rustin. But he failed to intercede.

But no one could have foretold my readiness to risk my career, no one could have prevented me from risking it, and no one could reasonably accept any responsibility for my having done so. Only I could stand up and take the medicine and I was prepared to do that.

The medicine, it was becoming clear, would grow more bitter. We began getting signals through the spring that the Justice Department was gearing up to prosecute me and, possibly, David. That meant legal maneuvers that could end up with me in jail. There was still plenty to worry about.

We got the bad news late in April that the Securities and Exchange Commission would be suing soon. Don Buchwald went to work trying to convince the SEC to leave David out since he'd been such a minor player.

David Clark warmed the seat of my old chair in the SEC examining room on three separate occasions during April. He spent nearly ten hours testifying. Clark portrayed himself as the innocent client. He intimated that Peter had transferred money from his account without authorization. He claimed he learned about my role in Peter's trading in December, well after he'd already participated in some fifteen different stories and had moved his account from Kidder to Bear, Stearns. Clark bobbed and weaved his way through the sessions, dodging direct answers. He claimed he wasn't worried about the SEC investigation and only accompanied Peter to the Brazilian consulate to try to talk him out of fleeing. He only mentioned that he had taken *his* passport with him as well after the SEC demanded to see it and he couldn't produce it.

David and I rode an emotional roller coaster as the SEC moved closer to filing its lawsuit. John Fedders, who'd promised not to forget our cooperation, abruptly removed himself from the case because of a conflict of interest with his former law firm's representation of David Clark. That was a blow we didn't expect. Gary Lynch, Fedders's second-in-command, was less pliant and hadn't made any promises he had to worry about breaking. Some days it sounded as though the SEC was willing to leave David out of the case because he merely followed my orders, as any spouse might. The intense publicity almost guaranteed that the Justice Department would bring a criminal case. It was just too juicy to pass up. The prosecutors could ride in on the SEC's coattails and share, or steal, the spotlight.

Don called me at home in the evening on May 16.

"Well, it's happening tomorrow," he said. "The SEC just

called and they will file their suit and issue a press release." David was in.

The lawsuit held few surprises for us and a minor concession for David. He was named as a defendant but not asked to pay any fines. The real shocker was that Peter had racked up nearly $700,000 in profits on our deal, most of which he had split with Clark and the rest with Ken and me.

"This is just incredible," I said to David after I got off the phone. "You want to hear something amazing? Peter and Clark made almost three-quarters of a million bucks out of this thing. The bum was lying to us the whole time."

The world learned about it the next day when the SEC filed its suit in New York. For the first time the press and public found out what I got out of the deal—$30,000 plus about $1,000 in British currency that Peter had given David for his vacation to London.

"You putz," a friend said. "You ruined your career for a lousy $30,000? I was hoping you had a million bucks in a Swiss account." It was a relief, in a way, to have the world know that I had penny-ante ambitions. The contrast between Peter and me became sharp and clear, and that was the way I liked it. In this rat-breeding contest, I wanted Peter to come out on top. Through Don I released my second public statement, which ran in the next day's stories reporting the lawsuit:

> There is much in my conduct during the last months at the *Journal* which was wrong. Whether by my action I have violated the federal securities laws is a matter my attorneys will address in court. Whatever that outcome, I stand in judgment of myself as having violated fundamental tenets of my profession and moral principles which extend beyond.
>
> For this, whatever the outcome in the courts, I feel great shame and ask the forgiveness of my friends.

I was thinking, of course, of Gary, George, Norm, and a host of other people at the *Journal* as well as a few friends I hadn't spoken to since the apocalypse. The *Journal* repeatedly asked me for an interview, but there was no way I could do that until the criminal side had been decided. If I had anything to say, I would say it in open court and the judge or jury would hear it at the same time as everyone else. It was like watching a crowd repeatedly hanging me in effigy and being powerless to stop it.

All the details as we knew them had become public. Now we could sit back and watch the press unravel what Clark and Peter were all about. Ken, Peter, Clark, David, and I were all defendants in the SEC suit. Clark, quoted in the *Journal*, swore his innocence. "I had no idea that any money changed hands between Mr. Brant and Mr. Winans," he said, adding that he had "cooperated fully" with the SEC. He did spend a lot of time testifying but the SEC didn't believe him. A lawyer with the agency claimed Clark had changed his story between the March 1 phone interview and his testimony in Washington, adding, "We believe he knew exactly where the information came from during the entire scheme."

The SEC told the judge that some of the money Peter and Clark had made was being moved to Switzerland and that Peter "may leave the country and take his assets with him." We had no way of knowing Peter's whereabouts, and it was a constant topic of speculation between David and me as to whether he had fled, blown his brains out, or turned himself in.

During the hearing the next day to freeze everybody's bank accounts and other assets, the SEC granted us another concession. We were exempted from the freeze. It was kind of elementary at that point. David and I had shot our wad on Don's retainer and we had to borrow money to live. We'd had a few strokes of good luck but our expenses had soared and my income had stopped. The *Journal* shocked me by paying me three weeks unused vacation pay and sent me about $4,500 I was due from a profit-sharing plan. I had expected them to keep the money and tell me to go screw myself. The *Journal* even honored its pledge to pay my legal expenses through my last official day on the job, my termination two days earlier notwithstanding. The bill came to more than $18,000. The tide hadn't exactly turned, but at least it seemed to have crested.

The Justice Department investigation was assigned to Peter J. Romatowski, a tall, slender, boyish-looking assistant U.S. attorney who wore round horn-rimmed glasses that kept slipping down his nose. He had a good reputation as a lawyer but this was to be his first big-visibility case. The word around the federal courthouse was that he was inexperienced as a trial lawyer. He also had worked for Don Buchwald when Don was deputy chief of the criminal division in the Southern District of New York. I'm not sure whether that worked for or against us, but Don was again wrestling with a government lawyer over the question of David's involvement. The publicity had just about guaranteed that I would be indicted. With David it was a closer question.

Romatowski interviewed Ken near the end of May, and Peter came in out of the cold in June. They hadn't spoken to each other since early April, right after Peter hinted he'd pin the rap on Ken. Romatowski spent hours and hours debriefing Peter on a whole range of subjects, from his deal with me to the money that disappeared from the Roger Wilson account.

Things settled down a bit after the SEC filed its lawsuit. David and I kept busy with his advertising business and I spent the rest of my free time working with Don. He had no helpers in his office, other than a secretary he shared with his partner and a third lawyer. I figured any work that I could do would reduce the bill and release him from drudge work, making him more effective on our behalf. Don was a stickler for detail, and I grew to appreciate how lucky I was that his name topped the list of three lawyers Sack had recommended back in March. For one thing, he knew all the players from his days working for the government and the years he'd spent defending clients. He always seemed to know where he was in the case, in spite of the growing reams of paperwork, documents, and minutiae that occupied his time and his mind. And, he liked to play the market, which meant not only that we could trade worthless opinions on stocks during breaks but that he understood all the issues in the case. He was very sensitive to my moods and tried to cheer me up when he saw I was down.

"You know, after this is all over, we should try to talk some discount broker into using you in their ads," he joked once.

"You mean like a bank robber doing an ad for a bank?"

Perhaps the single thing that impressed me most about him as a human being was his nervousness about sentencings. Most of his work was criminal, so he sometimes had clients who'd pleaded guilty or lost their cases and were up for sentencing. For two or three days before these events, he would grow increasingly jittery and irritable. He worried whether the sentences were going to be harsher than he expected and worried about his clients' reactions. I decided that he was more of a mess than the people who were going to jail.

I grew to dread these visits to his office, not because of Don or Alan, but because it reminded me of the nightmare and the overwhelming problems that remained to be resolved. And after the $15,000 retainer had been used up and the bill began to grow, it reminded me that I was becoming an indentured servant. It would have been different if I'd hooked up with a lawyer from a big firm that could afford to drag along deadbeats like David and me. But I knew Don was spending a lot of time working on this case and getting not even lunch money out of it. A few nights we worked until Don caught the last train home from Grand Central after midnight, having eaten only a few packages of cookies and a cup of tea to keep him going.

Spring gave way to summer and I grew detached from the process of the law. It was all happening to someone else. My role was limited to what I could do to help Don. Everyone else was pushing the buttons—the lawyers, the SEC, Romatowski, the *Journal*. David and I just nodded our heads obediently when decisions were made. We participated, of course. But in large measure, the script was written and we adhered to it.

One of the things that surprised me most about the continuing coverage was the occasional sympathy vote that came our way. None of it made me feel any less ashamed, but these were cool breezes on a sticky night. Ted Koppel devoted a portion of his "Nightline" program on ABC to the case in May. Dan Cordtz, the network's business reporter and a *Journal* alumnus, placed some of the blame on the *Journal*.

"The managers of the *Journal* do have more responsibility in this situation than they have been acknowledging so far. They took a very inexperienced man, put him in a highly sensitive job, paid him only thirty thousand some dollars a year, and he was an easy mark for temptation."

In June, we were the subject of a half-hour-long program on public television's "Inside Story," a TV magazine show about the press. Hodding Carter, President Carter's former press secretary, narrated the program and did a good job of dissecting the issues. But what I found most interesting was an interview, on camera, with Gary Putka. I had those same painful feelings when I saw him.

"He was a very engaging fellow," Gary said. "A great sense of humor. I relied on him for about 80 percent of my off-color humor. I think he was regarded as very friendly, very open, not very self-important, willing to share ideas, willing to share sources. I worked pretty closely with him for about a year and a half and there was no inkling that he was doing anything like that. Particularly because of the quality of his work, it came as quite a shock."

That night I dreamt I was in a small town in Alaska for some kind of exhibition. I was driving a jeep that could plow through snow and deep mud. I got to an inn where some guy wanted to buy the tires off the jeep. Suddenly, there was Gary. I started to cry, called out his name, and we fell into each other's arms. I touched his hair and his face and said over and over again, "I'm sorry. I'm sorry."

When I woke up, I had real tears in my eyes. I didn't even know it was possible to wake up crying.

The paranoia that had gripped the *Journal* infected the people I knew on Wall Street as well. Our finances were precarious, but we had a potential ace in the hole: our building was moving closer to going co-op. My mother somehow managed to scrape together the credit to buy it. But she could only get a loan for just long enough to take advantage of the 12-month holding period that would save us thousands of dollars in capital gains taxes when we sold the apartment. Without our expected profit from the sale, we were sunk and so were some friends who'd lent us their vacation money. But in the meantime, I didn't know how we were going to make it. I contacted several Wall Street sources I had been friendly with about short-term loans to get through the rest of the year. One of them, my favorite stock market guru and research director at a major firm, called me when he got my letter.

"Foster, I'm all for the underdog and personally I never felt victimized by you. But I had to ask the firm's lawyers about this and they told me no way should I get involved."

So many people had sent messages of cheer and support. But when it came down to paying our bills, we were pretty much alone with my mother's understanding banker waiting in the wings to bail us out—if we didn't go bust in the meantime.

We managed instead to borrow a little here and a little there, I took a few odd jobs, and somehow we made it through.

*   *   *

Peter Brant officially bit the dust on July 12. He signed a long agreement under which he pleaded guilty to three federal crimes. Brant pleaded guilty to one count each of securities, mail, and wire fraud. The plea deal provided that he would not be prosecuted for trading around *Journal* articles, for perjury in his March telephone interview with the SEC, for an inaccurate financial statement he supplied to Morgan Guaranty, for a questionable transaction in one of his client's accounts, or for any wrongdoing associated with his job at Kidder, Peabody.

The plea deal was more interesting, though, for the things it specifically stated he was not protected against—"any diversion, misappropriation, or embezzlement of customer funds." At the same time, he settled his part of the SEC lawsuit by paying the government more than $450,000. Ken settled with the SEC several months later, coughing up more than $160,000.

The government wanted us to plead guilty as well. In a wild four-day period, Don worked hard to convince Romatowski to leave David out. We were back on tenterhooks. We finally had the government convinced and we breathed a huge sigh of relief. Don said Romatowski finally gave in and agreed that David's involvement was more in the nature of a spouse's. We were elated. A few hours later, the phone rang again and it was Don.

"Now I don't want you guys to get upset but I think we have a little problem here." My heart was pounding. I still wasn't used to this knowing and then not knowing.

Some higher-up in the U.S. Attorney's Office had called and left a cryptic message to the effect that all deals were off. It was Friday afternoon and Don couldn't reach the responsible official. We waited like that, suspended in midair, all weekend long. Monday came and went. Finally on Tuesday the government came back with its final offer. David, we were told, would not be indicted if I agreed to plead guilty to three federal crimes and only if I did so within twenty-four hours. If I refused, we were assured that David would be indicted along with Ken and me.

"David, I want to do this," I said. I was wrung out and had had it. "It's not fair but I think it's even less fair that you should be involved in this for having been loyal to me. Besides, I'd like to have the goddamned thing over with and get on with my life."

"I can't go along with it," he said. "It isn't right. Everyone seems to think that there's no law against what you did, even if it was morally wrong. And I'd feel guilty as hell if you ended up going to jail when we might have won the case in a trial. We've got nothing to lose by fighting."

We debated for an hour or so and I finally came around. We gave Don the go-ahead to tell Romatowski to take his deal and, well, shelve it.

We heard through Don that Ken had also turned down a plea deal. At least we'd have company at our trial.

The tables had completely turned. David and I had been the first people to come in from the cold. We'd done it voluntarily and without any promises of immunity. We were cooperative and forthcoming. The SEC lawyers even described us in open court as fully candid witnesses. Now, somehow, we had become the bad guys and Peter, who had lied and had explored sixteen ways to run away, was now the government's star witness. Something was wrong with this picture.

In July I applied to get my license to drive a cab in New York. I had come full circle from my last cab-driving stint. In between, my career had soared and then crashed and burned. Dan Dorfman and I kept in touch during this period, and he lent us $500 to pay the rent one month. I told him about driving a cab again and he wrote a short item about it for the *Daily News*. Jim Hughes, owner of a courier service in Fort Lee, New Jersey, read the item that morning and phoned me.

"I know this may seem kind of off the wall," he said, "but I've had my problems in the past and I'm sympathetic. I need drivers for my courier service. If you're interested, why don't you come up and we'll talk? You could drive one of my vans but all you'll make is five bucks an hour. If you have a car, we pay a commission on the total value of the freight charges. It's better work than driving a cab, I assure you."

I went to work for him a week or so later, driving all over the New York area picking up and delivering documents and small packages. The commissions were respectable, anywhere from $250 to $500 a week before gas, tolls, and other expenses. It was lousy work, sitting on my butt all day, fighting traffic, looking for places to park and no time for breaks. But the worst part was picking up and delivering in the financial district in many of the same buildings I had haunted as a reporter for the *Journal*. I wore sunglasses into these buildings and kept my head low. I dreaded accidentally running into people I knew from Wall Street. It would have been embarassing for both of us. My friends loved the irony of it, though. Here I was, a defendant in a stock market scandal, entrusted to pick up and deliver stock certificates. One of my assignments was to deliver an advance copy of a manuscript to Sylvia Porter, the financial columnist, at her home in upstate New York. For a week I took over the job of picking up stock certificates from the New York Clearing House and delivering them to one of the downtown banks. It would've seemed funny to me except that I was crisscrossing painful territory, past the *Journal*'s offices, past the office of Standard & Poor's where I would have been working, in elevators I'd ridden as a reporter, and on streets filled with potentially embarrassing chance meetings.

One day I was sent out to Glen Cove on Long Island to deliver a parcel. When I looked to find it on my map I realized it was the town next to Locust Valley. It was a mild sunny day, so on my way back to the city I took a short detour and drove up Piping Rock Road to Peter's driveway. I was nervous as hell. In one sense I was dying to talk to him, but I was filled with dread as well. What the hell would I say?

But all I could see through the trees were some men in uniforms loading furniture into a truck. It looked like he was moving. I felt a wave of depression that stayed with me the whole day. I remembered the beautiful days out on the golf course and at the house when the future seemed so full of promise. I was torn. He had lied to me and even cheated on our deal. But I knew that his disgrace was keener than mine. By now it was public knowledge that Peter had changed his name and wasn't really a rich Wasp. He'd built up this image of himself—the name, the polo ponies, the fancy house, the club memberships, and the money. Now the image was gone. He was just the former Peter Bornstein, a flash in the pan, disgraced and drummed out of his profession, shunned and dropped by the social circle he'd spent his adult life infiltrating. Everybody said I was nuts but I really felt sorry for the guy.

Seeing the house in Locust Valley that day left me with my last fond image of Peter's life. He was no longer a part of my life after that.

Don warned us that the indictment was due near the end of August. But we didn't know exactly when. I was driving down

Broadway in the financial district on my way to deliver a package. I always listened to a newsradio station and I had the radio on when the bulletin came through. I looked around me as though everyone on the sidewalks could hear the radio and knew who I was. I was passing the *Journal's* offices at the time. It was unreal.

"Foster Winans, the former *Wall Street Journal* reporter who was involved in a trading scandal, was indicted today on sixty-one counts by a federal grand jury for payoffs he received from former stockbroker Peter Brant."

"They weren't payoffs!" I shouted.

"His roommate, David Carpenter, and a former stockbroker, Kenneth Felis, were also indicted on multiple counts. Arraignment is expected next week. In other news . . ."

I quit the job that day.

"Relax," Don told me when I called him later. "It doesn't get any worse." If only it had been true.

A week or so later, David, Ken Felis, and I appeared in a federal courtroom at Foley Square to enter our pleas of not guilty. The courtroom was packed with people, some of them there for our case, some for another insider-trading case against a guy named Thomas Reed that had just been announced in the papers. It was a civilized proceeding, and we were allowed to leave with the marshals out of handcuffs. Inexplicably, I winked at Reed on the way out.

First we were taken upstairs to a holding area inside the courthouse. We didn't speak to each other until we got settled—and before we were taken one by one into another room, through a prison sally port, to be fingerprinted and give our vital statistics to a clerk.

Ken looked tan and relaxed. I was a little angry when I saw how prosperous he still appeared. When the guards had left us alone, we looked at each other and he said, "Holy cow! How the hell did this happen?"

Next they dragged us across town to the main post office, where the Postal Service got a chance to book us also. It was political backscratching. We'd been charged with mail, wire, and securities fraud. The Post Office is mail fraud so, for their historical glory, the postal inspectors had the privilege of fingerprinting us. We were big fish, and everybody on the boat wanted a whack at reeling us part of the way in.

The indictment outraged the press establishment, in part because the indictment said that in addition to defrauding *The Wall Street Journal* I also defrauded the readers of the *Journal*. The indictment claimed I had a legal duty to disclose my investments to readers of the paper as well as to the *Journal* itself. That opened a real can of worms: a government official unhappy with press coverage could use such a legal theory to speciously discredit and harass a newspaper or a television news program. The government's legal theory, boiled down to its simplest form, was that I committed a crime because I violated a company policy. That irritated the hell out of me because I'd never seen the policy. I knew what I had done was wrong and I accepted that I deserved to be fired and probably banished from newspaper work. But I had not seen a conflict policy while I worked at the *Journal* and neither had Gary Putka, who laughed when he saw a mention of it in the *Journal*'s March 1 package of stories on insider trading.

The government even conceded that if the *Journal* hadn't had a policy, I wouldn't have been indicted. The legal theory was unique because, in effect, it allowed companies to establish criminal law by adopting internal policies. Media organizations feared that if the government won on this novel approach the press would be vulnerable in the future to politically motivated attacks.

The government, I decided, was trying to push a square peg through a round hole just to make its point: that the cop was on the beat.

Through the fall and holiday season David and I worked on his business. I taught myself how to do ad layouts and graphic artwork to save money. The business was growing, eating up any excess capital, and we still couldn't squeeze a profit out of the thing. It was doing too well to close and not well enough to support us. That summer my mother bought our apartment when it went co-op. We had had a big stroke of luck: Congress reduced the capital gains holding period to six months from a year. That meant we could sell the co-op soon after the first of the year and pay some of our debts.

In November we moved to an apartment in an old Victorian house across the Hudson River in New Jersey. We rented the New York apartment to a friend pending the co-op sale. It felt funny to be leaving that apartment where we'd been reunited, where we'd discussed my promising career with the *Journal*, and where we had spent an insane month with David running back and forth between Peter and me. It had served as a sanctuary during the worst period of both our lives and we were sorry to give it up.

As Christmas approached I spent more and more time with Don preparing for our trial, scheduled to begin shortly after the New Year. The government had already abandoned its theory that I owed a duty to the *Journal*'s readers. But that was a pyrrhic victory since it was the weakest prong of the government's case. The SEC suit had been put on hold until the criminal case was decided.

Don and I spent days selecting stories and documents we wanted to introduce as exhibits, lining up our witnesses and preparing for Don's cross-examination of Peter and the *Journal* people we expected the government to call. The only *Journal* person we were allowed to interview had been Rustin, way back in the spring. Since then, the *Journal* had advised its employees not to talk to us and wouldn't supply people like Gary. I found out that Gary had been back in the States for a week or so in December from his new home in London. But when we asked the *Journal* if we could interview him, they told us to go subpoena him in England. We couldn't afford it, of course. By now, Don had been laying money out of his own pocket to keep the case going. We tried to pare down our witness list so that we would be paying the least possible number of $35-a-day witness fees. It killed me to watch Don making out those checks, knowing I couldn't afford to do it for him.

One lawyer can't represent two defendants in a criminal trial, so Don persuaded two other alumni of the U.S. Attorney's Office to represent David pro bono. Jed Rakoff and Howard Goldstein, both hotshot criminal defense lawyers, partners in the big Wall Street firm of Mudge, Rose, Alexander & Guthrie, took over his defense. It was a major break, and made Don feel we'd have some big guns on our side if we needed them.

Our anxiety mounted as December slipped away. There were so many details to remember, and I worried about how I would do on the witness stand under attack by Romatowski in front of all those reporters. What would Peter say? What would Rustin say? What would Pinkerton say? Could we win? I wasn't sure, so I decided to plan on losing. That way, I wouldn't be disappointed. But I couldn't help myself. How could I be convicted, I kept thinking, for violating a company policy I had never seen and without the existence of which no crime could have been committed? The trial was scheduled to start in a few weeks in Room 1306 of the U.S. Courthouse a few blocks away from where I'd worked at the *Journal*.

Christmas morning, 1984, David and I awoke in a somber, spiritless mood. We were home alone and had no plans. We had no money for gifts and we sure as hell didn't feel like celebrating. We didn't even buy each other a present. We skipped the tree and declined all invitations. Instead, we sat at home mentally preparing ourselves for the second act.

16
My Turn

These trials have become media circuses, and that obscures the real reason for our fascination with them. [They] reveal to us the dark side of the American Dream . . . and the striving of Americans to elevate themselves both economically and culturally in society. The tragedy [is] the downfall of middle-class citizens who were victims of their middle-class lives.

—Letter to the editor, *The New York Times*, May 1985

I looked at myself in the full-length mirror and couldn't decide whether I liked what I saw. I was as nervous as a college senior on his first job interview. Something the mayor of Trenton once told me kept repeating in my mind: "I always wear a dark blue suit when I'm campaigning. Blue says sincerity, integrity." The mayor won five four-year terms. I figured he must know something.

I owned one dark blue suit and wore it that morning. As I looked at my reflection, I thought of the mayor. My mother was still in her room dressing and David was putting on his tie. I looked out the window at the Jersey City sprawl and the Manhattan skyline beyond. The day was starting out bright but bitter cold and windy.

It had been nearly ten months since the first wave of publicity. For ten months I had avoided having my picture taken, ducked the

285

press, and allowed the other teams—the SEC, the *Journal*, and the Justice Department—to have at me without response. Now it was my turn to tell the story in my own words to a captive audience of a judge and a gallery full of reporters. David and I expected the TV and newspaper camerapeople to ambush us outside the courthouse. We got haircuts and I pressed our good shirts.

Two hours later and just across the Hudson on the edge of New York's financial district, a white-haired judge with the face and wiry build of a New England fisherman stubbed out a cigarette in his private robing room. He stood and a clerk opened the door. He billowed past her into the ornate, Depression-era courtroom with its wood-paneled walls, concert-hall ceilings, and dark recesses. He hesitated a moment to look out at a dozen or so reporters in the audience and five sketch artists perched along the wooden rail that separated the gallery from the arena. The artists had been sitting in the jury box staring at David and me and scribbling madly on their pads. But the judge thought they would prove too distracting so he ordered them back behind the railing. When the judge sat down, a clerk who sat at a desk just in front of and beneath the judge glanced around the courtroom and then said, "United States of America versus R. Foster Winans, David Carpenter, and Kenneth Felis. Is the government ready?"

Romatowski rose halfway from his chair with his head bent forward toward the massive wooden table in front of him. He looked up at the judge over the rims of his glasses, which had slipped down his nose. "Ready for the government, Your Honor."

The three defense attorneys were sitting side by side at another massive wood table just behind Romatowski. They popped up in sequence, like ducks at a carnival shooting gallery.

"Ready for the defendant Winans."

"Ready for the defendant Carpenter."

"Ready for the defendant Felis."

Play ball! I thought.

The trial began January 21, 1985, before Judge Charles E. Stewart, a poker-faced man in his late sixties. We decided against a jury trial because a jury decides facts and the facts weren't much in dispute. The battle, we figured, would be fought over the law. Only judges can decide the law. We also guessed that the average man in the street has a built-in bias against Wall Street types: They are all crooks.

My mother came down from Massachusetts to stay with us for the duration. Everyone was sure it would be a short trial, five days or so. We expected lots of press and we weren't disappointed. A couple of film crews and a clutch of newspaper photographers waited out front on the steps of the courthouse, but we hadn't been photographed before so they didn't recognize us. We were able to slip up the side of the steps and into the building undetected. The camera people were doing triple duty. In the same courthouse two other big press trials were underway—General Westmoreland versus CBS, and Ariel Sharon, the former Israeli defense minister, versus *Time* magazine.

We arrived early at Judge Stewart's courtroom on the 13th floor and waited in the marble lobby outside smoking cigarettes. The press and hangers-on dribbled in. I recognized only a few of them. David and I were skittish. I knew better than to trust reporters. I'd been one. A tall man in jeans and a down jacket came up to me as we waited.

"Are you Foster Winans?"

"Yeah. Who wants to know?"

"I'm Fred Conrad, a photographer with *The New York Times*. How the heck did you guys get past us? I've been standing outside in the friggin' cold waiting for you."

"We just walked in. Simple as that."

"They all duck in and out the first couple of days but we get them eventually."

We went back into the courtroom where the crowd milled about waiting for Judge Stewart to finish a sentencing in his robing room. Two friends of ours arrived.

"How are you doing?" one of them asked.

"Nervous as hell," I said. "This looks like it's going to be a circus."

He looked around for seats in the gallery pews, divided by an aisle down the middle. He whispered to me, "Which side is for the bride's family and which is for the groom?"

The tension in the courtroom was palpable. I had no idea how the press viewed me. I was a rogue reporter, one who'd disgraced the profession. I expected no sympathy. Bob Sack milled about but wouldn't look me in the eye. A couple of reporters tentatively approached me.

"Foster, how do you feel?" one of them asked.

"I'll tell you when it's over," I said.

Finally we settled in our chairs. David and I sat next to each other behind Don at the right end of the defense table. To Don's left sat David's attorneys, Jed Rakoff and Howard Goldstein. To their left sat Michael Bradley, Ken's lawyer. Ken sat behind Bradley. I was glad to see Ken again. We didn't know each other that well. Almost all of my dealings had been with Peter. But I liked what I knew of Ken and now we had something in common— we were both on trial. He'd lost weight and looked good, full of self-confidence.

"How you doing?" I asked him. He smiled. "I feel great!" Ken was thoroughly convinced that we would win. He couldn't see any other outcome. I had convinced myself otherwise, a kind of self-defense mechanism. Since the day we decided to go to the SEC, I had contemplated the possibility of prison. That way, I could only be pleasantly surprised. There would be no disappointments.

As we waited in our seats for Judge Stewart, the windows rattled in their frames, buffeted by the wind. The temperature that morning was minus one when I got up. Ripples of teariness washed over me as I waited. But I wasn't frightened. This was going to be a unique opportunity. I had already told the truth to the SEC. The trial was not about whether I did these things. It was to be about whether the things I did were a crime. I had nothing to hide. There would be no dramatic courtroom confessions, no veiled accusations, no denials. This was to be my chance to publicly say all the things I couldn't say before.

But first the government had to have its crack at discrediting me. The defense always goes last.

Romatowski delivered a short opening statement that added nothing to the indictment. Judge Stewart listened with his head resting in one hand, his thumb propped against his left temple and his index finger rubbing his forehead and eyelids. He did this frequently and it gave the impression that he had a headache or that he was thinking or that he was bored or irritated.

Don went next and the contrast was sharp. He was animated, his voice clear and loud, whereas Romatowski's had been reedy and monotonous. We'll win, I thought, if the case is decided on oratory.

"I thought it would be a cold day in hell before the government brought a case like this, and they picked the right day, as it turned out," Don began.

Jed Rakoff, the shortest of the lawyers, with a magnificent full beard and bright blue eyes, opened for David:

"In the world's eyes he is the nobody in this case. He was never a reporter for a famous newspaper; he was never a broker for a large Wall Street firm. He got involved in the events that underlie this case only because of his personal relationship with Foster Winans. Nowhere is it alleged that David Carpenter agreed to do anything with anyone."

Mike Bradley, Ken's lawyer, was the only one of the three defense lawyers who really looked the part. He was tall, big-boned, and wore his hair short and slicked down. He had an aristocratic air and he punctuated his delivery with audible sniffs.

Pinkerton was Romatowski's first witness. It was the first time I'd seen him since that day in his office, ten months earlier, when he and Steiger told me the SEC had upgraded its investigation and I should get my own lawyer. It was so strange to see him sitting in the witness stand. He looked nervous and frequently glanced at Bob Sack, sitting in the gallery, during portions of his testimony. As he described the day I was officially hired by the *Journal*, I remembered why I didn't like him. He claimed he had an extensive conversation with me about the sensitivity of the "Heard" and how I shouldn't invest in the market. His recollection was tailor-made for the government's case, establishing for Romatowski that he had told me the rules, even if he hadn't given me a written copy of them. This was the meeting when he welcomed me to the *Journal* and told me I was getting a $50 raise. We had never discussed the things he was claiming.

But I shouldn't have expected anything different. Stew was a lawyer and a career *Journal* bureaucrat. He knew that he should have given me a copy of the conflict policy when I arrived. He knew he should have given me a lecture about the column. He covered himself by using qualifying phrases such as "I can't be terribly precise," and "I believe I told him." It was hard to sit there and listen to his orderly version of history.

Pinkerton also mischaracterized the famous "apology lunch"

about my errors: "The purpose of the lunch . . . was to reinforce the standards [and] to reassure him that as long as he was working hard and trying to turn things around we would support him."

I remembered every detail of that lunch because it was such a big disappointment. I was the one who brought up job perform-ance and we spent all of two minutes on the subject.

Pinkerton was on the stand all day and part of the next day. After a second *Journal* witness—David's former boss—Rustin was called later in the day. He slouched up to the witness stand with a smirk on his face and his head bobbing. He had the look of a street punk on trial for beating up an old lady. All of us at the defense table exchanged disbelieving glances. As he testified his head bobbed back and forth. His answers were long and he was so eager to answer that he cut off some of Romatowski's questions in midsentence. I was glad to see it. His cocky, arrogant attitude would make him an easy hit for cross-examination. He was on the stand only a short time before the judge adjourned for the day.

Romatowski must have given him a lecture that night because the next morning Rustin was more subdued and less arrogant.

His testimony was disturbingly similar to Pinkerton's. Rustin remembered all sorts of things he had told me about the company's policies and the "Heard," things he had in fact not told me. It really bugged the hell out of me. Rustin said he told me what was in the conflict policy, and even claimed he'd told me not to invest in options, a ban that wasn't even part of the conflict policy until after I was fired. I stared hard at him as he testified but he never looked at me. Neither did Pinkerton.

Because we had no jury, the defendants had the use of the empty jury room behind the courtroom, a real luxury. We were able to set up camp—file cabinets of documents and exhibits and a coffee pot. During breaks we hid in the jury room and parsed the day's testimony.

"Pinkerton's not coming across well," one of the lawyer's observed. "He has a sleazy look to him and his answers are vague. The judge looked like he wasn't paying attention."

After Rustin and Pinkerton had testified and been cross-examined, another lawyer whispered to me in the courtroom, "Now I know why you did it."

*   *   *

By the fourth day it was clear the trial was going to last more than a week. Peter was about to take the stand and his testimony would take as long as a week by itself. David had a stomachache and we were both feeling depressed. My pulse quickened when Romatowski called Peter to the stand. Would Peter look at me? Was he angry? What would he say?

Peter was well-dressed but he looked like he was doped up, in a stupefied state. His eyelids appeared heavy; he seemed disoriented and he moved in slow motion. He seemed unfocused. Both Ken and I felt pangs of compassion when we saw him, he looked so spiritless, a hollow husk of the energetic character we had known.

He answered Romatowski's questions slowly in a flat monotone and only after long painful pauses during which he seemed to drift off somewhere outside the courtroom. I concluded he was taking Valium or some mood drug to control his depression and anxiety. His voice was thin and weak. Romatowski had to ask him to speak up. He sat with his palms together in front of him and gently rocked in his chair. The sound of chimes outside somewhere echoed through the cavernous courtroom. The half-smile and the charismatic light were gone.

"Boy, he looks terrible," Ken said during a break. "I just wanted to cry."

"He's on drugs," I said.

"You think so?"

"Look at him," I said. "He's completely spaced out. He's way out in left field someplace. I feel bad for him."

One of David's lawyers overheard me.

"I don't feel sorry for him at all and you're crazy to. The guy's a bum. Look what he did to you guys. And you feel bad for him?"

We couldn't explain to people who didn't know Peter how it was possible to feel compassion for him. Sure, he was a user, climbing to the top of his profession by artifice. He tried to leave Ken holding the bag on our deal and he lied to me. But early in Peter's testimony, Ken and I remembered Peter's vigor and sense of humor. I thought of Peter as generous, colorful, and irreverent. More than that, I thought I understood the kind of intense pain he suffered with the revelation of his misdeeds. He was too attached to his lifestyle, his position and prestige, to suffer lightly these indignities. For all his wealth and prestige, for all his blustering against the stupid people of the world, Peter was the most fragile and vulnerable of us all.

We were all anxious to see how he would hold up under cross-examination. Romatowski gently coaxed him through questions. Our attorneys would be less sympathetic. They were prepared to beat him up.

The cross-examinations slowly peeled away the layers of Peter's fabricated life, his lies and misstatements. He admitted that he had overstated his net worth by several million dollars to Morgan Guaranty Trust in 1984, that he had lied to me, that he had transferred money out of the Roger Wilson account and into the joint trading account that he shared with Clark, and that he and Clark had discussed fleeing to Brazil.

Peter grew more self-confident and feisty as the three defense attorneys hammered away. Even as his credibility crumbled, he seemed to grow less interested in the proceedings, almost put out by it all. After five days on the witness stand, four of them under cross-examination, I had very little sympathy left. When Don cross-examined him about Clark's proposed drug deals, Peter was actually grinning and I could imagine him thinking, Those stupid fucking lawyers.

Don focused on the cocaine deals: "Sir, in response to, I believe it was Mr. Bradley's questions, you testified as early as January 1984 that you and Mr. Clark had discussions concerning some drug deals."

"No, I didn't."

"You testified that you never had such discussions, [that] Mr. Clark did?"

"That's correct."

"I always thought in order to have a discussion you needed two people. Did you just grunt?"

"Objection."

"Sustained."

"Were these discussions on the telephone or in person?"

"On the telephone."

"I mean how did he know you were still there if you didn't say anything?"

"I don't know. He probably figured I wasn't."

Peter grinned.

"And Mr. Clark, during the course of these discussions, told you, did he not, that his brother was working on setting up major cocaine deals that very moment during one such discussion, did he not?"

"Yes, he did."

"That he was going to South America?"

"Yes."

"During one discussion Mr. Clark told you about every week several hundred thousand dollars of cocaine would be brought in. Isn't that correct?"

"Something to that effect, yes."

"The discussions in which you say only Mr. Clark participated and you just listened silently: they continued even on March 6, did they not?"

"I don't believe so."

"March 6th was one of the days you were planning on going to Brazil?"

"I take that back. I don't remember."

"And throughout these various discussions . . . was there not one occasion when he told you there was an old airplane being fitted for the handling of dope?"

"Something to that effect, yes."

Peter flashed a small smile.

"And where did he tell you this airplane was?"

"I don't recall."

"Nasssau?"

"Possibly."

"Did he say that he had a pilot?"

"I think the pilot was from Nassau. I don't know whether the plane was there or not."

"Did [Clark] tell you on one occasion that the money from the drug deal would go to the Cayman Islands?"

"I believe so."

"Sir, is it not a fact that in late December of 1983 you went to the Bahamas?"

"Yes."

"You didn't take your wife with you?"

"No. My wife was pregnant."

"Your baby, your child was born on December 30th, your first child?"

"That's correct."

"You left your pregnant wife home and went to the Bahamas alone in late December?"

Peter had met an old girlfriend in Florida and flown with her to the Bahamas while Lynn was back home about to have her baby.

"In February 1984 you went to the Bahamas again, did you not?"

"Yes."

"As a matter of fact, it was right at that time, was it not, when Mr. Clark told you, 'You saved my life once. Now I'll save yours. We can make twenty to thirty million dollars a year through this cocaine deal'?"

"That's true. He said that to me, but it had no correlation. This was a vacation trip."

After two weeks of testimony, the trial was adjourned for six weeks. The judge had other cases he needed to attend to and he and a couple of the lawyers had vacations coming up. It was both a relief and a bother. Watching other people make fools of themselves on the witness stand made me worry I might do no better. But the delay pushed a final judgment further away and I wanted the thing to be over. We were cramming a five-day trial into ten weeks.

The second half of the trial began with a bombshell. Ken's attorney was lobbying the judge for a copy of the legal memo Bob Krantz, Kidder's general counsel, requested from an outside law firm when he noticed a correlation between David Clark's trading and *Journal* articles. Kidder's lawyers objected and the judge had to decide whether Ken could see it. Krantz had visited Clark after twelve trades around *Journal* articles. He then met with Ken and Peter who had asked Krantz whether the trading was illegal or if it would be reported to the SEC. Krantz had said no.

Ken's attorney was gambling that the memo, if he could persuade the judge to release it, explicitly stated a legal opinion that the trading was legal. It was a poorly calculated risk. Even if the memo said what he thought it said, the fact that Clark and Peter had misled Krantz tended to render the memo meaningless.

When we got back to court after the six-week recess, the judge had read the memo and granted the motion to release it. It was a disaster. The document read like a guilty verdict, with pages of legal citations and the conclusion that traders using advance tips on *Journal* articles probably would be subject to criminal as well as civil penalties. The judge had read it and might be swayed against us. The government would have the benefit of this helpful research as well. There was no way to undo this damage. Ken felt like he'd been mugged.

"Those bastards screwed us," he said later in the jury room. "Krantz told us point blank he didn't think this was illegal and now that we see the memo it's a completely different story."

On the third day back from the break the reporters finally got what they had been waiting two months for and what Don and I had been preparing for almost a year. I walked up to the witness stand and took my seat. I tried to pull the chair closer to the front of the box but it was bolted to the floor. I felt like I was perched on the edge of a cliff. I looked over at the judge's desk. He had a yellow legal pad out. I could see for the first time that he had been taking notes all along. He had a pile of pads full of handwritten notes. The courtroom looked even bigger from the stand. Don began his questioning. I concentrated on keeping my voice up so everyone could hear.

Don eased me in slowly, just as Romatowski did with his witnesses, asking me questions that required merely a yes or no answer. I was only on the stand a few minutes when the anxiety overcame me.

"Had you believed that what you were doing with Mr. Brant was a crime, would you have done it?"

A rush of sadness, regret and shame welled up inside of me. I choked out my answer: "No," and tears blurred my vision. I pulled out a handkerchief.

"Sir, following the March 1—" Don looked up and said, "Are you all right? Do you want a break?"

The rush was subsiding. I dabbed at my eyes with the handkerchief.

"No."

I tried to refute the testimony of Rustin and Pinkerton about the conflict policy but I didn't think we did a good job. Somehow, though, the *Journal* managed to turn that into another public relations mistake. In the *Journal*'s coverage of my testimony, the paper included a Dow Jones statement which read: "The testimony of both Mr. Pinkerton and Mr. Rustin makes it clear that Mr. Winans was aware of *Journal* policy in this regard." In other words, Winans is a liar. The statement continued: "If the question is whether to believe two distinguished editors or Mr. Winans, it should be remembered that he lied to the SEC and *Journal* editors about this matter and he is obviously eager to avoid conviction."

It was so bad, I was almost embarrassed for the *Journal*. The paper had no business using its columns that way to bolster its image. How flat can you squash a bug, anyway?

"This isn't an assignment I was happy to get," Jim Stewart, the *Journal*'s law writer, who got stuck covering the trial, told me.

My sixth and last day on the witness stand, Romatowski was winding up his cross-examination. He had mellowed since his first few questions when he seemed all wound up and excited. It was kind of funny, watching him wave his arms and deliver questions in a sarcastic tone usually reserved for jury trials. He settled down further into his cross-examination. Near the end, he asked me about our cooperation with the SEC.

"So you did, you cooperated for a time, right?"

"For a time?" I asked. What's he talking about? We poured our guts out to those people.

"For a time," he repeated.

"As I recall, we cooperated after that as well." The SEC asked for additional information after our testimony. We held nothing back.

Romatowski pressed his attack and I began to get a sense of where he was going.

"You cooperated right up until that point that it became clear that you weren't going to get away with this just because after you were caught you confessed, right?"

Don jumped up and objected. As he was talking, I remembered we had discussed whether to raise the subject of the U.S. Attorney's threat to indict David unless I pleaded guilty to three federal crimes within twenty-four hours. Don had said it would be bad form for us to raise the subject. "It would just open the door for Romatowski to beat you up about considering pleading guilty. Don't bring it up unless it seems perfectly appropriate." I wasn't sure, as Don continued his objection speech, but it sure as hell sounded like Romatowski had handed me the perfectly appropriate place to bring it up. If nothing else, the judge would realize that David had almost escaped being indicted.

Finally Don finished his speech. The judge looked at Romatowski.

"You want to repeat the question, Mr. Romatowski?"

"Can we have it read back?" he said.

"All right," the judge said. The reporter read the question back.

"You cooperated right up until that point that it became clear that you weren't going to get away with this just because after you were caught you confessed, right?"

That sure sounded like the right question for the answer I had in mind but I wanted to be absolutely sure. I was breathing fast now. I didn't want to screw it up.

"I'm sorry," I said to the reporter. "Could you read that again?"

He read the question again. Now I was sure.

"We cooperated up to the point that the U.S. Attorney's Office . . . threatened to indict David unless I pleaded guilty in twenty-four hours."

Romatowski took a step back, as though he'd been slugged. This kind of strong-arm threat makes the government look bad. Now I had spilled the beans in front of a courtroom full of reporters.

Romatowski did a funny kind of little dance thing with his feet and started to speak. But he was still in shock. He was talking very rapidly.

"Let me ask you something, Mr. Winans. Let me ask you one last thing—" He paused and looked at Don who shrugged his shoulders. Don had a look of serene satisfaction on his face. Then Romatowski said, "Your Honor, I am going to move to strike that last answer, Your Honor."

Don, now with a perfect poker face behind which I knew he was doing a jig, looked out the window and said, "Perfectly responsive."

The quicksand deepened and if anybody missed the answer or its significance, the judge fixed that. He looked up and said, "I didn't get the answer. I'd like the reporter to repeat it please."

The reporter pulled the tape out of his machine and read it.

"We cooperated up to the point that the U.S. Attorney's Office . . . threatened to indict David unless I pleaded guilty in twenty-four hours."

Every reporter in the room was scribbling like mad. The next day it was the lead news in their stories. "Winans Tells of Plea Deal."

* * *

Like popular songs that recall significant events, periods or people in our lives, there were occasions during my friendship with Peter that drew strong responses from both David and me. The meetings on the golf course on those perfect fall days were emotional memories for some reason. David was there for only one of them but that golf course, the beautiful weather on both occasions and all that flowed from them elicited powerful feelings in us. It all began on that golf course. As Don walked me through that first day on the golf course, David started to weep and, finally, was so overcome he fled the courtroom.

My weak point was the first public statement of apology that I gave to *The Wall Street Journal* during the chaotic hours before we traipsed off to testify at the SEC. The statement captured in just a few words the overwhelming shame I felt. Toward the end of my testimony, Don handed me a copy of this statement. He hadn't warned me he would use it and when I saw the words my heart sank.

"Would you read that and tell us what you meant, sir?"

I took a deep breath and read it.

"What did you mean by that, sir?"

I took another deep breath. I barely had control of myself. Here beat the heart of my misery.

"I meant that—I meant that many people that I cared about would be reading about this and hearing about it for the very first time in the pages of *The Wall Street Journal*, that my mother, my brother, that people I cared for and worked with at the *Journal* would be finding out that I had violated journalistic ethics and they would be reading about that in the paper, they wouldn't be hearing it from me, I wouldn't be able to explain it to them.

"I meant that—I meant to apologize to people like Gary, who—"

I had to stop and compose myself.

"—who was the best friend I ever had in a professional position, and that I didn't get a chance to explain to him that I had misled him about my conduct."

The judge could see I was coming unglued.

"Is this a good time to break for lunch?"

"Yes, Your Honor," Don said.

I sat there for a few seconds, sort of stunned and confused. But the dam had burst. I turned in the chair so that I faced away from the courtroom, doubled over, and, for the first time since the whole mess began, exploded in deep, uncontrollable sobs. The tension of the trial overflowed and it felt good to let some of it out. David ran up to the witness box and put his hand on my shoulder. It took a half minute to regain enough composure to thread my way through the desks, the lawyers, and a crowd of reporters, past the gallery rail and down the aisle to the jury room. The courtroom was absolutely silent.

The trial finally ended March 28. David and Ken decided not to testify.

Because no one was sitting in jail waiting for a decision, and there was no jury to deliberate, the judge took his time reaching and writing up the verdict. I continued to help David with his business and worked a couple of weeks in Don Buchwald's office answering the phone and typing letters while his secretary was on vacation.

Three months later, near the end of June, a news clerk ripped a piece of paper off a teleprinter in the glass-enclosed wire room on the sixth floor of *The Wall Street Journal*. He added it to the pile of pieces of paper he held in his hand and walked out the door, around a corner and into the large newsroom where two dozen editors sat at desks organizing stories for the next day's paper. He dropped the stack on a desk. The editor moved it in front of him and began sorting out the pieces. He stopped over one of them, scanned it, and called out, "Well, we got the verdict in the Winans case."

That same day I was sitting at the reception desk in Don's office. The phone rang.

"Buchwald & Kaufman. Can I help you?"

"This is Judge Stewart's clerk. Is Mr. Buchwald in?"

A flutter of anxiety. This had to be it.

"Just a moment." I put her on hold. "Don," I called out. "Judge Stewart on the phone."

I wanted to listen to Don's side of the conversation but the phone rang again. As I hung up, Don emerged from his office. He put a hand on my shoulder and gave me the news.

Epilogue

Judge Stewart found everybody guilty of everything, with one exception, to David's benefit.

    My verdict:
- One count of conspiracy to defraud. Maximum possible sentence—five years in prison and $5,000 in fines . . . . Guilty
- Twenty-two counts of securities fraud. Maximum possible sentence—110 years in prison and $110,000 in fines . . . . Guilty
- Eighteen counts of wire fraud (based on the fact that *Journal* stories are wired from New York to the printing plant in Massachusetts). Maximum possible sentence—90 years in prison and $90,000 in fines . . . . Guilty
- Eighteen counts of mail fraud (based on the fact that the *Journal* is mailed to about 20,000 subscribers in Manhattan and the Bronx). Maximum possible sentence—90 years in prison and $90,000 in fines . . . . Guilty

    David's verdict:
- One count of conspiracy to defraud . . Not Guilty
- Twelve counts of securities fraud. Maximum possible sentence—60 years in prison and $60,000 in fines . . . . Guilty

Ken's verdict:
- One count of conspiracy to defraud. Maximum possible sentence—five years in prison and $5,000 in fines. . . . . .Guilty
- Sixteen counts of securities fraud. Maximum possible sentence—80 years in prison and $80,000 in fines. . . . . .Guilty
- Fourteen counts of wire fraud. Maximum possible sentence—70 years in prison and $70,000 in fines. . . . . .Guilty
- Fourteen counts of mail fraud. Maximum possible sentence—70 years in prison and $70,000 in fines. . . . . .Guilty

Neither David nor I was particularly shocked by the verdict, contained in a forty-five-page written decision. Ken, however, had whetted his appetite for victory. He may yet have it, but the verdict left him a little bewildered and struggling to adjust.

Judge Stewart decided to believe that Pinkerton and Rustin told me about the conflict of interest policy. It was an important decision because it helped him to find me guilty. There was no evidence or even suggestion that I had ever seen the policy. But to convict, the judge had to decide that I had been told or learned of its prohibitions, which included one against trading in stocks of companies about which employees know stories that were being prepared for publication. The policy said employees are supposed to "bend over backwards" to avoid any appearance of a conflict of interest.

That question seemed kind of moot because I knew, as any journalist does, that it was unethical to have an undisclosed interest in the subjects I wrote about. It's like having your car mechanic recommend a particular brand of tire without telling you that the only place in town to buy that brand is the tire distributorship owned by his brother. They might be great tires, but the customer ought to know about the relationship so he can make an informed choice. But the standard journalists aim for is much higher, and that is the shame I will live with the rest of my life—having failed to uphold that standard and, in the process, having misled and let down a lot of newspeople, sources, readers, and friends.

We were convicted, essentially, of violating a company policy.

Actually, we were convicted of damaging the *Journal*'s reputation by defrauding it of something its policy said it owned: the content and publication schedule of its articles. It was our duty, under the policy, to tell the *Journal* about the trades.

Many newspapers don't even have a conflict of interest policy, let alone one as detailed as Dow Jones's. And they are all different. That means the acts required to break the law under the government's theory would be different at each newspaper or television news program. Furthermore, the Feds admitted that if the *Journal* hadn't had any policy, we couldn't have been prosecuted. I'm not a lawyer, and I'm not very objective, but that sounds crazy to me.

The guys in the white hats say they are protecting the public from unscrupulous journalists. But the real issue, in the words of the SEC's John Fedders, is that investors know "the cop is on the beat." I accept that a celebrity hanging helps keep investors honest. That's a tough thing to take when you are the person being hung.

Fedders, meanwhile, learned firsthand what it is like to wake up one morning and find you are the guest of honor at one of those celebrity hangings. One year after my phone interview with Joe Cella in Pearlstine's office, the *Journal* published, on page one, a long, biting feature story about Fedders that focused on his personal life, including a grim account of his drawn-out divorce proceedings, and allegations that he physically abused his wife and that he lived beyond his means. It was a cruel irony: the guy who promised never to forget our cooperation, the "cop on the beat," now was as tainted as we were.

Many of the allegations were history, disclosed in papers filed in his divorce case, and known to members of the press. But the *Journal* presented it as a major story, maybe because it showed the Reagan administration, which was under fire from the women's movement, was ignoring a wife-beater in its own back yard. The article drew a round of reader criticism—similar to what had followed the page-one story about David and me—taking the paper to task for overkill. But Fedders's SEC career was fatally wounded. He resigned within two weeks of the story's appearance.

Some people thought the *Journal* had done a job on him to balance the job it had done on us. Or that the *Journal* was "getting back" at the SEC for mucking around in the *Journal*'s affairs in the first place. Fedders had expressed a belief that the kind of thing I did was widespread in the business press. Maybe the *Journal* thought it time to put a hypocrite in his place. I was embarrassed for the paper. The story was unnecessarily cruel.

After the verdict, David and I prepared for sentencing. We assumed, but couldn't be sure, that Judge Stewart would sentence Ken and me to some prison time, the possibility I had anticipated even before our trial began. David—we assumed but couldn't know—would get probation for his limited involvement. While we waited, Paul Thayer, the former Defense Department official and LTV Corporation executive who was caught spilling the corporate beans to his dozen or so best pals, drew a whopping four-year sentence—the longest we'd ever heard of in an insider-trading case. (Actually, Thayer's judge said he was being tough because Thayer lied and encouraged others to lie. But the press missed that part and declared it a landmark insider-trading sentence.)

Judges were trying to prove they were tough on white-collar crooks. Government lawyers argued in favor of the "deterrent" effect of longer sentences on anyone else who might be thinking about doing the same thing. We worried that we would be further penalized by this trend.

We had six weeks to gather letters from friends and relatives to the judge asking that he give us probation instead of prison. The government could have raised the same legal issues in the SEC civil case alone, under which the penalty for losing is that you pay money to the government—just as when one citizen sues another for damages. Here, the government threatened the ultimate penalty, loss of liberty, for doing something that had never before been considered a crime under federal securities laws. Our friends argued in their letters that we had suffered enough.

The day of sentencing, August 6, 1985, the courtroom was again packed with reporters and other hangers-on. The day before, I marked my 37th birthday. The room seemed unfamiliar, which was strange because we'd spent so much time in it—four weeks in all—that by the end of our testimony I felt that we practically owned it. But it wasn't our courtroom anymore and now it was just Don and I at the defense table. Romatowski argued some law, Don said a few things about what a nice guy I am, and I made a short statement about my shame, my public punishment, the destruction of my career and the volunteer work I was doing on behalf of people with AIDS. I asked the judge for a sentence of community service continuing to work for people with AIDS instead of sitting in jail. A few months earlier, a close friend of 13 years had died of AIDS. I was learning that because of public misunderstanding, many patients found it difficult to obtain basic care. I was willing to empty bedpans.

I sat down after finishing my statement and waited to be told to stand again to hear the sentence. But instead, the judge announced a short recess. Don and I sat there stunned for a few seconds as the judge swept off the bench and into his robing room. If his mind had been made up, wouldn't he have passed sentence when I sat down? Did this recess mean he'd realized the waste of jail and just needed a couple of minutes to reconsider a lighter sentence? It seemed like a good sign but we had few clues as to what was going through his mind. The judge took a probation officer with him into the robing room who had interviewed David and me. But he didn't take Romatowski.

The reporters milled around the courtroom talking to each other like hardware salesmen at a convention. They couldn't wait to interview me and a few tried. But I waved them off, thinking only about whether or not the judge would let me remain free pending the appeal we would file. I had butterflies in my stomach but was calm otherwise. In a sense, the trial ended when I left the witness stand. That was the hardest part—telling my story in public. This seemed anticlimactic by comparison.

Finally the judge came back and we resumed our seats. He looked up to see if anybody else had anything to say. The courtroom was very quiet. He started to speak and Don nudged me to stand up.

"I'm going to do what's best for you and the community," he said. Then he looked down at something in front of him:

"On counts 1 through 6, 26 through 30, and 44 through 48, the defendant is sentenced to imprisonment for a period of 18 months. On counts 1 through 6, the defendant is fined $5,000. On counts 26 through 30, the defendant is fined $1,000 on each count to run consecutively with each other but concurrently with the sentence imposed on counts 1 through 6. And the defendant is fined $1,000 . . ."

It went on and on like this as I stood trying to remember the difference between concurrent and consecutive and, at the same time, calculating the subtotal. I was prepared to hear a tough sentence and resolved not to give any reporter any reason to write in tomorrow's editions that I "sagged" or "sobbed" as sentence was pronounced.

The judge granted our motion for me to remain free pending an appeal, he was out the door and it was over. I huddled with Don long enough to learn that my sentence added up to 18 months in prison, fines totaling $5,000, five years' probation after my release from jail, and 400 hours of community service. With good behavior I'd be eligible for release after 13 months.

I wasn't happy but I was also determined not to say anything that would sound stupid or arrogant in print. All I could think of to say to the reporters when I got outside the courtroom was that it was a fair sentence.

David was sentenced a couple hours later but the courtroom was empty. He declined to give a statement. The judge gave him three years' probation, $1,000 in fines, and 200 hours of community service.

Ken Felis was sentenced the next day. He got six months' imprisonment, to be served on weekends—which would allow him to run his business and support and raise his children. He was also fined $25,000, and sentenced to five years' probation after prison and 500 hours of community service. I thought his prison sentence actually was worse than mine. It translated into a year's worth of weekends when he'd have to leave his family and report to a correctional facility. I'd have a hard time choosing between spending six months confined to a cell or driving myself to prison every Friday for a year, while the rest of the world heads home, or to the mountains or the beach, for the weekend.

We faced a wait of as long as a year before we'd know the result of our appeal to the next highest court—the Second Circuit Court of Appeals in New York.

The summer we were sentenced, 1985, I sank into an emotional swamp for nearly three months. Until then I had managed to keep myself too busy to reflect on the chaos our lives had become. It was a form of self-defense. Once the verdict was in, my job was over and I collapsed in a heap. I lived on the sofa, irradiating my brain with television, smoking cigarettes, and watching a beautiful, mild summer waste away just outside the window. I knew all the commercials by heart and the names of all the game-show hosts. I even knew how many days each contestant had been on and the total of their winnings. I hated feeling like that but I also realized that it was part of the healing process. I kept telling myself, This is just something you have to go through. It'll be over soon enough and you can go on with your life.

It finally was over in September and I began working on this book.

In the fall of 1985, David and I settled with the SEC. We agreed not to do it again. I paid the government $4,500, which I borrowed.

David gave up his small advertising business in return for repayment of the $9,000 or so he'd loaned it. It never earned him a salary. In October 1985, he decided to become a real estate salesman. It's a field all his friends thought he'd be terrific at. He took the required four-week course, paid all his tuition and license fees, passed his state boards, and then was denied a license because he checked "Yes" where it was asked if he had ever been convicted of a crime. That decision was appealed and reversed, but his stride and his spirit were broken. In the spring of 1986, he moved to the Midwest to be near one of his brothers and try to get a fresh start on his life.

Ken Felis loved to hunt, and owned a collection of shotguns he had acquired over the past thirty years or so. He discovered much to his chagrin that convicted felons aren't allowed to own guns.

His company submitted competitive bids in hopes of landing a big government label-printing contract. He discovered that companies owned by people with criminal records can't bid on government contracts.

He lured a top salesman away from a competing company. Two days after accepting Ken's offer, the guy changed his mind. In between he'd learned of Ken's legal "problem."

Otherwise, Ken has continued to prosper in his business, fathered a fourth child, and spent a lot of time recalling and mourning the end of a great friendship. He has not spoken to Peter since that last time on the phone, right after his trip to Florida when Peter hinted he might try to pin the blame on him.

Peter J. Romatowski's resume began turning up at selected private law firms a few months after our sentencing. In early 1986, he accepted a partnership in the Washington, D.C., firm of Crowell & Moring.

Gary Putka finally made it to London in 1984. He covers the financial markets. I see his byline infrequently. I have written to him several times without a response.

George Anders returned to the New York bureau from his London post and has been covering the investment business. He is one of the few people still writing for the *Journal* who knows how to cover the markets.

Norm Pearlstine is still managing editor of the *Journal* and is thought to be in line to become chairman of Dow Jones someday.

Two of the bosses who testified against me have since seen their careers advance. Stew Pinkerton's name began appearing directly under Norm's on the daily masthead of the paper. His title is deputy managing editor and his responsibilities tend toward personnel matters. Paul Steiger, the white knight who rescued me from Rustin, is another deputy managing editor. His name also appears on the masthead, just under Pinkerton's. Steiger's job focuses more on news gathering.

When Rustin's rescue mission to "restore credibility" to the "Heard" column was over in 1984, he became one of four submanagers in the New York bureau. He is responsible for financial news other than the markets columns.

The *Journal* overhauled its advertising campaign in 1984 from its hard-sell call-this-number-now ads to a softer, image-creation theme wrapped around a new slogan: "If the American Dream had a diary, *The Wall Street Journal* would be it." In the winter of 1985–86 the company also upgraded its physical plant, moving from the battered offices at 22 Cortlandt Street to a brand-new building a couple of blocks away in Battery Park City, a complex of apartments and offices on reclaimed Hudson River bottom. Now visitors can't miss the home of America's best-read daily newspaper: over the door it says THE DOW JONES BUILDING.

Pearlstine began his tenure as managing editor in 1983 with a hiring binge, in part to handle the *Journal*'s planned expansion, which would require more people turning out more stories. After the disclosure of my misconduct and my salary, there also was a flurry of raises.

By 1985, the paper had declared in effect an "austerity" program. Some employees were offered and took early retirement. Attrition was permitted to winnow the staff further. But the *Journal* seemed to have weathered its embarrassment by my conduct unscathed.

Chris Winans, my brother, remains a *Journal* employee and his career flourished even as mine died. The celebrity gossip page of the *New York Post* reported his promotion in 1985 to assistant news editor. "He's one of the best copy editors we have," a Dow Jones spokesman was quoted as saying.

Kidder, Peabody had a little trouble of its own with the SEC, but on matters not related to my scheme. The firm settled out of court, without admitting or denying, charges that it used customers' accounts as collateral to guarantee loans to the firm. In the spring of 1986, General Electric agreed to acquire 80% of Kidder, one of the oldest and last remaining independent securities firms on the street.

David W. C. Clark was the only defendant left in the stalled SEC suit, and he reportedly remains a target of a criminal investigation at this writing. We were all waiting for his indictment after we were convicted, but the government was silent and there was no movement in the SEC suit. We assumed that the government was waiting to see if its legal theory held up in the appeals of our conviction. It did. In May 1986, nine months after the appeals were filed, the three-judge panel announced it had voted two to one to uphold the convictions of all three defendants. It was better than three to nothing. David, Ken and I all planned appeals to the Supreme Court, which may be heard in 1987.

May 1986 also was a busy month for the SEC and insider-trading cases. In just a few weeks the SEC and the Justice Department brought parallel cases against seven individuals. Dennis Levine was accused of misusing inside information about companies to make $12.6 million in the stock market over a six-year period. It was the biggest such case ever and suddenly the country

was again talking and reading about insider trading, only this time
it was front-page news.

The SEC, in a separate case, accused five young men, all in
their twenties, of misusing inside information that had been leaked
from a law firm to make about $250,000 in the market. The *New
York Post* playfully dubbed it "Yuppiegate."

On June 6, five of the seven defendants—who had been
charged with crimes as well as civil violations—pleaded guilty in
the same courtroom before the same judge. Dennis Levine, who
had been a successful investment banker on Wall Street, agreed to
give up most of his fortune, about $11.5 million, and to cooperate
in continuing investigations of insider-trading abuses. The investment community was nervous that Levine would talk too much and
expose to public scrutiny the whole network of information trading
that fuels the Street. I could just imagine the paranoia I would have
been running into if I had still been a reporter covering the stock
market.

A week later, the U.S. Department of Commerce reported
that several of its employees misused advance knowledge of sensitive economic statistics, such as the quarterly Gross National
Product figure, which often moves bond prices when the agency
makes it public. The department said some of the employees would
be fired, but they would not be criminally prosecuted because there
is no law against what they did. The SEC wasn't pursuing the case
either, yet it was just like our case. I hope the Supreme Court
would notice this discrepancy.

David Clark, meanwhile, has filed a lawsuit against Kidder,
Peabody claiming Peter stole money from him. We've all had a
good laugh over that one. Clark has reportedly quit New York and
moved to Fort Lauderdale.

Summer 1986 marked the second anniversary of the guilty
pleas to three federal crimes by the government's star witness,
Peter Noel Brant. He admitted guilt to one count each of securities
fraud, mail fraud, and wire fraud. He agreed that if any other
defendants should win a reversal of a conviction on those same
charges, he would come back to court and plead guilty to something else.

But he had yet to be sentenced and may not be for some time.
When witnesses like Peter cop a plea, they understand that the

sentence will reflect their degree of cooperation in the subsequent prosecution of others. If they get cold feet and decide not to cooperate, the government holds over them the potential of recommending a harsher sentence.

Peter performed his duty as it related to us. But Clark's status remains an open question. It's an educated guess that Peter won't be sentenced until Clark is either indicted and his case disposed of, or a decision has been made not to indict him.

Peter sold the Locust Valley house for about $1.3 million in 1984 (he paid $700,000 and put an estimated $400,000 into it) and made his new home the apartment he owned in Wellington, Florida, at the polo club where he lived with Lynn and their infant daughter. The co-op apartment in New York was sold in April 1985, and $1.2 million of the proceeds paid to Roger Wilson as partial settlement of Wilson's $12 million lawsuit. The *Journal* reported at the time that Clark's lawyer said Clark "always agreed that the money belonged to Mr. Wilson." Peter's lawyer said Peter settled "to get a major issue in the case resolved."

The rest of the lawsuit remains to be tried in court.

In November 1985, I found the *Finesse*, the 52 foot sailing vessel Clark bought and Peter was supposed to refurbish, riding at anchor where it had been when Peter's world fell apart: in a boatyard on the inland waterway in West Palm Beach. It belonged by then to the Spencer Boat Co., which completed the refurbishing work and was offering the yacht for sale at $175,000.

Peter's father claims he learned his son was a millionaire stockbroker from the newspapers. He says the last contact with him was in 1976. Morton Bornstein in 1984 told a reporter that his son is a *chazzer* (Yiddish for pig) and declared of Peter's conduct, "He didn't learn it from me. If I knew then what I know now, I'd never have a child."

Peter talks from time to time to some of his friends from his Kidder days. They report he tells them he works for a company in the long-distance telephone business and commutes every day to an office where he has a secretary. He complains that by writing this book I have betrayed him.

I receive my *Wall Street Journal* every day in the mail. From my kitchen and my bedroom I can see the Dow Jones Building, across the Hudson River, where the *Journal* is produced every day. I can also see the taller buildings of Wall Street and the rest of the financial district, buildings I used to haunt as a reporter.

Sometimes I sit on the porch of my apartment and wonder: What would I be doing today over there if I had never met Peter Brant?

I can imagine floor clerks, in their brightly-colored smocks, on cigarette breaks from their posts at the stock exchanges, loitering on the crowded streets in the spring light.

Somewhere, in a poshly decorated office, a stockbroker is glued to his quote machine, telling a client on the phone that he has found a stock to change his lifestyle.

Harry is yelling at some new editor on the ticker who has garbled an important headline.

In the *Journal* newsroom, reporters are flitting up and down the aisles as deadlines grow closer.

The ticker machines are grinding away.

The Quotron machine seductively winks its numbers.

And a young reporter is on the phone at his desk, learning the difference between a stock and a bond.

Index